POLAND

An Illustrated History

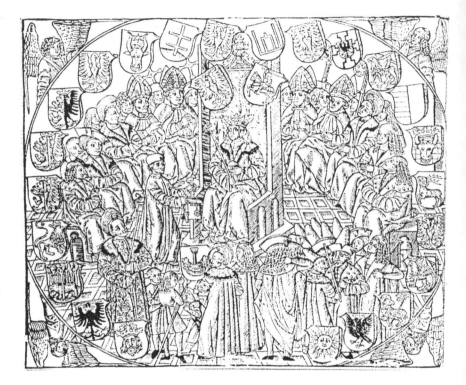

The first Polish constitutional law of 1505, entitled
Nihil Novi or Nothing New About Us Without Us.
Passed in Radom by the Seym or the LowerHouse of
the Polish Parliament, which was the supreme power
in Poland until 1795. The Polish Parliament became
bicameral in 1493.

POLAND

An Illustrated History

IWO CYPRIAN POGONOWSKI

HIPPOCRENE BOOKS INC.
NEW YORK

ISBN 0-7818-0757-3

For information, address:
HIPPOCRENE BOOKS, INC.
171 Madison Avenue
New York, NY 10016

Cataloging-in-Publication Data available from the Library of Congress

Printed in the United States of America.

To my wife Magdalena and
to our daughter Dorota

TABLE OF CONTENTS

LIST OF MAPS AND DIAGRAMS

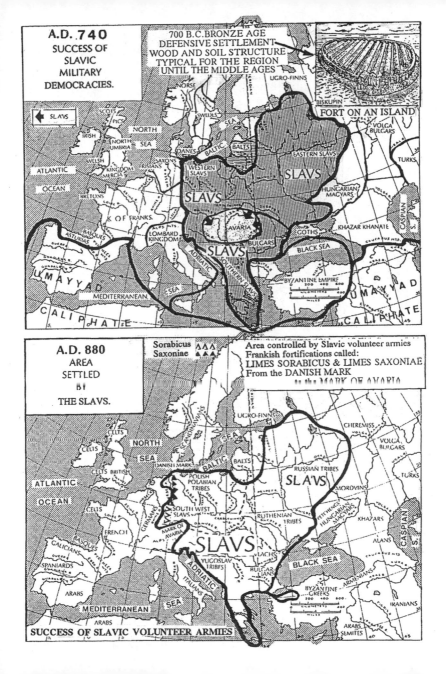

Poland in Western Civilization

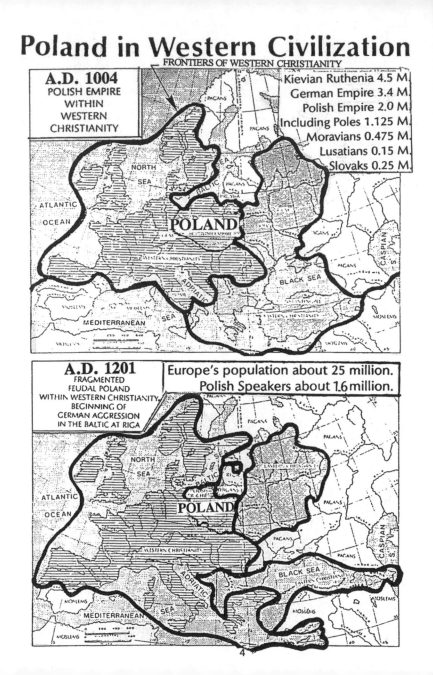

FRONTIERS OF WESTERN CHRISTIANITY

A.D. 1004
POLISH EMPIRE
WITHIN
WESTERN
CHRISTIANITY

Kievian Ruthenia 4.5 M.
German Empire 3.4 M.
Polish Empire 2.0 M.
Including Poles 1.125 M.
Moravians 0.475 M.
Lusatians 0.15 M.
Slovaks 0.25 M.

A.D. 1201
FRAGMENTED
FEUDAL POLAND
WITHIN WESTERN CHRISTIANITY,
BEGINNING OF
GERMAN AGGRESSION
IN THE BALTIC AT RIGA

Europe's population about 25 million.
Polish Speakers about 1.6 million.

A.D. 1493

POLISH JAGIELLONIAN
REALM
THE SHIELD OF
WESTERN CHRISTIANITY

POLISH
JAGIELLONIAN
REALM

Europe 77 Millions	
Poland – Lithuania	7.5M
Polish Jagiellonian Realm	14.5M
France	14M
Germany	10M
Spanish Domain	8M
Italy	8M
European Turkish Empire (Christians 5M + Moslems 1M)	6M
England	3.5M
Russia	3M
Netherlands	2.75M
Kingdom of Denmark	2M
Portugal	1M
Tartars and Turkmen	0.5M
Irish	0.75M
Scotland	0.5M

Poles 3.25M		Ukrainians	2.5M
Byelorussians	1.25M	Lithuanians	0.5M
Kingdom of Hungary			3.5M
Hungarians+Slovaks+Croats+Serbs			
Czechs Kingdom			2.75M
Czechs+Moravians+Lusatians+Silesians			
Moldavian Fief			0.75M

A.D. 1618

REPUBLIC OF POLAND,
THE
BASTION OF
WESTERN CIVILIZATION

POLAND

"Freemen with free. Equals with equal"

Population of Europe:97 million	
France 15½M.	Habsburg
Germany 12M.	Austria 7M.
Republic of Poland 11½M.	Netherland 1½M.
	Belgium 1½M.
Italy 11M.	Portugal 1½M.
European Turkey 9½M.	Scotland 1M.
Russia 8M.	Sweden 1M.
Spain 8M.	Ireland 1M.

"POLISH EYES ON PARIS;
POLISH HEARTS ON ROME;
POLISH SABRES ON RUSSIA."

Republic of Poland 11.5M.
Poles 4 M.
Byelorussians 1.5M.
Lithuanians 0.75M.
Prussians 0.75M.
Livonians 0.5M.

5

Poland in Western Civilization

Poland, the Athens of Slavic Europa 1370-1795

A.D. 1717

REPUBLIC OF POLAND
IN CRISIS OF
SOVEREIGNTY.

Frontier of Western Christianity

Population of Europe: 120 Million

France 19M	Republic of Poland 9M
Russia 15M	Portugal 2M Spain 9M
Italy 14M	Netherlands 2M
Germany 13M	Belgium 1½M
Austria 11M	Swiss 1½M
European Turkey 10M	Sweden 1½M
Great Britain 9½M	Denmark 1½M

Republic of Poland 9M
Poles 4½M, Jews 0.5M
Ukrainians 1½M
Byelorussians 1.2M
Lithuanians 0.8M
Others 0.5M

Decline of Poland, the Athens of Slavic Europe in face of the rise of Russian Sparta

A.D. 1922

POLAND
AS THE MAIN
BARRIER AGAINST
COMMUNISM.

Communist Revolutions
in Germany and Hungary

Population of Europe 485 Million	
(Eur.)Soviet	Holland 7M.
Russia 120M.	Greece 6M.
Germany 64M.	Portugal 6M.
U.K.(Britain)45M.	Bulgaria 5.5M.
France 40M.	Sweden 5.5M.
Italy 39M.	Swiss 4M.
Poland 27M.	Finland 3.5M.
Spain 20M.	Denmark 3.2M.
Romania 16M.	Norway 2.5M.
Czechoslovakia 13M	Lithuania 2.3M.
Yugoslavia 9M.	Latvia 1.7M.
Hungary 8M.	Eur. Turkey 1.9M.
Austria 8M.	Estonia 0.9M.
Belgium 7.7M.	Albania 0.8M.

Republic of Poland 27M.
Poles 17M. Ukranians 4.5M.
Jews 2.5M. Byelorussians 2M.
Others 1M.

POLITICAL DOMAIN
OF THE WESTERN CIVILIZATION

6

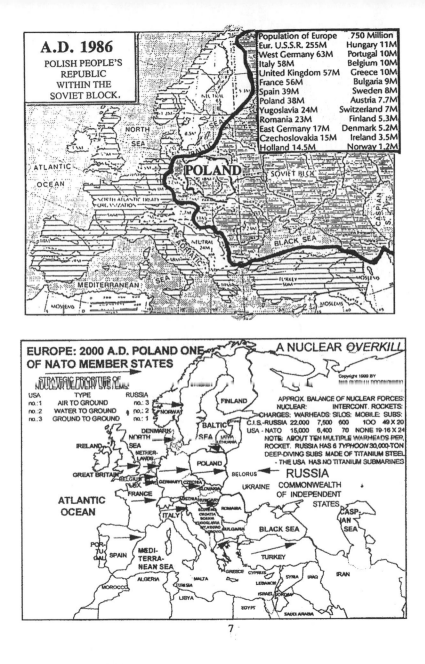

A.D. 1986

POLISH PEOPLE'S
REPUBLIC
WITHIN THE
SOVIET BLOCK.

Population of Europe	750 Million		
Eur. U.S.S.R.	255M	Hungary	11M
West Germany	63M	Portugal	10M
Italy	58M	Belgium	10M
United Kingdom	57M	Greece	10M
France	56M	Bulgaria	9M
Spain	39M	Sweden	8M
Poland	38M	Austria	7.7M
Yugoslavia	24M	Switzerland	7M
Romania	23M	Finland	5.3M
East Germany	17M	Denmark	5.2M
Czechoslovakia	15M	Ireland	3.5M
Holland	14.5M	Norway	1.2M

NORTH
SEA

ATLANTIC
OCEAN

NORTH ATLANTIC TREATY
ORGANIZATION

POLAND

SOVIET BLOC

CASPIAN SEA

BLACK SEA

NEUTRAL

ADRIATIC

MEDITERRANEAN
SEA

TURKEY
SUM

MOSLEMS

MOSLEMS

**EUROPE: 2000 A.D. POLAND ONE
OF NATO MEMBER STATES**

A NUCLEAR OVERKILL

Copyright 1989 BY

STRATEGIC PRIORITIES OF
NUCLEAR DELIVERY SYSTEMS:

USA	TYPE	RUSSIA
no.:1	AIR TO GROUND	no.: 3
no.:2	WATER TO GROUND	no.: 2
no.:3	GROUND TO GROUND	no.: 1

FINLAND

APPROX. BALANCE OF NUCLEAR FORCES:
NUCLEAR: INTERCONT. ROCKETS:
CHARGES: WARHEADS: SILOS: MOBILE: SUBS:
C.I.S.-RUSSIA 22,000 7,500 600   100 49 X 20
USA - NATO 15,000 6,400 70   NONE 19-16 X 24
NOTE: ABOUT TEN MULTIPLE WARHEADS PER
ROCKET. RUSSIA HAS 6 TYPHOON 30,000-TON
DEEP-DIVING SUBS MADE OF TITANIUM STEEL
- THE USA HAS NO TITANIUM SUBMARINES

NORWAY

BALTIC
SEA

DENMARK

NORTH
SEA

NETHER-
LANDS

IRELAND

GREAT BRITAIN

BELGIUM
LUX

POLAND

GERMANY CZECHA

BELORUS

UKRAINE

RUSSIA
COMMONWEALTH
OF INDEPENDENT
STATES

FRANCE

AUSTRIA HUNGARY

SLOVENIA
CROATIA
BOSNIA
YUGOSLAVIA
MT. NEGRO KOSOVO

ROMANIA

ATLANTIC
OCEAN

ITALY

CASP-
IAN
SEA

BULGARIA

BLACK SEA

PORTUGAL

SPAIN

MEDI-
TERRA-
NEAN SEA

TURKEY

GREECE CYPRUS

SYRIA IRAQ

IRAN

LEBANON

MOROCCO

ALGERIA

TUNISIA

MALTA

ISRAEL JORDAN

LIBYA

EGYPT

SAUDI ARABIA

Timeline of the History of Poland

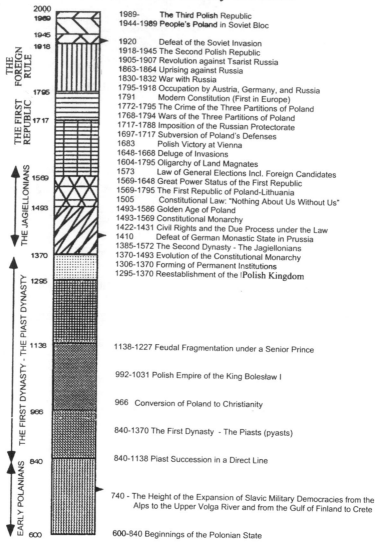

1989-   **The Third Polish** Republic
1944-1989 **People's Poland** in Soviet Bloc

1920   Defeat of the Soviet Invasion
1918-1945 The Second Polish Republic
1905-1907 Revolution against Tsarist Russia
1863-1864 Uprising against Russia
1830-1832 War with Russia
1795-1918 Occupation by Austria, Germany, and Russia
1791   Modern Constitution (First in Europe)
1772-1795 The Crime of the Three Partitions of Poland
1768-1794 Wars of the Three Partitions of Poland
1717-1788 Imposition of the Russian Protectorate
1697-1717 Subversion of Poland's Defenses
1683   Polish Victory at Vienna
1648-1668 Deluge of Invasions
1604-1795 Oligarchy of Land Magnates
1573   Law of General Elections Incl. Foreign Candidates
1569-1648 Great Power Status of the First Republic
1569-1795 The First Republic of Poland-Lithuania
1505   Constitutional Law: "Nothing About Us Without Us"
1493-1586 Golden Age of Poland
1493-1569 Constitutional Monarchy
1422-1431 Civil Rights and the Due Process under the Law
1410   Defeat of German Monastic State in Prussia
1385-1572 The Second Dynasty - The Jagiellonians
1370-1493 Evolution of the Constitutional Monarchy
1306-1370 Forming of Permanent Institutions
1295-1370 Reestablishment of the lPolish Kingdom

1138-1227 Feudal Fragmentation under a Senior Prince

992-1031 Polish Empire of the King Bolesław I

966   Conversion of Poland to Christianity

840-1370 The First Dynasty - The Piasts (pyasts)

840-1138 Piast Succession in a Direct Line

740 - The Height of the Expansion of Slavic Military Democracies from the
       Alps to the Upper Volga River and from the Gulf of Finland to Crete

600-840 Beginnings of the Polonian State

THE MIDDLE GROUND OF EUROPE: THE STAGE FOR THE HISTORY OF POLAND

The Republic of Poland is located at the physical center of the European continent. Warsaw is midway between Paris and Moscow. Poland lies on the open, relatively flat northern European plane between the Baltic Sea in the north and the Sudety and Carpathian Mountains in the south. The present area of Poland is 120,665 square miles, about the size of New Mexico. The maximum distance in Poland from east to west is 405

The White Eagle on a Red Field.

miles, while from north to south it is 430 miles. Its Baltic coast is 310 miles long.

The country's lowest elevation is sea level in the north and the highest is Rysy Peak, which ascends to a height of 8,212 feet in the south. Most of Poland is flat or gently rolling with the countryside rising gradually toward the mountains in the south.

Poland's main river, the Vistula, flows north through the capital city of Warsaw to the port of Gdańsk. Its basin drains four-fifths of Poland. The second largest river is the Odra (Oder). Canals link the two main river systems.

The current estimated population of Poland is about 40 million, or some 330 persons per square mile. Over ninety-six percent of its people are ethnic Poles. The largest of the ten minorities are the German population of more than 550,000 persons; the Ukrainian of 400,000; and the Belorussian of over 250,000.

The country's climate results from its location on the border between the Atlantic moist and east European continental climates. The typical Polish meteorological configuration consists of a barometric high over the Azores and an Icelandic low. In winter a Eur-Asian high often dominates the climate of Poland. However, the temperature in January averages 30 degrees F; in July it averages 70 degrees. Sixty-percent of days are windy, with winds blowing from the west. Most of Poland receives 20 to 30 inches of rain per year.

A third of the Polish population earns its living in agriculture. Poland grows more rye and potatoes than any other country in Europe. Other important crops are sugar beets, oats, wheat, barley, and flax. Besides farmland, Poland is rich in resources. After World War II, Poland was one of the leading coal, lead, and zinc producers in Europe. Copper, iron ore, potassium salt, rock salt, and sulfur are also mined.

Polish industries are still adjusting to the market economy and the privatization process. They are coping with the problem posed to all post-communist states by the survival of economically useless but politically powerful state enterprises -- the legacy of a communist command economy. The main industries undergoing this reorganization include shipbuilding, steel mills, the manufacturing of heavy machinery, and the building of locomotives and farm equipment. The same situation exists in Poland's chemical industries, as well as in its cotton, wool, and silk textile mills.

Electric power is generated in hydroelectric plants and in steam plants fueled with coal. Oil is imported and refined in Poland to fuel the ten million cars and trucks that travel its roads.

Recently the tenth anniversary of the democratic revolution was celebrated in Poland and in other former Soviet Bloc countries. The results of this revolution are easily seen in Warsaw, the capital of Poland. Its shops resemble stores in the United States, full of imported goods, of meat, and exotic and domestic fruit. Shiny skyscrapers, shopping malls, cinemas, expensive hotels, and luxurious private homes are becoming commonplace.

POLAND IN EUROPEAN HISTORY: AN OVERVIEW

Poland's Culture and Slavic Roots

Poland acquired the traits of Western Christianity more than one thousand years ago and became a land of many diverse forms of art, architecture, and styles. It provided a home for many foreign influences, as did all the other countries of Europe; in fact each national culture, to a considerable extent, became a cosmopolitan conglomeration. So despite all of its originality, the culture of Poland was a part of a commonly-shared European culture to which its citizens made a permanent contribution.

The originality of Polish culture is tied to its language and to its Slavonic roots. Linguistic studies indicate that as late as 4,000 years ago the Balto-Slavic languages were part of the Arian or the Eastern Indo-European languages. Over 3,500 years ago, the languages of the Balto-Slavs separated from the Arian languages; some 3,000 years ago, the Baltic and Slavic languages separated from each other; and for the next 1,500 years, the Slavic languages evolved parallel to the Greek, Latin, Celtic, Germanic, and other languages. The evolution of the Polish language occurred during the following 1,500 years.

Polish language reflected the intellectual and material culture in spoken words and later in literature. Early Polish vocabulary contained much earlier cultural information than did written records. The adoption of foreign words grew with the passage of time. During the present information age, new European and American terms related to fashion, sports, arts, politics, and technology are being adopted by the modern Polish language. Unabridged Polish dictionaries presently contain some 200,000 entries; one-third of these are foreign adaptations, while about one-fourth are still close to Old Slavonic words.

Travelers to Poland can visit many representative sites of the twelve historical periods of Polish culture:

11

1. The Prehistoric Period (700 B.C. to 966 A.D.)
2. The Middle Ages:
    a. Romanesque (1040-1200)
    b. Gothic (1200-1500)
3. Renaissance (16th century)
4. Baroque (17th century)
5. Enlightenment (18th century)
6. Romanticism (early 19th century)
7. Positivism (late 19th century)
8. Young Poland Movement (turn of the 20th century)
9. Inter-war Modernism (1918-1939)
10. German-Nazi Devastation (1939-1945)
11. Social-realism (1945-1955); Modernism (1956-1989)
12. Post-Modernism (1989-present)

The Rise of a Center of Civility

The country of Poland was an early outgrowth of Slavic or Slavonic civilization in Europe, which at one time encompassed the eastern two-thirds of the European continent. From ancient times the Slavs governed themselves in self-ruling communities. They often formed large volunteer armies led by elected commanders who had conquered most of central Europe by 740 A.D., and had started forming individual Slavic states. One of those states, Poland, was formed *c.* 840 A.D., when a leader named Piast established the royal dynasty that would rule Poland until 1370.

During the time of the Piast Dynasty, the Polish state evolved into a great civilizing entity whose influence spread widely beyond its borders. It established Western Christianity as Poland's official religion in 966 A.D., an affiliation widely accepted and devoutly followed by its people. The University of Kraków was founded in 1364. One of its future professors, Paulus Vladimiri (Paweł Włodkowic, 1370-1435), formulated the first modern rules of international law in 1413, and defined the *Prussian Heresy* as a violation of the principle that "the license to convert is not a license to kill or expropriate." Nicolaus Copernicus (Mikołaj Kopernik), who would graduate in astronomy at the University of

Kraków, founded modern astrono-my in 1543 by establishing the theory that the earth rotates daily on its axis, and that the planets revolve in orbits around the sun.

Nicolas Copernicus (1470-1543).

In 1385, Poland formed a voluntary union with Lithuania, forming a huge commonwealth that extended from the Baltic to the Black Sea - the largest united territory in Europe at the time. Poland-Lithuania defeated the attempt to impose German political and economic domination on east-central Europe in the crucial battle at Tannenberg-Grunwald-Dąbrowno in 1410. Also at stake also was the permanent loss of Polish coastal provinces and Poland's access to the Baltic Sea. Victorious Poland subsequently undertook a great civilizing role in Balto-Slavic Europe, and its language became known as the language of civility, elegance, and diplomacy throughout the entire region.

The country itself became a land of innovations in law and tolerance among its peoples. It was the first European state to adopt the concept of due process under law - nearly three centuries before England would do so. Poland also established the principle of Habeas Corpus, in which a person detained by the state has the right to a prompt trial under an official court of law. Its people accepted the idea of "No taxation without representation" long before the English Colonies were founded in North America. Furthermore, Poland provided a homeland for the Jews who grew in number and thrived, eventually saving them from extinction in medieval and early modern Europe, when Jewish people were persecuted, evicted, and killed in other European countries. At one time, over 80% of all Jews worldwide lived in Poland.

Although Polish was the national language of Poland, the influence of the Roman Catholic Church introduced Poland to Latin - the

13

lingua franca of western European culture. Polish translations of Latin texts and other Polish publications were the only source of the eastern Slavic peoples' knowledge about Western civilization. Thus nearly all ruling members of the Russian Romanov Dynasty (1613-1917) were fluent in Polish.

Changes in the Eastern Frontiers of Poland.

Poland's second dynasty, the Jagiellonian (1386-1572), originated in Lithuania and required parliamentary approval of each royal succession. During their reign, traditional Polish regional legislatures, or *sejmiki,* established the first national parliament in 1454. A bicameral national parliament was constituted in 1493, in which the king presided over the Senate, and the Marshal presided over the Chamber of Deputies. The first Polish constitutional law, famous for its democratic motto "Nothing new about us without us," was passed by the parliament and instituted in 1505. This law made the Chamber of Deputies the supreme power in the commonwealth.

The Polish Renaissance of the 16th century was the country's "Golden Age." Its culture and arts blossomed, while the Polish population was among the best fed and healthiest in Europe.

The First Modern Republic in Europe

The law of 1573 guaranteed religious freedom. The civil rights of free citizens lay at the root of religious toleration in Poland. Paradoxically, the desirable qualities of democracy such as liberty and acceptance of diversity contained the seeds of weakness in the face of absolutist neighbors. After the Jagiellonian Dynasty, Poland proclaimed itself to be "The Republic of Good Will ... Free Men With Free... Equals with Equal...."

Thus did it pioneer the first modern European republic. There was a widespread pride in Polish citizenship throughout the new republic. Of its ten million inhabitants, one million were full-fledged citizens. Within the 10% of Polish citizens, all males could offer themselves as candidates in general elections for the office of the head of state -- a unique situation in Europe in 1573. The head of state kept the title of "king," but in reality he functioned as a chief executive with legal limits on his powers. The motion by the Chancellor Jan Zamoyski to restrict the candidacy to natives of the Polish-Lithuanian Commonwealth was not acted upon. Thus, since Polish law permitted acceptance of foreign candidates for the throne, Polish general elections (called *viritim* because the electorate had to appear in person) generated anxiety in neighboring countries. None of them wanted an unfavorable change in the European balance of power that might result from Polish elections. Taking advantage of the legality of foreign campaign contributions, bribery and subversion were used by foreign governments to promote their interests in Poland.

The Polish democratic process further suffered at the hands of the strong political machines formed by the wealthiest landowners. These political machines caused Cossack uprisings for civil rights in 1594, 1648, and 1768; they also introduced the first use of the *liberum veto* that, after 1652, often paralyzed parliamentary proceedings with the vote of a single dissenting deputy. Foreign agents paid huge bribes to prevent the removal of the *liberum veto* by the Polish Seym.

The Allied Christian Armies under the command of the King of Poland, John III Sobieski, saved Europe from invasion by the Muslim Turks in 1683 at Vienna. The comfort of this victory was short-lived, however. Fourteen years later, a serious calamity was inflicted on the Polish Nobles' Republic by Peter the Great of Russia: he militarily engineered the fraudulent inauguration of a Saxon candidate, as King August II, who had lost the general elections in Poland in 1697. This event started a twenty year period of decline in the early 18th century and ushered in the beginning of the "Saxon Night," which was a low point of education and civil virtue in the republic. Capped by the ruin of Poland's defense establishment, it was the most wretched and humiliating time in Polish history.

A reestablished Polish leadership then started a campaign of reforms. Europe's first Ministry of Education was established in Warsaw in 1773, through which Poland's school system was modernized. Poles voted to institute the first modern constitution in Europe in 1791, and started to rebuild their army.

The reforms in Poland alarmed the neighboring absolutist regimes and led them to fight three wars of partitions. The rulers of Russia, Prussia, and Austria committed the international crime of annexing of all of the republic's territory between 1772 and 1795. Criminal destruction of the Polish state converted its provinces into bones of contention in a European search for a balance of power, and for the creation of new empires. The robbery of Polish provinces made Prussia the largest among the 350 German states and principalities, putting it in a position to unify Germany in the 1870s, and to organize a short-lived German Empire.

Poles reacted by organizing an army on the side of Napoleon of France, who thoroughly exploited them militarily and financially. After Napoleon's defeat, the 1815 Congress of Vienna established a much smaller constitutional Kingdom of Poland with the Tsar of Russia as its king. Thereafter, the Polish constitution was frequently violated by the

Russians, leading the Kingdom of Poland's army to rebel against the absolutist Russian Empire in a bid for national independence (1830-1831). Polish veterans emigrated and fought in most struggles for national freedom in Europe and in America. During the next Polish uprising, in 1863-1865, some 1,230 partisan battles were fought throughout the Polish lands annexed by Russia.

The Second and Third Polish Republics

After World War I, the Poles declared their independence on Nov. 11, 1918, thereby creating the Second Polish Republic. To keep its independence, the new republic had to win six borderland wars. By far the most important was the Polish victory, led by Marshal Józef Piłsudski, over the Red Army in 1920. Lenin had attempted to overrun Poland and form a Moscow-Berlin alliance in order to proceed with the communist world revolution. Many Germans had been ready to accept a communist government in return for the acquisition of western Poland and the Gdańsk

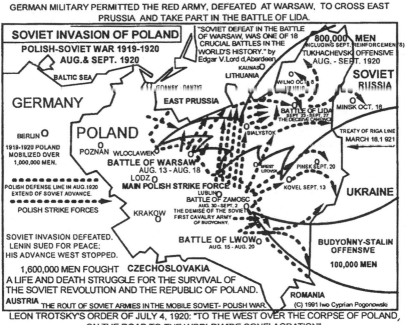

GERMAN MILITARY PERMITTED THE RED ARMY, DEFEATED AT WARSAW, TO CROSS EAST PRUSSIA AND TAKE PART IN THE BATTLE OF LIDA.

LEON TROTSKY'S ORDER OF JULY 4, 1920: "TO THE WEST OVER THE CORPSE OF POLAND, ON THE ROAD TO THE WORLDWIDE CONFLAGRATION".

Pomerania region, once those lands were occupied by the Soviets. The Polish victory destroyed Lenin's hope for world revolution, and resulted in retaliation against the Polish minority within the Soviet Union. Twenty years later, the Soviets would avenge this defeat.

From Oct. 25, 1938 to Jan. 27, 1939, Germany pressed Poland to join the Anti-Comintern Pact. The Germans wanted 3,500,000 Polish soldiers to join with Germany and Japan in the conquest of the USSR and its oil and fertile lands. When Poland refused, however, Hitler and Stalin became allies in 1939 and invaded Poland (Sept. 1 and Sept. 17 respectively), thereby starting World War II. Poland mobilized nearly one-and-a-half million soldiers in 1939. During the six-year war, over twenty percent of its citizens were killed, nearly half of them Jews. Poland was the only country to organize an underground state with a *Home Army* (*Armia Krajowa*) of 400,000 soldiers. Polish resistance triggered a more vicious response by the Germans than was visited upon any other nation; it resulted in massive manhunts, torture, and the killing of ordinary citizens by the Gestapo. Poland had 200,000 soldiers, sailors, and airmen fighting against the Germans on the Western front in Norway, Italy, and Africa. Polish pilots played an important part in the Allied victory in air battles over Great Britain. 400,000 Poles served in two armies of the new People's Poland. They were recruited and controlled by the Soviets, and fought the Nazis on the Eastern front in 1944-1945.

Despite large Polish contributions and sacrifices for the Allied's victory, Poland was betrayed by Roosevelt and Churchill at Yalta; it was handed over to become a Soviet satellite state, after a ruthless pacification by the communist terror apparatus.

The Pope from Poland, John Paul II, helped in Polish Solidarity's effort to start unraveling the Soviet communist cloth in 1989, bringing independence to Poland and other satellite states that had been part of the Soviet Bloc.

The Third Polish Republic, created after the elections of 1989, embraced the free market in the 1990s, and became a member of the NATO alliance in 1999. Poland has been lauded for the rapidity of its reforms, compared to many other countries attempting to rise from the rubble of their subjugation by the Soviets.

THE SLAVONIC AGE
The Prehistoric Period

Early Slavonic History

The Slavs of antiquity were called "Scythian farmers" by Herodotus in the 5th century B.C. About 550 A.D., ecclesiastic and historian Jordanes wrote that the Slavs were of "one blood" and lived in three groups: Vednedic (western), Antic (eastern and southeastern), and Sklavinian (southern). Slavic volunteer armies led by elected commanders were described by Byzantine historians after the Slavic victory over Byzantine forces at Adrianapolis in 551 A.D. The western Slavs pressed the Germanic tribes out of the basin of the Elbe River after 512 A.D.

In the 8th century, Slavic agriculture was based on ploughing with horses; the area between the Rhine and the lower Elbe River became Christianized; and the Teutons, benefitting from improved organization and discipline, started "the push to the East to conquer Slavic lands." This would be known as the "Drang nach dem Slawischen Osten," or simply as the "Drang nach Osten" and would become a German tradition. Its best known recent exponents were Frederic II, King of Prussia, and Chancellors Bismarck and Hitler.

In the 9th century, the "Bavarian Geographer" wrote the earliest known report about western Slavs. He described the Slavic area (c.844) north of the Danube River, and east of the Elbe River and the upper Main River, including the Polanian or Polish language area. The Polanians spoke Old Polish, a part of the Lechitic language group that extended from the lower Elbe River to the Bug River. Polish cultivated fields were fertile clearings created by burning of forests.

The name of Poland, in Polish "Polska," originated from the name of Polanians. Linguistic data of the highly diversified early Slavic vocabulary proves familiarity with elaborate abstract ideas. In Slavic self-perception the ethnic meaning of the word "Slav" or Słowianin (swo-vyah-ñeen) in Polish was derived from the term for the spoken word, or "słowo" (swo-vo). Thus, to the Slavs, their name testified to their mastery over spoken words, in contrast to others, whose languages they did not understand. Even in modern Polish vocabulary, Germany is called *Niemcy* or the land of the mute or dumb.

Prehistoric Structures in Poland

Thousands of Neolithic flint mine shafts still exist in Central Poland. Flint, amber, and cattle were used then for barter trade.

During prehistoric times, wood - often combined with soil - served as the main building material. Characterized by logic and simplicity, ancient dwelling constructions were dug into the ground.

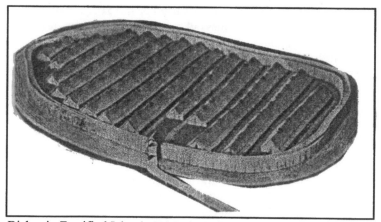

Biskupin Fortified Island, 650 B.C. Soil and Wood Construction.
Lusatian - Proto-Slavic Culture.

Modern Slavic languages have kept many construction terms from that period. In Polish, for example, a wall is called ściana (śhćhah-nah), meaning "a cut ground face"; stairs are schody (skho-di) meaning "the steps down"; a floor is podłoga (pod-wo-gah), meaning "a layer laid under"; and a ceiling is powała (po-vah-wah), meaning "a layer thrown over the ground."

Biskupin provides an example of a fortified proto-Slavic or Lusatian village built of wood and soil *c.* 650 B.C., during the Bronze Age in the region. It includes about 100 houses of similar size and contains no large house of a chief, a fact indicating communal self-government. This type of functional wood and soil construction was used in Poland until the 11ᵗʰ century.

The Indigenous Slavonic Pagan Religion

Before their conversion to Christianity, Slavs believed that the god of the thunderbolt and war called Perun lived in the sky. The cult of Perun (pe-roon) dominated during wars and migrations. The god of peaceful life, work, and home was Wołos (vo-wos) - a word that meant hair or furs and related to the idea of warmth and protection from the cold. Swarog (sfah-rog) was the god of fire and father of Darzbog (dahzh-bog), the sun-god. The name Swarog contains the root word "war" (vahr), which meant heat or fire. Countless modern Polish words contain this root word; they range from cooking to quarreling and fighting. The name Darzbog was derived from the verb "darzyć" (dah-hzić) which, meant to grant, bestow, or provide. The sun-god's name described him as the source of the life-giving rays of the sun.

There were also tribal gods such as the other son of Swarog, Swarożyc (sfah-ro-zhits), a deity of the Elbe River Veleti. The Rugian Slavs worshiped Świętowid (śvyan-to-veed), whose statue with four faces faced the four directions of the world. The name Świętowid meant giving a "holy look" or "blessing the world," and he occupied the temple in Arkona on the Baltic Ruegen Island.

Each family, clan, tribe, and region had its own guardian deity. The dead were cremated and their ashes were buried in urns in cemeteries, along with cremated objects to be used in the afterlife. According to the Slavonic religion, the deceased were forever united with the eternal fire of the sun-god Darzbog through the fire of cremation. The souls of ancestors were also worshiped.

Generally, the statues of gods were made out of wood; occasionally, also out of stone. Many of them can be seen today in museums in Poland, and in neighboring countries.

21

Romanesque Rotunda in Strzelno
12th Century.

Romanesque Sculptured Columns
in Strzelno, 12th Century.

12th Century Romanesque Door
in Olbin.

12th Century Romanesque Door
in Tum.

HEREDITARY MONARCHY
THE PIAST DYNASTY (*c*.840-1370)

The Middle Ages:
Romanesque (1040-1200)
and Gothic (1200-1492) Periods

Conversion to Western Christianity

Mieszko I (*c*. 921-992), the fifth member of the Piast dynasty, established Western Christianity as Poland's official religion in 966. Mieszko's alliance with the Czech ruler, Bolesław I the Severe, resulted in his marriage to Czech Princess Dobrawa, a union that facilitated this conversion. German Emperor Otto I declared his support and confirmed the appointment of Jordan as the first bishop. The new diocese was, however, directly subordinated to the Pope of Rome. Bohemia, still without a bishop of its own, helped the Poles to translate the Church terminology into Slavic words. By 989, Mieszko's dominions included about the same lands as modern Poland. In the same year, the neighboring Slavs of Kiev converted to Byzantine Christianity.

Mieszko's decision to convert to Western Christianity was of fundamental importance to the eventual fate of Poland as a shield of western civilization, as well as a religious and cultural middle ground between the Slavs and the Germans; the western and eastern Slavs, western and eastern

Romanesque Rotunda in Cieszyn, 11th Century.

23

Christianity; Christians and Muslims; and between the Roman and Greek alphabets. In 991, Mieszko issued the oldest surviving Polish state document, which describes Poland for the purpose of concluding an alliance with the Pope against the German Emperor of the Holy Roman Empire. It was entitled the Dagome Iudex.

St. Adalbert and the Spread of Christianity

St. Adalbert (Święty Wojciech) was one of the surviving members of the abolitionist Sławnikowics - a Czechian family who fled their native land for Poland, after losing a power struggle with the slavery advocate, Boleslaus II. As Bishop of Prague, St. Adalbert wrote a treatise, entitled "Infelix Aurum," that condemned slavery and the slave trade.

He baptized the population of Gdańsk in 997, and then carried his evangelical mission to the Balto-Slavic Prussians. The mission ended two years later in his martyrdom - a sacrifice that would be recognized with his election as the patron saint of Poland in the 11th and 12th centuries. His Latin popular biography marked the beginning of Polish literature written in Latin.

11th Century Polish Empire

A friend of St. Adalbert, Bolesław Chrobry (Boleslaus the Brave, 967-1025), also called the Great in early chronicles, was the oldest son of Mieszko I. He created the short-lived Polish Empire - a kingdom that included Bohemia, Moravia, Slovakia, Lusatia, and Milsko (Milzenland). In 1018 Boleslaus I Chrobry conquered Kiev and sent triumphant letters to the Byzantine and Roman Emperors. The same year, he signed a peace treaty with the German Emperor Henry II (1002-1024), who recognized the western Slavic provinces of Łużyce (Lusatia) and Milsko (Milzenland) as a part of Poland, thus formally fixing the furthest western border of Poland in history.

In 1025 Bolesław I Chrobry was formally crowned and became the first King of Poland shortly before his death. His son, Mieszko II (990-1034), then succeeded to the throne. Six years later (in 1031), he was defeated by the coalition of the Holy Roman Empire of the German Nation and Kievian Ruthenia. The Polish state recovered under the son of King Mieszko II, Kazimierz Odnowiciel (Casimir the Restorer, 1016-1058), who rebuilt the early medieval monarchy. At that time Poland was entering a period of economic, social, and political transformation. The political center of Poland shifted from Poznań to Kraków.

The Arts in Medieval Romanesque and Gothic Periods

Upon the arrival of Christianity, Polish builders used limestone, sandstone, and brick masonry in fortified sacral construction. Master builders determined that the flying buttress construction popular in western Europe was not practical in Poland. For this reason, Polish Gothic or Vistula Gothic architecture included buttresses built into the walls of the structures. A number of original Polish-style arrangements of bricks were used in these early masonry walls. Monumental Gothic cathedrals, huge ecclesiastical buildings, and ornate town halls were built throughout Poland, as well as defense castles and some of the largest fortified complexes in Europe.

The stone Rotunda of Our Lady was built on Wawel Hill in Kraków before 1040 A.D., when a large Benedictine monastery was built in nearby Tyniec. Romanesque architecture blossomed in Poland in the 12th century. It included ornamental sculptures in stone and in wood. The Dominican church and monastery built in 1277 in Sandomierz shows the first Gothic tendencies in form of pointed arches. The high Gothic period in Polish architecture occurred from 1320 to 1500.

Craftsmanship attained a high level very early in Poland. Goods included pottery, ceramics, woven linen and woolen fabrics, silver jewelry, furniture and tailored fabrics.

Early Polish festivities were accompanied with music. Polish musical instruments included bagpipes, called "dudy" (doo-di) and the four-string "gęśle" or "skrzypce," the forerunner of the modern violin. The latter means "squeaker" - a term indicative of the instrument's poor sound box. Ancient regional dances were a part of Polish folklore. Centuries later, many of them would inspire the compositions of Frederic Chopin (1810-1849) and other modern composers.

The earliest written polyphonic religious music by anonymous Polish composers can be traced back to the 12th century.

Gothic Painting of St. Maciej
Trzebinia.

Gothic Painting of St. Jadwiga
Trzebinia.

Schools and Old Chronicles

The growth of Polish intellectual culture was evidenced by the formation and development of ecclesiastical education at the end of the 10th and during the 11th and 12th centuries.

Dominican Monastery in Kraków.

Polish cathedral schools taught the seven Liberal Arts: Grammar, Rhetoric, Dialectic, Arithmetic, Geometry, Music, and Astronomy. In addition to these subjects, Theology and Canon Law were taught in Gniezno, Poznań, Wrocław, Płock, Sandomierz, and Kraków.

The year 1136 marked the beginning of the literary period of the Polish language, when the papal Bull of Gniezno included over 400 names of Polish people and places in a description of the estates belonging to the archbishopric of Gniezno. At the beginning of the 14th century, the Świętokrzyskie Sermons (kazania Świętokrzyskie) were written. They are the oldest Polish medieval texts. They served as a basis to estimate that the Polish of the time consisted of approximately 15,000 words.

Polish literature and state documents written in the Latin language by priests date from the end of the 10th century until the beginning of the 15th, and include diplomatic and legal correspondence.

Gallus Anonymous (11th-12th centuries) wrote the oldest chronicle that presents the political, social, and economic situation of Poland starting from the beginning of the Polish State.

Wncenty Kadłubek (c.1150-1223) wrote a chronicle in the contemporary style. Though it was less factual than Gallus', it served as a textbook for the teaching of eloquence.

The chronicle of the Cistercian abbey at Henryków (1227-1310) includes the oldest preserved sentence written in Polish.

Bolesław II the Bold, or Generous (1058-1079) (Jan Matejko).

European Feudal Fragmentation Reaches Poland

Bolesław Śmiały (Boleslaus II the Daring, c.1040-1081), son of Casimir the Restorer, allied with Pope Gregory VII, revived Poland's military strength, and crowned himself as King of Poland in 1076. Thus ended the direct line of succession to the Piast throne.

King Boleslaus II the Daring faced a conspiracy that involved his brother, Władysław Herman (1040-1102), and the Bishop of Kraków Stanisław of Szczepanów. The King sentenced the Bishop to death and later had him executed. With the support of the Church, Duke Władysław

Bolesław III the Wrymouth
(1102-1137) (Jan Matejko).

Herman then ruled Poland. However, under German pressure, he had to surrender his claim to the royal crown and pay a tribute for Silesia to Bohemia, which was included in the German imperial sphere of interest.

More successful was Herman's son, Duke Bolesław III Krzywousty (Boleslaus the Wrymouth). He extended his rule to Western Pomerania and Ruegen Island, once the center of Slavic pagan religion. In 1135, however, he had to pay a tribute for these territories to the Emperor Lothair III.

Recurring European crises of feudal fragmentation soon reached Poland. After the death of Duke Boleslaus III, the feudal disintegration was formalized by his will, in which he divided Poland into duchies that were inherited by his sons. The oldest son was to be the General Duke in charge of foreign policy, friendly relations with the Church, and resistance to German expansion.

Act of Cienia Similar to the Magna Carta

The 12th and 13th centuries were marked by the evolution of settlements, economic growth, and social transition as Poland became consolidated and fully Christianized. In 1228, the Act of Cienia was issued by Duke Wladyslaw III (Ladislas III, 1161-1231). The duke promised to preserve "just and noble laws according to the council of bishops and barons," in return for succession to the throne of Kraków. It was an act similar to and contemporary with the Magna Carta of 1215 (issued by the King of England, John Lackland of Anjou of the Angevin or Plantagenet Dynasty, after he lost the Duchy of Normandy).

Economic Growth and Social Transition

New settlements were established on the basis of the customary

The Market Place of Kraków.

Polish law of the right of free settlers, which strictly defined a rent in kind or money. Generally, the position of knights who owned land was strengthened. However, in areas exposed to foreign invasions, such as Mazovia, it was necessary to organize a permanent defense force of a large number of knights of lesser rank, who did not own serfs.

Class differentiation began to develop and slowly take the form of feudalism. However, in the Slavic tradition, every descendant of a nobleman was himself considered a nobleman and all his children were entitled to an equal share of the family inheritance. Thus, Polish nobility became more numerous than in other countries. Eventually, it reached ten percent of the population and became the political nation of Poland.

Early Stage Plays and Science

At the beginning of the 13th century, municipal schools were founded in parishes and collegiate churches. School theaters started to form shortly thereafter - a development that marked the beginning of the Polish stage. In 1207, Pope Innocent III issued an edict critical of Polish Catholics who were staging unholy theatrical performances in churches. The earliest Polish text for staging the Visitation of the Tomb by the Three Marias originates from Kraków in the middle of the 13th century.

In this period many Poles studied and worked abroad. Paris

Star Compass the Torquetum of Jan Bylica, 1493.

attracted theology students, and Montpelier medical students, while Bologna and Padua attracted law students from Poland. From 1275-1314, twelve Poles served as presidents (rectors) at the University of Bologna.

An eminent Polish mathematician and physicist, Witelo of Silesia (*c.*1230-1314) published an important work on optics entitled *Perioptike* in 1270. Polish astronomer, Franko of Poland, authored a 1286 treatise on the newly invented instrument, the torquetum. Marcin Polak became famous by publishing compendia of law and history. Western knowledge of geography and the ethnography of Eastern Europe and Asia was advanced by writings of Benedykt Polak, who was sent on a diplomatic mission to Mongolia in 1245-1247.

New Town Law and the Rule of General Dukes

German town law was introduced in the 13th century as the immigration of Germans, Flemings, Walloons, and Jews increased. The immigrants were allowed to prosper and to preserve their language. Free peasants settled in villages founded on the principle of the rent law and became trading partners of the burghers. The peasants supplied grain, cattle, and pigs in exchange for articles produced by the artisans. The towns conducted trade on a local and regional scale and tried to obtain total or partial exemption from customs duties. Early ramparts and town walls provided adequate room for new construction. As trade increased the Hansa Trade Organization was established (a. 1241), first in German ports and then in other Baltic ports.

The General Dukes ruled until the 1295 coronation of King Przemysław II. Five years later, Wacław II (1271-1305) King of Bohemia and Hungary was crowned King and Poland. The following year, King Władysław I Łokietek (Ladislaus the Short, a.1260-1333) ascended to the throne, from which height he consolidated the Polish State and restored the process of Poland's unification. His son Kazimierz III Wielki (Casimir III the Great, 1310-1370), the Builder, was the last king of the Piast dynasty(c.840-1370).

Konrad I of Mazovia (1187-1247) (Jan Matejko).

German Aggression in the Baltic (13th and 14th cent.)

In 1201, German monastic orders began an aggressive campaign to establish missionary enclaves on the southern and eastern coasts of the Baltic Sea near the deltas of the Rivers Dvina, Memel, Narva and Vistula. They did so to monopolize the trade on these rivers and eventually dominate and Germanize the entire region. They become the richest Hanseatic grain merchants, who used rivers as the highways of transport and trade. The conquest and conversion of Lithuanians, Latvians, and Prussians would lead to the eventual creation of a dominant German monastic state in the region. In 1228, armed German monks of the Teutonic Order of the Cross (or Krzyżacy) succeeded in obtaining the Act of Kruszwica from Duke Konrad I of Mazovia, who gave them a temporary fief of Chełmno. The temporary fief was established for the time needed to convert the Balto-Slavic Prussians to Christianity.

By 1233 German aggression in the East Baltic had spread yet further. The unification of the armed monks of the Order of the Knights

The Castle of the Teutonic Order in Malbork, 14th Century.
The Largest Gothic Fortification in Europe.

of the Sword of Riga with the Monastic State of the Teutonic Order was completed in 1237. The Monastic State annexed the Brethren of Dobrzyń in 1235.

The towns of Toruń and Chełmno were founded by the German Brethren on the Magdeburgian model and built as Gothic fortresses. The Teutonic Order thus became a growing threat to Livonia, Lithuania, Novgorod, and Poland.

Duke Konrad of Mazovia's temporary grant was falsified in 1234 by the German Armed Brethren to read as "permanent," and thus became the "legal" foundation of the independent German Monastic State in Prussia. This forgery resulted in protracted international legal and military conflict between Poland and the German Armed Brethren.

The Massacre at Gdańsk

In 1308, German armed monks committed the mass murder of Polish people and knights after a treacherous entry into Gdańsk and Tczew. Pope John XXII appointed inquisitors in Poland in 1318, but they were inactive. However, a Church court held a trial in 1320-1321 in Inowrocław and subsequently ordered the Armed Brethren of the Teutonic Order to pay damages to Poland and evacuate all of Pomerania. This order, however, was not obeyed.

In 1325, the first common defense treaty between Poland and Lithuania against the Teutonic Order was concluded. It led to the marital alliance of the Crown Prince of Poland, soon to be crowned as King Kazimierz III, and the Lithuanian Princess Aldona, daughter of the Grand Duke Gedymin.

The Brethren had an ally in King John Luxembourg of Bohemia, who invaded Poland and occupied most of Silesia, taking advantage of the war between Poland and the Armed Monks of the Teutonic Order (1327-1332). Despite a Polish victory in the battle of Płowce, the Brethren occupied the provinces of Kujawy and Dobrzyń. In fact, Poland was engaged in a life-and-death struggle with Germans encircling the country from three sides: the Teutonic Order from the north, Brandenburg from the west, and German-dominated Bohemia from the south.

Invasion by the Mongol Empire

A new disaster simultaneously loomed in the southeast of Poland. While the Teutonic Order created a serious problem for Poland, the Tartar invasion was a more devastating calamity for both eastern and central Europe. The Mongol Empire captured Kiev and conquered Ruthenia in 1240. The invasion of Poland by the Mongol Empire in 1241 was short but devastating. The battles of Chmielnik and Legnica were lost by the Poles. Henry the Pious, Prince of Silesia and the Polish commander of assembled Christian defense forces, died on the battlefield. The main defense force consisted primarily of Polish knights of Silesia and Greater Poland, the miners of precious ores, and the peasants of Silesia with minor detachments of knights of the Templar, Joannite, and Teutonic Orders.

During these battles, the Mongols used rockets with incendiary warheads, as well as sulfuric fumes which choked both men and horses. The Margrave of Berlin in Brandenburg took advantage of the Mongol invasion and occupied the Polish province of Lubusz.

In 1259, the second Mongol invasion devastated and burned the towns of Lublin, Sandomierz, Kraków, and Bytom. In 1287, only the fortified towns of Kraków and Sandomierz resisted the Mongol invaders. Prussians (also called Pruthenians) and Lithuanians joined in pillaging the frontier lands of Poland. The trickle of German immigration became a flood into depopulated Poland.

The Reign of the Builder King Casimir III the Great

After the 1333 coronation of King Kazimierz III Wielki (Casimir III the Great, 1310-1370), the papal Nuncio conducted a trial of the Teutonic Order in Warsaw. The Teutonic Brethren were again ordered to evacuate all Polish lands, including Pomerania, and pay damages to Poland.

The Brethren unsuccessfully appealed the sentence of the Warsaw Tribunal to the Vatican. The Treaty of Kalisz followed in 1343, in which the monastic state of German Brethren recognized the King of Poland as its founder, and returned Kujawy and Dobrzyń to Poland.

King Kazimierz III Wielki is known as the Builder-King. He built some eighty major castles, two hundred commercial and sacral buildings for all rights, and city wall fortifications with ornate gates. These structures were built in the Vistula Gothic style combining stone and bricks adorned with stone sculptures. These were splendid examples of Gothic architecture. During the reign of the Builder-King the high quality of Polish art was due to the fact that in late medieval Poland, craftsmen as well as painters and sculptors had to include a trip abroad as an obligatory element of their apprentice education.

The Seal of King Casimir III the Great (1310-1370).

Prosperity under King Kazimierz Wielki reached its peak thanks to his brilliant administration, currency reforms, codification of laws, protection of peasants from exploitation, and strengthening of the country's defenses.

The first Polish invasion of Halicz in Ruthenia (1340) was conducted in competition with Lithuania during Poland's war with Bohemia over Silesia (1341-1345). In the Treaty of Namysłów (1348), Poland ceded Silesia to Bohemia in exchange for Bohemia's renunciation of its claims to the Polish throne. German immigrants in Silesian towns supported the Bohemian claim.

In 1349, King Kazimierz III Wielki (Casimir the Great) annexed the two Ruthenian principalities of Halicz and Vladimir, thereby extending Poland eastwards to modern-day Ukraine.

Codification of Laws and Progress in Civil Rights

Codification of the Polish Common Law, the first in Europe, was accomplished in 1346-47 by Casimir III the Great. In addition, the King uniformly extended Jewish liberties throughout Poland; he recognized the Jews as a distinct legal, national, religious, and cultural group.

Jewish refugees continued to arrive from Germany. Gradually, the Jews in Poland created the world's largest Jewish community, as the country's law protected them. Punitive fines for towns were established in case of anti-Jewish activities; half of the money was used to pay for damages to the Jews, and half went to the state treasury. The new law also banned the accusations of ritual murder against the Jews brought to Poland by German immigrants.

The Polish economy became capable of supporting a rapidly growing population and provided a steady surplus for trade. It should be noticed that such a situation was not reached in central Russia until the middle of the 19th century.

Further limitations on the power of the throne were promised in the 1355 Act of Buda. It was issued as a part of dynastic politics of Ludwik I, Louis I of Anjou, King of Hungary (1326-1382). The Act of Buda confirmed all previous constitutional acts and privileges in order to secure Louis' succession to the Polish throne, and to overcome the weakness of his female connection to the Piast dynasty. A Polish succession treaty between King Ludwik I of Hungary and King Kazimierz III was concluded. At the same time in 1356, the Supreme Court for Urban Affairs was founded in Kraków by King Kazimierz III.

In 1364, King Casimir presided over the Congress of Kraków in which the Emperor, the kings of Denmark and Hungary, and the dukes of Silesia and Western Pomerania reconciled their differences and promoted a crusade against the Turks headed by Peter of Lusignan, the King of Cyprus.

The First Polish University Founded In 1364

In 1364, the first Polish university was founded in Kraków by Casimir the Great. The king was helped by Poles who taught at the University of Prague such as Mateusz of Kraków, a theologian who later served as president of the University of Heidelberg and Bishop of Worms. It followed the Italian model, in which law was the principal subject. The university included colleges of liberal arts, medicine, and law. The Law School was to be especially strong because of Poland's legal entanglements with Germany and the German Armed Brethren over Prussia. Reforms in 1400 followed the models of the Universities of Paris and Prague, and the study of theology was added. The school of astronomy and mathematics was added in the middle of the 15th century. Many illustrious Polish scholars acquired European recognition.

Casimir the Great (1310-1370).
(Jan Matejko).

The University of Kraków is one of the oldest universities in central Europe; it was founded one year before the University of Vienna (1365), and twenty-one years before the University of Heidelberg (1385). (The oldest in central Europe was the University of Prague founded in 1348.)

The founding of the university in Kraków strengthened upward mobility in Polish society. Prior to its founding, a bright child of a poor peasant could hope to obtain an education sufficient only for the ranks of the clergy; but the university gave him a chance to become a scientist or a university professor. Often clerical and university careers were combined and resulted in the powerful political position of a bishop, or even the Primate Bishop of Poland.

First Diaries and Newsletters

The chronicle of Jan of Czarnków (a.1320-1387) is regarded as the first diary in Polish literature. It describes the social problems current at the time. Around 1400, etiquette instructions were published in poetic form by a man named Słota. The poem is didactic in nature, providing lessons on good table manners and on showing due respect towards women.

Latin was the international language of law and science, and influenced Polish legal and scientific vocabulary. Czech literary language was more advanced at the time, and also influenced Polish literary expressions. Generally people spoke Polish; however, German and Yiddish were spoken in enclaves. Some borrowed German terms were used in trade. German and Latin were used in Poland in 15th century newsletters called "ephemeral letters," which contained news, notifications, reports, communications, and stories that described wars, international conflicts, famous court cases, commercial news, religious celebrations, and visits of foreign dignitaries. Most Polish newsletters originated in Kraków, and were delivered handwritten to subscribers. They are considered to be the origin of press in Poland.

EVOLUTION OF THE CONSTITUTIONAL MONARCHY (1370-1493)

Five hundred years of the rule by the Piast dynasty ended. "...the Kingdom of Poland was set fair to found one of the most original civilizations of early modern Europe, which, in union with Lithuania, spread out from sea to sea, and lasted for more than four hundred years." (Norman Davies, *God's Playground, A History of Poland*, Columbia University Press, New York (1982, p.105).

An Electoral Monarchy

The death of King Casimir the Great ended the period of hereditary monarchy in Poland under the Piast Dynasty. For over two hundred years, the succession to the Polish throne was negotiated. Poland became an electoral monarchy between 1370-1572. A constitutional monarchy evolved in this period (1370-1493). During this evolution, due legal process was established in Poland; Polish became a language of elegance, diplomacy, and civility in east central Europe, as Poland acquired a civilizing role between the Baltic and the Black Seas.

Christianization of Lithuania

The leadership in Kraków perceived a great historic opportunity in arranging a peaceful conversion of Lithuania to Christianity. The Poles hoped that the union of Polish and Lithuanian Christian forces would put an end to the invasions and pillage of the Teutonic Order, which conducted the predatory wars under the cover of missionary activity. Poles were about to achieve the greatest missionary deed of the late Middle Ages by peaceful means and adroit diplomacy. Thus, as the relations with Lithuania became closer, the foreign policy of Poland had to focus on the problems in the North and the East. Poland's strategic

Wawel -- Poland's Pantheon, the Royal Castle in Kraków.

position· on the borders with Western Pomerania and Brandenburg improved as the Polish state grew more powerful.

Concessions in the Act of Koszyce

The first personal union between Poland and Hungary lasted for twelve years (1370-1382) during the reign of King Ludwik I, the successor of Casimir the Great. Ludwik I of Anjou, King of Hungary and Poland, issued the Act of Koszyce in 1374, which further limited the royal power by giving taxing authority to regional legislatures, reducing taxes, and promising to nominate local people to territorial offices. From that point on the royal succession was possible only with the assent of the entire nobility, which was represented by the regional legislatures.

The act of 1374 limited the obligation of military service and provided compensation to soldiers for injuries suffered outside the national territory. It also guaranteed the inviolability of the territory of Corona Regni Poloniae, as the Kingdom of Poland was known in Latin. All of this was granted by King Ludwik in return for his and his

King Władysław II Jagiełło
(*c.* 1350-1434).

Queen of Poland Jadwiga I
of Anjou (1374-1399).

daughter's right of succession to the Polish throne. The Act of Koszyce started the country on the path to becoming the main scene of development of civil liberties in Europe, especially when England drifted in the direction of absolutism, and the Magna Carta Libertatum became ineffectual for several centuries.

The power of regional legislatures called "Sejmiki" (sey-mee-kee) was also strengthened, the noble estate of about ten percent of population was defined; and the estates system was crystallized. Thus, the Polish parliamentary system was reconfirmed in the form of regional legislatures based on the indigenous democratic process. Immunities for nobles were granted in exchange for military service in the defense of the country

Polish nobility had the function of a warrior caste known as szlachta (shlahkh-tah). The coats of arms were held in common by whole clans whose heraldic designs were unlike those of western European chivalry. Many of them originated from property markings, the *Tamgas,* of the Sarmatian Alans, who were assimilated by the Polanian Slavs in the sixth century A.D.   There was no college of arms and sometimes imposters abused the rights of nobility.

The class identity of Polish nobility, the backbone of the armed forces, evolved during a struggle with the Crown based on the principle of "no taxation without representation," and during the subsequent development of a fully-fledged parliamentary system.

In 1381, Ludwik I signed the Act of Kraków, in which he reduced Church land taxes in return for the acceptance of the succession of his daughter to the Polish throne. The reign of Jadwiga d'Anjou, Queen of Poland, followed from 1374 to 1399.

The Emblem of the Kingdom of Poland-Lithuania.

Unions of States for the Common Defense

The aggression by the orders of German armed monks on the Baltic coast caused the formation of two unions of states: in the south, Poland and Lithuania united at Krewo in 1385, and in the north, all of Scandinavia united at Kalmar in 1397.

In the Union Act of Krewo, Jogaiła or Jagiełło, the Grand Duke of Lithuania, committed himself to convert Lithuania to Latin Christianity and to unite all Lithuanian and Ruthenian lands with Poland. He also promised to recover Polish territories lost to the Germans, in exchange for both his marriage to Polish Queen Jadwiga of Anjou, and his coronation as the Catholic King of Poland. Before his coronation in 1386, Władysław Jagiello, (Ladislas Jogaiła, c.1350-1434), confirmed the 1374 Act of Koszyce.

The Union of Kalmar was concluded during the coronation of Polish Prince Eric Pomorski (c.1382-1459), great grandson of Casimir the Great, as King of Denmark, Sweden, and Norway in 1397. King Eric VII fought against German expansion in the Baltic, concluding an alliance with Poland against the Teutonic Order in 1419.

During the reign of King Władysław Jagiełło (1386-1434), Polish missionaries converted Lithuania to Roman Catholicism. The Act of Wilno followed in 1387. In it King Władysław Jagiełło bestowed hereditary ownership of land and freedom from taxation on the local princes of the newly converted Catholic Lithuanian nobles. Moldavia also became a fief of Poland. In the 1388 Act of Piotrków, King Władysław Jagiełło increased the civil rights of the nobility and clergy, further limiting the royal power in Poland. In 1400 the king assigned an important role in the conversion of Lithuania to Christianity to the University of Kraków, which in the 15th century attained a high standard of learning.

The union with Lithuania opened new political, economic, and cultural prospects for Poland. The territory of the Polish-Lithuanian state had an area three times larger than Poland had before the union. Making it the largest state in Europe with a population of about ten million, or twice that of England. The union also turned a homogenous nation into a multinational state; it changed Poland's orientation from West to East.

The tyrannical rule of the German monastic orders resulted in the founding of the "Salamander Society" or "Reptile Association" in 1397. It was a forerunner of the Prussian Union that would be organized for the overthrow of the rule of the Teutonic Order, and for the unification in freedom of Prussia with Poland. In 1401, in the Union Act of Wilno and Radom, the Lithuanian knighthood received the same civil rights as were enjoyed by Polish *szlachta*. Poland guaranteed the safety of Lithuania against aggression by the Armed Brethren of the Teutonic Order in 1409.

Victory and a New Union Act

The Great War against the Teutonic Order by Poland and Lithuania lasted two years (1409-1411). On June 30, 1410, a decisive victory in the battle of Tannenberg-Grunwald was won by the Polish and Lithuanian forces with the assistance of Czech Hussites and auxiliaries from Smoleńsk. The chief of the Teutonic Order, Eric von Jungingen, was killed on the battlefield.

A second victory on October 10, at Koronowo, led to peace negotiations. The terms of the Peace Treaty of Toruń included the return of the Dobrzyń province to Poland, the province of Żmudź to Lithuania, and payment to Poland in the amount of 6,000,000 groszes by the Teutonic Order. The victory transformed the Polish-Lithuanian union into a great power and put an end to the expansionist plans of the Teutonic Order and the Luxemburgers, the emperors of the Holy Roman Empire; it also stopped German aggression in the Baltic area.

The Union Act of Horodło (1413) was concluded by King Władysław Jagiełło, following the victory over the German Monastic State of the Teutonic Knights in 1410. It was a personal union of Poland and Lithuania in which the two were to remain separate states. The King established the territorial office of *wojewoda* (vo-ye-vo-da), or provincial governor, and initiated new administrative and defensive organizational models, which were followed in central and eastern Europe. Polish noble families extended the use and privileges of their coats of arms to the Lithuanian and Ruthenian nobility.

The frontiers of Western civilization were shifted considerably to the northeast, and Polish social and political institutions penetrated Lithuania, Belarus, and Kievian Ruthenia. New towns were founded and granted a wide measure of self-government. Considerable prosperity was achieved by Polish towns in the 14th and 15th centuries. Those that were members in the Hanseatic League shared in the profitable Baltic and Levantine trade.

The European balance of power changed as a result of Poland and Lithuania's union. Bohemia started to cooperate with Poland. Moldavia became a Polish Fief as the Turkish empire became a threat to Balkan Slavs and Byzantium. Thus, Poland had to reorient itself to the problems of the Lithuanian-Ruthenian Empire.

The License to Convert is Not a License to Kill

The military triumphs of the union of Poland and Lithuania were soon paralleled by successes in diplomacy. After their defeat by the Polish king, the armed monks of the Teutonic Order accused Poland of killing German missionaries and allying itself with pagans. These accusations

The Coat -of-Arms of Paulus Vladimiri-Paweł Włodkowic.

were to be investigated at the Council of Constance (1414-1418), one of the great diplomatic conferences of the Middle Ages. Paweł Włodkowicz, (Paulus Vladi miri) of Brudzewo, was the Polish Ambassador at the Council of Constance. It was there that he proposed the first seventeen basic theses of international law founded on justice and toleration. His proposal was based on natural law, the premise that the license to convert is not a license to kill or expropriate, and that only vo-luntary conversion is valid. He defined the principle of national self-determination, the international society, its functions, organs, and laws. He began to formulate these laws for use by an international tribunal, which he proposed. He justified only purely defensive wars. Włodkowicz advocated international mediation and arbitration, and an international tribunal for the peaceful solution of conflicts among nations. He argued that the Teutonic Order of armed monks lost its missionary character by committing mass murders and pillage. Therefore, in reality, the German Order constituted a "Prussian heresy." The Council of Constance accepted the arguments of the Polish Ambassador.

Establishment of Due Process and Royal Elections

In 1422, King Władysław Jagiełło issued the Act of Czerwińsk, which provided for a permanent ban against the confiscation of private property, known as the law *Nec Bona Recipiantur*. This act promised not to allow the confiscation of privately held property without a court sentence based on a written law; it also excluded officials of the crown from judgeships and made the refusal to answer a call to arms punishable by the confiscation of property. The Act of 1422 was the beginning of the formulation of due process under Polish law. In 1423 in the Statute of Warka, King Władysław Jagiełło extended the Act of Czerwinsk of 1422 to include burghers and free peasants; he also abolished the hereditary rights of bailiffs. King Władysław Jagiełło spread uniform civil rights to all provinces in the Act of Brześć of Kujawy (1425) in return for the recognition of the succession right of his sons to the Polish Crown

A fundamental law in the Act of Jedlno od 1430 was known as *Neminem captivabimus nisi iure victum.* It was a guarantee against illegal imprisonment equivalent to the English act of Habeas Corpus of 1679. King Władysław Jagiełło further strengthened the civil rights of the nobility and clergy in return for a promise to elect one of his sons as King of Poland and to incorporate the Grand Duchy of Lithuania into the Polish Commonwealth. The provincial government of Podolia was organized at Kamieniec Podolski.

In 1432, the Union Act of Grodno was concluded. The Grand Duke Zygmunt Kiejstutowicz was recognized as the ruler of Lithuania for life. After his death, Lithuania (including Belrus and Kievian Ruthenia) was to be incorporated into Poland.

King Władysław Jagiełło guaranteed the personal freedom of citizens under protection of the courts in the 1433 Act of Kraków; it was thus a reconfirmation of the protective law against illegal imprisonment.

The due legal process guaranteed the inviolability of citizen's person (who was not caught in the act of committing a crime). It was formulated for the first time in Europe in Poland in the acts of 1422-1433. Thus due process was the basis of the legal system in Poland when absolutism reigned in the rest of Europe. This legal development happened in Poland because the middle nobility, allied with the royal court, won the power struggle against huge land owners. The democracy of nobility was led by the middle nobility, which had acted as "the middle class" of the political nation of free citizens in the Polish Commonwealth. In the 1434 Act of Troki, the Grand Duke of Lithuania, included the gentry of Halicia (Galicia) and Podolia within Polish civil rights, thus further spreading due process under the law.

Defense of Christianity and the Prussian Union

King Władysław III (1424-1444) was crowned at the age of ten, and became King of Hungary six years later. The power of the Polish-Lithuanian union was reflected in the fact that the Hungarian and Czech crowns were offered to the King of Poland. Important political events faced the court of the young king.

An alliance of Poland and Hungary with Pope Eugenius IV against the Turkish Empire was signed. In 1440 the Act of Confederation of Prussian Nobility and Towns was concluded in protest against the yoke of the German Monastic State of the Teutonic Knights. Its purpose was the free incorporation of Prussia into the Polish Commonwealth. The confederation was known as the Prussian Union (it was later condemned by papal anathema, which was issued as a result of intrigues of the Armed Brethren of the Teutonic Order at the Vatican).

The Polish-Lithuanian Union was terminated (for six years) in 1440 by the Act of Wilno. It was a short-lived victory for the Lithuanian aristocracy which wanted to establish an oligarchy in Lithuania. At the same time, a personal union of Poland and Hungary (1440-1444) was again established under King Władysław III. The union was concluded in the face of the threat of the invasion by the Turkish Empire. King Władysław III

King Kazimierz IV Jagiellończyk
(1427-1492) (Jan Matejko).

won a brilliant victory over the Turks in Bulgaria, and signed a highly favorable truce. However, a year later, the Pope, fearful about the possibility of the fall of the Byzantine Empire pressed King Władysław III to break the truce. The Pope, anxious to consolidate the merger of Eastern and Western Christianity, urged an immediate attack on the Turks without proper preparation. Had King Władysław III succeeded - freed Constantinople and driven the Turks into Asia Minor - the union might have succeeded. Unfortunately, the King of Poland and Hungary was killed leading the Hungarian army and Polish knights into the battle of Varna (1444). The victorious Turks were now free to conquer Constantinople in 1453, solidify their rule over the Balkan Slavs, and became a threat to central Europe.

The Incorporation of Prussia

The interruption of the Union of Poland and Lithuania ended in 1446, when the Grand Duke of Lithuania was crowned as King of Poland Kazimierz IV Jagiellończyk (1427-1492), and issued the new Act of Wilno. In it he agreed to reign in Poland and Lithuania as two equal countries (in a "brotherly union") and to confirm the existing civil rights and due process under the law in both countries. In 1447, in the Act of Grodno, the king further insisted on enforcing Polish-type civil rights among the Lithuanian and Ruthenian nobility in order to limit the political power of Lithuanian aristocracy. In 1453 the King signed the Act of Confirmation of Jewish Liberties, first issued in 1264. One year later he proclaimed the Act of Incorporation of Prussia into the Polish Crown during a rebellion against the yoke of the German Monastic State of the Teutonic Knights. The insurrection broke out after failed tax negotiations between the brethren of the Teutonic Order and the Prussian Confederation of the knights and burghers of Prussia, at the time of growing prosperity in Poland.

The Thirteen Year's War fought by Poland against the Teutonic Order ended in 1466 with the treaty of Torun. Malbork along with the province of Warmia or Warmland became a part of Poland, while Królewiec or Koenigsberg became the new capital of the Polish Fief of Prussia. The Grand Master of the Teutonic Order was obligated to pay homage and taxes to the King of Poland. Ulryk Czerwonka, the Czech mercenary commander of the Malbork garrison, surrendered the main castle and capital of the Teutonic Order to Poland. In the Act of Gdansk (1457), King Kazimierz Jagiellończyk bestowed self-government and trading privileges on Gdańsk, Elbląg (Elbing), and Toruń - cities recently freed from domination by the German Monastic State of the Teutonic Knights (or German Armed Brethren). Lithuania was not involved in the Thirteen Year's War against German Armed Brethern.

Late Gothic Parish Church in Gasławice. Built in 1440.

THE FORMATION OF THE NATIONAL BICAMERAL PARLIAMENT (1454-1493)

The Indigenous Polish Democratic Process

An original Polish civilization was maturing in early modern Europe. The formation of the feudal republic of Polish nobility started in 1454 with the Act of Nieszawa, which some call the Magna Carta of the masses of Polish *szlachta* (nobility). King Kazimierz IV Jagiellończyk officially confirmed the legal power of each Seymik (sey-meek) or regional legislature in each district. The regional Seymiks had the power to approve every military mobilization, and the right to nominate four candidates for the local judiciary, of which one would be chosen by the king to fill a vacant post. Thus, the power of aristocracy was limited in favor of the middle and lower nobility. It also marked the transformation of unicameral regional legislature with an open attendance into an orderly system of representation in a national parliament. Thus, the maturity of representative form of government was achieved in Poland. Starting in 1468, representatives of the Seymiks, which constituted regional assemblies of the nobility (the *szlachta)*, met annually as one parliament, known as the Seym.

The indigenous Polish democratic process was based on Scymiks, or regional legislatures, where ordinary citizens had a dominant voice. The Seymiks themselves evolved from the prehistoric Slavic institution of *wiec* (vyets), which were the basis of Slavic military democracies and the organization of Slavic volunteer armies. In 740 A.D. these Slavic armies dominated central Europe from the frontiers of the Empire of Charles the Great in the west to Byzantium in the east (as illustrated on the first map at the beginning of this book).

Seymiks become platforms for political emancipation; a source of information about the affairs of state for the ordinary citizen; and created the means for mutual consultations through duly elected representatives equipped with a real and clear mandate. It was the beginning of the reshaping of the Polish monarchy into a republic of the nobility. By the 1630s, the Polish nobility would number one million citizens. Polish democratic processes would be successful as long as the lower and middle nobility won the power struggle against landed aristocracy.

Economic Expansion and Culture

In the middle of the 15th century, the population density of Poland was estimated at about 10 persons per square kilometer, or a total of about two-and-a-half to three million people. The three field system of field rotation was becoming generally used in Polish agriculture. (The peasants paid rent for the fields they cultivated.) From 1466 on, the Vistula River carried Polish grain export through Gdańsk. Thus grain was produced for new and expanding markets, while western Europe suffered an agrarian crisis. The cereal prices were high and the land became more valuable. New deposits of iron ore, copper, lead, zinc, sulphur, and rock salt were discovered and mined. Hundreds of towns were granted municipal charters. Money was in general use in trade involving manufactured goods and farm products. During the 14th and 15th centuries, trade and the use of money reached the highest level of activity during the feudal period in Poland. A large number of craft guilds were formed among leather and metal workers, covering all kinds of specialties.

The towns were surrounded with defense walls. The multi-story artillery bastion in Arabic style, the barbican, was built in front of St. Florian's Gate in Kraków at the end of the 15th century. It was the largest structure of its kind in Europe Gothic style prevailed in architecture. Monumental cathedrals, huge ecclesiastical buildings, and ornate town halls were built, as well as some of the largest fortified complexes in Europe. The city of Gdańsk was closely associated with the new burgher architecture exemplified by Antwerp in the Netherlands. Built in 1345-14987, St. Mary's Basilica in Gdańsk is the largest church in Poland.

Art works such as stained glass windows, murals, plaques, paintings, sculptures in stone and wood, gold jewelry, and textiles attained perfection in form and design. The monumental wooden altar of St.

Mary's Basilica in Kraków was produced in 1477-1485 in the Late Gothic style. Cardinal Zbigniew Oleśnicki founded the castle of Pinczów (1426-1454) built in a style which shows the transition from the Medieval into the Renaissance. Master Benedykt, a Pole, was the architect of the arcaded courtyard of the Collegium Maius, a university building in Kraków. The Volhynian school of Ruthenian mural painting flourished. The royal capital of Kraków became an important cultural and political center in Europe.

One of the oldest relics of Polish prose, known as *The Bible of Queen Zofia* (the fourth wife of the King Władysław Jagiełło), is the translation of the Old Testament into Polish *c.* 1455. Latin texts of statutes were translated into Polish. The first book on Polish orthography was published in 1440. Poetry was written in Polish. Secular music was written for one voice, and songs were composed in the vernacular. The song *Bogurodzica (The Mother of God)* was sung before battles with the Teutonic Order in 1410. Musical compositions of Mikołaj of Radom of the first half of the 15th century had high artistic value. Stanisław of Skalbmierz, a professor at the University of Kraków, developed an advanced doctrine of just war *de bellis iustis* in 1411.

A history of Poland was written in 1455-1480 by Jan Długosz (1415-1480). His work represented an outstanding example of European historical studies of the period. The twelve-volumes of Polish history up to 1480 are a monument to the early Polish Renaissance and the best Polish historical work before the 18th century. Among other historical works by Jan Długosz is *Banderia Prutenorum*. In it, he describes the German banners of the Teutonic Knights captured at the battle of Grunwald.

A documentary Polish poem describes the murder of the Castellan, Andrzej Tęczyński, in 1461 by rebellious townsmen of Kraków.

In 1473, the first printng and publishing firms were established in Kraków. The same year Nicolas Copernicus (1473-1543), the founder of modern astronomy, was born in Toruń. In 1475, the first Polish text was printed in Wrocław by Kasper Elyan. It included The Lord's Prayer, The Hail Mary, and The Creed in Polish. Polish printers also worked abroad. Jan Adam of Poland worked in Naples in 1478; and in 1492-1495, two Polish printers, Stanisław of Poland and Stefan Polak, worked in Seville.

Archbishop of Lwów, Grzegorz of Sanok (*c*.1406-1477), was the first prominent humanist writer in Poland. He wrote poetry in Polish and in Latin. He was a historian and a patron of literature. Many scholars found hospitality in his manor. Among his guests was Filippo Buonaccorsi, who described the life and works of his host as those of an ideal humanist.

In 1474 the wojewoda (governor) of Poznań and doctor of law, Jan Ostroróg (*c*.1436-1501), published a political program entitled *Pro Republicae Ordinatione* or On An Orderly Republic (or Commonwealth). In it the author defends the sovereignty of Poland against the power of the Pope; supports the right to appeal sentences of local Church courts; and advocates taxing the Church for the national defense, as well as the improvement of the civil rights of the burghers and peasants. He furthermore insists on the limitation of the power of aristocracy, and the strengthening of the alliance of the throne with the middle nobility.

By the end of the 15th century, national and regional parliaments became catalysts of social and cultural life in Poland - a role played in the rest of Europe by the royal court and the town. The Act of Kraków of 1485 regulated the standing of Jewish craftsmen in the guilds. The first Digest of Polish Law was printed in Kraków in 1488; it included a royal guarantee against searches and seizures. Approximately 15,000 different Polish words were used in these preserved medieval texts.

Social consciousness was strengthened by the expressions of

A Page of Polish State Records, the Metryka Koronna of 1463, with the Text of an International Peace Plan Similar to the United Nations.

Polish nationalism in Renaissance writings. In addition to works in the Latin alphabet, books were also printed in the Cyrillic alphabet, for the first time anywhere, in Kraków.

The Polish Commonwealth was a social and political union of many ethnic groups, among whom forty percent were Polish speakers. There was a broad support for the Polish State. Turkish and Tartar threats produced solidarity among all the ethnic groups of the Commonwealth, and the belief that the mission of Poland was to serve as a shield of Christianity.

An International Peace Plan of 1462

Polish State Records known as Metryka Koronna include a unique copy of a remarkable proposal for an international charter for peace, similar to that of the United Nations. It was co-sponsored by Poland, Hungary, and Bohemia, and was the earliest proposal for an international peace organization in Europe's history. The project was based to a considerable extent on the works of Paweł Włodkowicz (Paulus Vladimiri), Polish ambassador at Constance (1414-1418). The actual text was prepared at the Bohemian court of King Jiri of Podjebrady. It included a General Assembly ruled by a simple majority, and an international force controlled by its secretariat. It was to follow a procedure for an international judicial arbitration; it did away with the idea of a universal medieval empire and outlawed aggression (especially by the Muslim Turks and the "hornet's nest" of Crimean Tartars who staged yearly raids in the Ukraine in order to rob and kidnap people for ransom. Their activity turned the southern Ukraine into the "Wild Plains.")

The project was to create a new international authority in view of the declining power and the ineffectiveness of both the fragmented Holy Roman Empire and the Papacy. The peace project was a subject of negotiations between the European states for two years (1462-1464), but was ultimatelty wrecked by Papal opposition. King Jiri of Podjebrady of Bohemia named Polish Crown Prince Władysław as his successor. In 1471, the Czech legislature elected Władysław King of Bohemia. When Władysław became King of Hungary (in 1490), the Jagiellonian realm extended from the Baltic to the Black and Adriatic Seas.

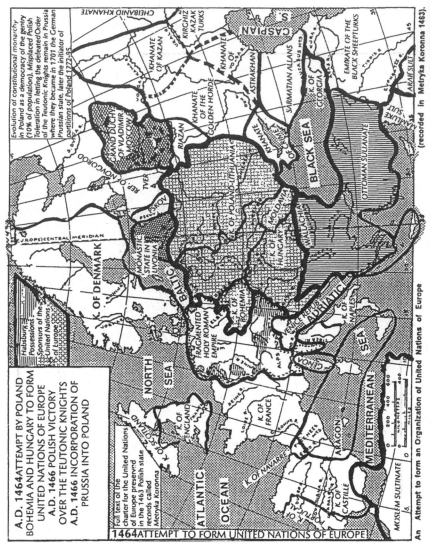

Incorporation of Prussia into Poland after the Polish Victory over
the Teutonic Knights; and an International Peace Plan.

54

A CONSTITUTIONAL MONARCHY IN EARLY MODERN EUROPE (1493-1569)

The Bicameral Parliament

During the reign of King Jan Olbracht (1459-1501), son of King Kazimierz IV, the Polish parliament became bicameral in 1493. Thus, the year 1493 marked the maturity of the Polish Constitutional Monarchy: the Bicameral National Parliament or the Seym Walny (seym val-ni). It defined itself as three estates: the king, the senate, consisting of bishops and dignitaries, and the lower house or the Seym proper. It was called the Izba Poselska (eez-ba po-sel-skah), or the Chamber of Deputies. It was presided over by a speaker called the Marshal, while the Senate was presided over by the King. It was an important step in the indigenous Polish development of the representative form of government, which would last uninterrupted for 300 years.

The year 1493 also marked the beginning of 160 years of successful parliamentary activity of the Seym. During this period a proverb was coined: *Polska nie rządem stoi ale cnotą*, meaning that the well being of Poland depends primarily on the virtue of its citizens. Each deputy to the Seym represented his own region and was theoretically obliged to veto legislative proposals that violated his mandate. When unanimity was not achieved, less important matters were postponed while more urgent matters were attended to by persuasion or by forming a confederation in which the majority ruled.

In Muscovy Russia, Ivan the Great consolidated his power by crushing the independent republic of Novgorod in 1476; and in 1480, by conducting mass deportation of 10,000 Novogrodians to the Urals. It was the maturity of Muscovy political engineering and the beginning of a 500-year tradition of empire building by coercion, deportations, and despotism. It would eventually become the foundation of a Russian colonialism that proved to be disastrous for Poland.

The Basic Polish Constitutional Law
In 1501, King Aleksander Jagiellończyk issued the Union Act of Mielnik. In doing so, he yielded to the aristocracy and assigned to the Senate the exclusive right to elect and control the king. If the king should try to establish a "tyrannical rule" in violation of the will of the Senate, he could be legally impeached; an election ordinance was also established in the Act of Mielnik. Vigorous action by the members of the Seym of Piotrków (1504) led to the abolishment of the Union Act of Mielnik. It was a victory of the middle nobility in its power struggle with the aristocracy. The Seym placed crown estates and properties under the partial control of the Chamber of Deputies. No person was to hold more than one office. The office of the grand hetman was defined as that of the defense minister and the administrator of the armed forces, who also was to serve as the head of the military court.

In 1505, the Constitution Seym of Radom passed the first Polish constitutional law called *Nihil Novi* or "nothing new about us, without us," meaning that nothing new would be decided in Poland without the concurrence of the Chamber of Deputies.

The Chamber of Deputies was composed of representatives of the provincial legislatures, or the regional or county diets known as the Seymiks. The new constitution prohibited the political nation of free citizens to occupy themselves with commerce and crafts under the penalty of loss of their civil rights.

The first constitutional law of 1505 made the Chamber of Deputies the supreme power in Poland. The kings, elected for life, became successive heads of state and chiefs of the executive branch of the Polish government.

Starting in 1507, the laws passed by the Seym were published in Latin at the end of each session under the title of Constitutions. (Polish would replace Latin in the Seym records beginning in 1545.)

Political Moves Leading to the First Prussian Homage
The Hohenzollerns of Berlin conspired with the Muscovites against Poland. However, the situation changed adversely for the Hohenzollerns when the Muscovy soldiers fared badly in war against Poland-Lithuania. Thus, starting in 1512, during the three-year long siege of Smoleńsk, they suffered ten thousand dead each season. Russia's bloodiest losses of 30,000

dead, including 1,500 boyars, occurred in the battle of Orsza on the upper Dnieper River in 1514. There, the Muscovy cavalry army of 80,000 fought 20,000 Polish regulars and 15,000 Lithuanians. Konstanty Ostrogski won the battle by skillfully using artillery and cavalry; for the first time, Husaria (later known as Polish winged knights) were used. Despite their defeat at Orsha; the Muscovite troops later took the city of Smoleńsk in 1514.

The King of Poland Sigismund I the Old, brother of King Aleksander I, met in Vienna in 1515 with Władysław II Jagiełło, the King of Bohemia and Hungary, and the Emperor Maximilian Hapsburg. The Hapsburgs received the guarantee to succeed to the Bohemian and Hungarian throne in case of the extinction of the Jagiellonian Dynasty, in exchange for Hapsburgs' acceptance of Poland's ownership of the Fief of Prussia. Also facing the loss of Muscovy support, Albrecht von Hohezollern, former Grand Master of the Teutonic Order and recent convert to Lutheranism - paid homage to the Catholic King of Poland out of the Polish Fief of Prussia in 1525.

In the same year, the Seym accepted the secularization of the Monastic State of the Teutonic Order and committed a political blunder by not evicting the remnants of the Teutonic Order from Prussia. A 116-year long series of homages to Poland paid out of the Fief of Prussia by the Hohenzollerns began; they delivered their payment kneeling before the Polish throne. Albrecht von Hohenzollern paid the first act of homage to Poland in the market of Kraków and recognized the control of the Polish king over Prussia; it was the first pact in Europe, torn by religious conflicts, between a Catholic king and a Protestant vassal duke.

The Copernican Revolution

The Polish Renaissance was the Golden Age of Poland. The arrival of the Renaissance coincided with the formal establishment of the parliament (the Seym) as the supreme power in the land.

Among the native leaders of that period was Nicolas Copernicus (1472-1543) - Mikołaj Kopernik (mee-ko-wahy ko-per-ńeek) - the father of the modern astronomy. His alma mater, the University of Kraków, had an excellent college of astronomy, then the best in Europe. There, Copernicus discovered the structure of the solar system and conceived his heliocentric

Copernican Universe
Sphere of immobile stars
Saturn 30 years orbit
Jupiter 12 years orbit
Mars 2 years orbit
Earth 1 year orbit
Venus 9 months orbit
Mercury 80 days orbit
Sun at the center

Signature:

Nicolaus Copernicus
Mikołaj Kopernik
(moo-ko-way ko-per-neck)
1473 1543

The Universe of Copernicus, 1543.

astronomical theory about 1504. The Copernican calendar was subsequently proven to be accurate within two minutes of the correct year's length - an amazing accuracy considering the condition of European science in early 16th century.

The Copernican heliocentric theory - the earth rotates daily on its axis and that the planets revolve in orbits around the sun - was circulated in *Commentariolus* (1510) and published in *De Revolutionibus Orbium Coelestium* (1543). While Luther and Calvin condemned this theory, the Catholic Church approved its development. After three years of studying Copernicus' text, it encouraged its publication as early as 1536. Eighty-six years later, however, the Church placed Copernican works on the index of forbidden books, where it would remain until 1828. (The Church's use of the Copernican calender, on the other hand, continued uninterrupted throughout this period.)

Copernicus, a true Renaissance man, served in many capacities. He was an administrator of Warmia on the Baltic in northern Poland, a military commander, and a finance minister; he was also a trained astronomer, mathematician, economist, lawyer, and medical doctor. Copernicus published the *Monetae Cudende Ratio* on the stabilization of currency in 1526. There he states the law of currency that "bad money drives the good money out of circulation," a law that was later named in England after Thomas Gresham. Copernicus then combated fraudulent schemes by the German House of Hohenzollerns, who were minting debased Polish currency and tampering with the Vistula River grain trade. Copernicus served on the legislative committee for the reform of Polish currency.

During the German siege of the Mazurian fortress of Olsztyn (1519-1521), while serving as a commanding officer, Copernicus successfully combated an epidemic by designing world's first epidemiological study.

After discovering that bread was the vector, he ordered that all loaves of bread be coated with butter at bakeries, so that foreign matter, accumulated during delivery, could be readily detected and discarded. The plague was subsequently checked. This event is known in the history of medicine as the inception of bread-buttering by Nicolas Copernicus.

Copernicus moved the leadership of western civilization's philosophical thought from the Mediterranean basin into the northern middle ground of Europe. The philosophical implications of the great Copernican discoveries were fundamental. The idea that the Earth is a stationary and flat central area in the universe, on which the human drama of personal salvation goes on without privacy under the eyes of God and His angels, was shaken irreparably. Eventually, it became apparent that life on earth is a thin surface-effect on a minor celestial body traveling through cosmic space at a high speed.

The age-old human yearning for safety and stability was destroyed by the realization that the Earth was neither immovable nor the largest celestial body, central in the cosmos. The Copernican universe brought home, as no other idea in the history of the human thought, the frightening realization that all of existence is in a permanent flux of ever-changing and ever-becoming.

In 1523 Erasmus of Rotterdam, impressed by Polish achievements, wrote the following passage: "I congratulate this nation ... which now, in sciences, jurisprudence, morals, and religion, and in all that separates us from barbarism, is so flourishing that it can rival the first and most glorious of nations."

Economic Notes

The export prices for Polish wheat were weakening as Muscovites subsidized their exports. This situation resulted in the 1520 passing of Statutes of Toruń and Bydgoszcz, which obligated the peasants to work one day a week without pay as a form of rent for the use of land. It was the beginning of the return of serfdom to Poland, and was soon accompanied by a drop in agricultural efficiency. The European price revolution reached Poland, bringing towns to the peak of their importance, while inflation grew to 300 percent and wages doubled over the next 100 years.

A further serious drop in grain prices resulted in 1543, due to the passage of the Act of the Seym that attached the serfs to the land and then denied their right to free themselves from servitude by cash payments. The serfs were proscribed to the land of their origin, which was a form of slavery.

The Act of Monetary Reform in Poland (1526) introduced a system based on the Polish unit złoty (zwo-ti), meaning golden coin. The Polish monetary system was adopted in Prussia in 1528 and in Lithuania in 1569. The same year, the Seym ratified the incorporation of Mazovia into Poland.

Standardization of Legal Procedures

The codification of the electoral functions of regional legislatures was accomplished; a joint artillery and military engineering command was established. In 1521, the Act of Seym approved a Code of Law for Prussia.

The Act of Seym of 1523 formulated the Formula Processus, a code that standardized legal procedures in the courts of law throughout the Polish Commonwealth. It was the earliest standardization of legal procedures in Europe (in France, for example, such a code was first instituted some 270 years later during the French Revolution). Roman letters replaced Gothic, thus making printing more readable. In 1524, an Act of Seym revised the instructions for tax collection; and one year later, it established courts for the mining industry.

Defeat at Mohacz, Hungary

The Polish Jagiellonian realm was diminished and suffered a serious decline in 1526. The battlefield death of Ludwik II Jagiełło (1506-1526), King of Hungary and Bohemia at Mohacz, was the second death of a Jagiellonian king in a battle against the Muslim Turkish Empire. This time the victor was Sulejman the Magnificent (c. 1496-1566), who expanded the Ottoman Empire to include in its territories the Hungarian capital Budapest, as well as Belgrade, Rhodes, Tabriz, Baghdad, Aden, and Algiers. Poland had to face the threat of Muslim invasion, while all of central Europe was thrown into turmoil.

In 1527, the reorganization of the Polish defense establishment was started by the Decree on Subordination of Hetman Polny, or the field commander, to the Grand Hetman (defense minister); separate appropriations for the artillery; and the mass production of gun barrels in in the foundries of Kraków, Lwów, and Wilno.

Poland Saves Jews from Extinction

Jewish immigrants, persecuted in the west, were permitted to continue to settle and prosper in all parts of Poland. They were allowed to elect their own elders and to administer to their own affairs. It was the rebirth of Jewish people in Polish Commonwealth. Thus, Poland saved Jews from extinction, while Polish parliamentary life flourished. The autonomy of the Jews was strengthened when the Jewish Supreme Tribunal was established in 1530 in Lublin. It had jurisdiction over the entire European Jewry. The Royal Decree (1549) gave the Jewish Autonomy the authority to assess and to collect their own poll tax, which was determined in bargaining sessions with officials of the Polish treasury. Maturity was reached by the autonomous Jewish legislative institutions in Poland. The *Congressus Judaicus* (1592-1764) in Lublin, was patterned after the Polish parliament. It was unique in the history of Jewish Diaspora. The 16th and 17th centuries were the period of spiritual hegemony of Polish Jews over world Jewry.

Portrait of a Rabbi.

Codification of Laws Based on a Public Debate

In 1532, a committee of the Seym was formed for the codification of all Polish common and written laws. It was the earliest such legislative project in Europe; the codification procedure was based on a public debate. Printed proposals were made by the National Seym and sent to every one of the regional legislatures for examination and evaluation. A written report from each Seymik was then sent back to the National Seym to be processed by the Law Codification Committee.

An act of the Seym prohibited the peasant serfs from moving without the consent of their landlord; prohibitions included the employment of runaway serfs and their citizenship in towns, and penalties for runaway serfs were specified. However, the runaway serfs were able to escape to join Ukrainian Cossacks. The possibility of the escape to Ukraine was a limiting factor in the exploitation of the peasant serfs. The status of free peasants, meawhile, remained unchanged.

The *"Respect for the Law"* - a political program known as the "execution-of-the-law" movement - was organized (1535-1538) for the strict execution of laws and for the reformation and modernization of the government. Related legislation was effective in producing manifold results: lords were forced to return illegally held crown lands; the holding of more than one office by one person was again prohibited; a closer union with Lithuania was encouraged; and the establishment of a national church was among the other proposals.

In 1537, a Protest Seym was in session during the mobilization for a war with Moldavia; demands were made there for adoption of the Respect of the Law Program by the King's government. An Act of the Seym (1538) ordered the sale of farming properties by the burghers, and passed taxes for the expenses of the war against Moldavia. In 1540 an act of the Seym revised electoral apportionment. Four years later, a Seym Act codified the ordinance for courts.

Banning of the Inquisition, the Incorporation of Livonia

The reign of the last Jagiellonian king was to bring the final shaping of the republican system of government in the Polish-Lithuanian Commonwealth. King Zygmunt August (1520-1572) was a Renaissance man and one of the founding fathers of the Polish Nobles' Republic.

In 1552, an Act of Seym suspended the execution of Church court sentences by county chiefs for a year; a resolution against heresy was also passed and the Holy Inquisition was banned from Poland in all its forms. There was no burning at the stake, and Poland was free from activities of the Inquisition. In 1553, an act of the Seym established the ordinance for the procedure of the Impeachment Tribunal by the Seym. The ecclesiastical jurisdiction was further constrained by the Act of the Seym (1556).

Two years later the Seym established the Post Office. In 1560, the Act of Gdańsk founded a privateer navy for the blockade of the Russian Narva River grain trade.

The Act of Wilno (1561) ratified the treaty with Livonia that made Kurland Poland's fief in exchange for protection against Russia and Ivan the Terrible. The secularization of the German Armed Brethren of the Sword, formerly a part of the Monastic State of the Teutonic Brethren (or Knights), followed. The incorporation of Livonia into the Polish Commonwealth was accomplished. It was a choice of the Livonian leadership to unite in freedom with Poland. The income of royal estates (demesnes) was earmarked for the defense.

Renaissance in Literature, Architecture, and Political Science

The first modern description of eastern Europe was published in 1517 by a professor at the University of Kraków, Maciej of Miechów (Miechowita,1457-1523), under the title *Tractatus de duabus Sarmatiis*. Miechowita was a historian, physician, and geographer. In 1519 he published the first printed history of Poland: *Chronica Polonorum* which dealt with events up to 1506. Its Polish translation was printed in 1535. The best known among Polish burgher writers was Biernat of Lublin (*c.* 1465-*c.*1530). His prayer book, *The Soul's Paradise*, was published in 1513. The first leading poet of the Polish Renaissance was Klemens Janicki (1516-1543). A peasant's son, he wrote patriotic political poems about Poland in Latin. After his death his poetry was translated into Polish (1563) and became very popular. Janicki gave the first truthful description of his own life in Polish poetry.

The Reformation in Poland was not primarily a spiritual movement. It was used to further the process of intellectual and political emancipation that had started long before. The masses of Polish nobility, which were so successful in limiting the power of the throne, were attracted to the ideas of Reformation. They broke the power of the Church. The Reformation helped to crystalize the absolute primacy of personal freedom in the Polish Commonwealth. Thus, neither the throne, nor the Church, could take precedence over the sacred right of citizens to personal liberty. Hetman Jan

Hetman Jan Tarnowski
(1488-1561).

Tarnowski said, "It is not a question of religion, it is a question of liberty." An excellent biography of Hetman Jan Tarnowski was written by a political writer, Stanisław Orzechowski.

In Calvinism, *szlachta* found the confirmation of its superiority over the crown, and its administration as Calvinism gave the leading position in Church matters to lay elders rather than to the reigning monarch. Polish nobles treated the Calvinist ministers as tools and never as equal partners in Church affairs. Lutheranism, on the other hand, because of its alien national character and its submission to the throne, did not appeal to Polish nobles. Lutheranism in Poland remained predominantly the religion of the burghers. The Reformation did not improve the situation of the peasants and very few of them adhered to the new creed.

City Hall in Poznań.

The Renaissance brought with it an interest in history, geography, and customs. It influenced the 1551 publication of the *Chronicle of the World* by Marcin Bielski (1495-1575), which became the first textbook of world history written in Polish. During the Renaissance and up to the Enlightenment, Kraków was the leading center of printing in Poland, both in quality and in quantity. Mikołaj Szarffenberg invented a portable "camp-printer" for publication of proclamations and mandates during the king's travel.

A political program, republican in nature and advanced for its time, was published in 1551 under the title of *Commentariorum De Re-publica Emendada* by Andrzej Frycz Modrzewski (1503-72)- called the father of Polish de-mocratic thought. Modrzewski 's work is composed of five books: On Customs, On Laws, On War, On the Church, and On Schools. In them he calls for the legal equality of all; for ending the oppression of the serfs and the inadequate laws that protected them; and an opposition to all wars and schemes of aggression Modrzewski advocated a strong central government, strictly controlled by laws; an efficient administration; and an independent court system to guarantee social justice. He also advocated a high quality education independent from the Church. He was one of the pioneers of European political science. (His works were translated into German, French, Spanish, and Russian.)

City Hall in Poznań.

The Fortress of Kamienic Podolski. Etching by Napoleon Orda.

Western Europe exerted the main cultural influence on Polish architecture. Renaissance architecture blossomed. Old buildings were embellished in the Renaissance style. Residences of the elite Polish nobility had a form derived from medieval castles. Eventually, the development of artillery brought predominance of magnate residences in the form of a palace surrounded by bastion fortifications. These palaces were often built by Italian architects.

In Poland, the royal castle of Kraków is the prototype of Renaissance architecture, as it was before with the Romanesque and Gothic styles. Sepulchral chambers on Wawel Hill were built in the Italian Renaissance style in 1502. Gothic structures, like the castle of Pieskowa Skała, were easily remodeled in the Renaissance style, which was soon followed by Mannerism and its delicate garden structures. The first ecclesiastical building in Poland based on the new architectural style in the age of humanism was the Sigismund Chapel (*Kaplica Zygmuntowska*) in the Wawel Cathedral. It was designed according to the "perfect temple" of Leon Battista Alberti (1404-1472). It won universal acclaim and influenced later sacral architecture in the country. Renaissance-Mannerist style blossomed in the architecture of town halls, town houses and fortified residences, castles, and manors.

Polish painters were influenced by Flemish realism. Jan Albert executed sacral paintings with landscape backgrounds in 1501-1506; Erasm Ciołek included an aerial perspective in 1515. A high quality guild book, the 1505 *Code of Behem* of Kraków, was illustrated with twenty-seven scenes from the lives of the guilds and burghers, painted with realism all in beautiful color. Stanisław Samostrzelnik - a monk, fresco and portrait painter, miniaturist, and illustrator - was an outstanding artist who worked in 1519-1541 in the Polish Mannerist style. Portrait of dignitaries and university professors were also painted in the second half of the 16th century. Marcin Kober from Wrocław painted a number of portraits of King Stephen Batory in 1563-1583.

The huge Sigismund Bell of Kraków is a masterpiece of Polish craft of the first half of the 16th century. It was made by Hans Beham in commemoration of the Polish-Lithuanian victory over Muscovy in 1514. Ornamental metalworks were also executed in this period including the beautiful Cock of the Kraków Marksmen's Fraternity. Polish kings commissioned a large collection of Arrases to be made in Brussels for the walls of the royal castle. Ornamental metalworks including coffins were made in this period in Gdańsk and in Nuremberg. Polish manufacturers produced elegant dress sashes of oriental design used as a part of the costume of Polish noblemen. Fine, richly decorated wooden altar-pieces were produced in southern Poland.

Polish Theater in the 16th Century

Early Polish theater had a form of mystery plays staged in the 15th century. On Jan. 12, 1578 in Jazdów, a very carefully prepared production of *Odprawa Posłów Greckich (The Dismissal of the Greek Envoys)* was staged by Jan Kochanowski in the presence of King Stephen Batory. It was a political play that forced the audience to make a personal judgement of the events shown on the stage - a novelty in Polish stage plays.

In 1580, Mikołaj of Wilkowiecko wrote the oldest dramatic text that still plays an important role in contemporary Polish theater. It contains numerous stage directions for actors, as well as description of the costumes. It was used on a Warsaw stage in the mid-20th century.

Jan Kochanowski, (1530-1584).

The satire of everyday life has a long tradition in Poland and it was the origin of Polish comedy. Satirical performances started with medieval jugglers, and were also used during lengthy interludes within mystery plays. Some humanist writers attempted to write comedies patterned after the Roman works. One such example is *Potrójny (Treble)*, written by Piotr Ciekliński and performed about 1595 at the castle of Stanisław Tarnowski against a background of painted scenery.

Western dramas with mythological themes were staged at the beginning of the 16th century by the students of the University of Kraków, under the direction of their professors. The first performances of the humanist theater staged at the royal court were in Latin, soon to be replaced by Polish. These plays were commissioned by rich burghers. The tickets were sold at a price equivalent to the value of twelve gees. At the same time, the secular popular theater flourished.

Music in 16th-Century Poland

Polish Renaissance music blossomed in the 16th century, with Kraków as its principal center. Polish composers wrote mainly polyphonic music for liturgical texts. Jan of Lublin compiled a *Book of Organ Music (c.* 1540), that evidences a high artistic level and a very varied musical repertoire in Poland at the time. In 1580, published psalms were composed by Mikołaj Gomółka to a text written by Jan Kochanowski. A long list of Polish composers who studied the theory of music at the University of Kraków is well documented in the university library, which has many handwritten treatises on music and their first printed editions. Music for the lute was widely played. It was composed for preludes, fantasias, dances, love songs, and other vocal pieces. Valentine Nakfark (1507-1576) was the best known lutanist at the royal court in Kraków. His compositions were printed in Lyons (1552), Paris (1564), Kraków (1565 and 1568), and Antwerp (1569). Among other well known composers were Wojciech Długoraj, and Jakub Polak (also known as Jacob de Reys). Secular music by anonymous artists dealt with historical themes and was composed to commemorate victorious battles, events at the royal court as well as to uplift the morale of the people.

The four string violin is mentioned in Polish records in the second half of the 15th century, some fifty years earlier than in Italian archives. Marcin Groblicz (c.1530-c.1610) apparently adopted the acoustic box of 15th-century Italian seven-string *lira da braccio* to the Polish four-string gęśle and made one of the first violins in Kraków. He made a new type of head with four pegs for the instrument. The head itself was

The head of the first violin in Kraków by Marcin Groblicz.

sculptured in shape of a lion head. Today, Grblicz's violins sell for more than $50,000.

Jesuits and Polish Rationalists

During the 16th century, fine arts and learning flourished in Poland. Poles were widely recognized for their advancement in legislation, religious tolerance, science, and their contribution to European culture. The University of Królewiec (Koenigsberg) was founded by an act of King Zygmunt August in 1544. It played an important role in the Polish and German culture.

Twenty years after the Copernican revolution, the rationalist philosophy was founded in Poland in 1562. It was spread by Polish Brethren also called Arians, Anti-Trinitarians, or Socinians. They were pacifists opposed to all forms of serfdom, to the possession of wealth, and to the use of money, as well as to the tenure of any civic office. The Polish Brethren contributed to the rise of educational and cultural level in Poland. Their largest educational center in Raków had an attendance of 1,000 students per year. Their literature also reached a high standard. The Church responded by bringing the Jesuits to Poland in 1564, and by using the political argument that the multinational commonwealth needed the Church to unite it. Jesuits equated Catholicism with Polish reasons of state and the interests of the political nation of the nobility.

The Popularization of Printing in Poland

Printing was done on a large scale, which fact helped the gradual Polonization of the leadership communities of Lithuania, Latvia, Belarus, and Ukraine. Polish continued to be the language of civility, elegance, and diplomacy in Slavic Europe. The number of schools increased. New academies and universities were founded. Progress was made in geography and cartography. A map of Poland was prepared by Bernard Wapowski in 1526 using the scale of 1:1,000,000. It was printed under the title of *Map of Sarmatia* because it was fashionable during the Renaissance to use Roman geographic names. Wacław Grodecki (Grodecius) published a map of Poland in 1558; it was included in the *Atlas of Ortelius* of 1570. Two important works for the propagation of the knowledge of Poland abroad were written by Marcin Kromer (1512-1589). The first, published in Latin in 1555, was entitled *De origine et rebus gestis Polonorum*. It was an adaptation of the works of Długosz,

Miechowita, and Wapowski. The second was an encyclopedia published in Latin in 1577, containing information about the Polish form of government, army, clergy, villagers, townsmen, customs, climate, flora, fauna, and natural resources. It was reprinted many times in the West and translated into German and Spanish.

Jan Mączyński published the first extensive Latin-Polish dictionary *Lexico Latino-Polonorum* in 1564. A pioneer of cardiology, a professor of medicine and philosophy, Józef Struś (1510-1568) published a 1555 treatise on the pulse entitled *Sphygmicae artis libri quinque.* In 1583, Andrzej Patrycy Nidecki edited and published the partially preserved writings of Cicero. His *Fragmentorum M. Tulli Ciceronis* was very popular among European humanists.

Printing houses were also opened in provincial areas. Polish orthography was standardized chiefly by printers who helped the development of the Polish language by encouraging the publication of Polish books and dictionaries. A Polish grammar book for foreigners was printed in 1568 by Piotr Stratotius-Stojeński; his book was in French. During the first one hundred years of Polish printing some three-and-half million books were printed. By 1550, printers in Kraków had reached the highest European level.

Widespread polemics on the religious questions often resounded throughout Europe. Protestants contributed to the wider use of the Polish language. Mikołaj Rey, called the father of literature in the Polish language, first wrote moralizing dialogues published in 1543. In them he criticized overspending, luxury, and drunkenness. He wrote the best 16th-century Polish satire and gave an excellent picture of everyday life in Poland. His *Life of an Honorable Man* gave a

Mikołaj Rej (Rey) z Nagłowic (1505-1569).

vivid picture of the customs of Polish country squires.

The level of financial sophistication in Poland *c*.1540 is evidenced by an engraving entitled "The Lament Over The Death of Credit." It also shows a letter of credit and a traveler's check, as well as the clothing used in 16th-century Poland. Polish culture was greatly influenced by humanism, the Reformation, and the republican movement of the masses of Polish nobility, which contributed to the rapid development of political prose.

The Flowering of Polish Literature.

Polish literature was flowering. Some of the greatest poetry of all times was created by Jan Kochanowski (1530-1584). He was the first to use a sophisticated and artistically perfect language. He reached lyrical perfection in a collection of 300 poems of various length. He wrote on political subjects suited to the times.

Prose was written in beautiful Polish by Łukasz Górnicki (1527-1603). In 1566, he published *Dworzanin Polski (The Polish Courtier),* an adaptation of an Italian work by Baldassare Castiglione, *Il Cortegiano* (1528). Górnicki also wrote a critical political dialogue, *Rozmowa Polaka z Włochem (A Dialogue between a Pole and an Italian).* In it he criticizes the notion of Polish "Golden Freedom."

Polish was made into a medium of refined literary expression. Its writers also contributed to reforms in orthography. Republican political writings in Latin continued. However, starting in the middle of the 16th century, Polish displaced Latin in public life. The majority of sermons were delivered in Polish; religious polemic was conducted in Polish; and Polish Protestants used Polish in their schools to a much greater extent than did the Catholics.

In 1568, Wawrzyniec Goślicki (1530-1607) published *De Optimo Senatore,* a program for a Polish republican system based on a pluralistic society with perfect equilibrium between power and liberty. He defined the responsibility of the King as a head of state and a chief executive officer. He wrote about people's right to the pursuit of happiness. His work was translated and published three times in England starting in 1568. Its English title was *"The Counselor Exactly*

Portraited."   Each printing was summaily banned and confiscated; William Shakespeare gave the name of *Polonius* (a Pole in Latin) to the chief counsellor of Hamlet, a man who tried very ineptly to follow Goślicki's program. One hundred and fifty years later, *The Counselor* was highly praised by Sir Robert Walpole.

Calvinism kept spreading among the nobles, and Lutheranism among burghers. The perfecting of Latin poetry continued as a long tradition in Poland. Plebeian humanist comedy about soldiers, beggars, etc. was popular because of its humorous, lively, and natural language.

Prosperity and "The Sarmatian Roots"

A unifying "low brow" Sarmatian myth explained that the noble citizens of the Polish Commonwealth descended from the Sarmatians, the legendary invaders of Slavic lands in antiquity. Roman maps, fashionable during the Renaissance, had the name of *Sarmatia* written over most of the territory of the Polish-Lithuanian Commonwealth and thus "justified" interest in "Sarmatian roots."

In the 16th century, Sarmatism was visible primarily in manners and taste. The Sarmatian myth of the "noble warriors" was much more familiar to Polish nobility than were western European traditions of chivalry such as vassalage, homage, service, and humility. Sarmatism eventually became a form of culture typically Polish. It radiated in the entire area of East and Central Europe from the Baltic to the Black Sea and to the North Balkans. Gradually it became not only an all-embracing ideology but the essence of the Polish culture. Polish lifestyle was becoming extravagant. Horses were symbol of the Polish warrior tradition. Fine horses dressed in beautiful trappings were a status symbol in Poland, as well as ornate weapons and expensive clothing influenced by eastern fashions and suitable for the cold Polish winters.

The rediscovery of ancient Rome and its cultural and political legacy fascinated the Poles who noticed the similarity of their own institutions to those of the ancient republic. Polish political and scientific vocabulary included many Latin terms. The masses of Polish nobles thought of themselves as heirs of the Roman civilization. Everyday Polish language became full of Latin expressions.

Poles benefitted from rising cost of Polish agricultural products, which went up more than three hundred percent during the 16ᵗʰ century. Increasing numbers of Poles studied in western European universities and brought back new ideas. Intellectual life was enriched. There was a flowering of music and the arts. Polish editions of classics of European literature introduced western culture to the eastern Slavs who were outside the influence of Latin Christianity.

Legislative Activity and an Offer of Emancipation

In 1562, the Act of Seym made the Respect for the Law Program into a law. Consequently, all the lands illegally held since 1504 were returned to the state; the gentry was exempted from the jurisdiction of Church courts; and the execution of sentences of the bishop's court by territorial officers was prohibited.

Laws passed in 1563 defined the control of town administration and prices charged by territorial officers of the government; separated the defense treasury from the royal treasury; and compelled the Church and peasantry to pay the land tax and to contribute to the costs of national defense.

A major political blunder was committed by the King of Poland when he granted, by an executive decision, the right of succession in Prussia to the Brandenburgian branch of the Hohenzollerns. It was done in return for promises of support in the war against Muscovy It was one of the most unfortunate executive decisions in Polish history, as the Hohenzollerns of Berlin eventually initiated the crime of partitions and the destruction of Poland.

The Seym passed an act in 1565 on the codification of commerce regulations. It exempted the gentry from custom duties, terminated the towns' privileges to store goods, and prohibited the free export of goods from Poland by local merchants; while no limitation on imports was enforced. This was exactly contrary to the prevailing European policy of mercantilism, under which exports were encouraged and custom duties were imposed on imports. The large land owners who also owned private towns were in conflict with burghers and operated their business in alliance with Jewish financiers, who benefitted from the sale of imports, alcoholic beverages, land leases, etc. The landowners had a monopoly on alcohol production and marketed vodka through Jewish agents (who, in turn, were accused of encouraging drunkenness).

In 1568, the Act of Gdańsk was passed. It founded the Maritime Commission under the authority of the central government. It was to control maritime commerce, shipbuilding, coastal defenses and enforce the maritime blockade of Russia. Soon, the first Polish warship was launched.

A royal decree on

Chancellor Jan Zamoyski, (1542-1605).

the incorporation of Ukraine into Poland was confirmed in 1569 by the Act of the Seym, convened in Lublin. (Ukraine was previously a part of the Grand Duchy of Lithuania.) The admission of Prussian senators and deputies into Polish parliament was accompanied by an offer of emancipation to the Armenian, Moslem, and Jewish minorities without obligation to convert to Western Christianity; the offer was accepted by the Armenians and Moslems.

The offer of emancipation was rejected by the Jews, however, who were satisfied with an autonomy governed by Talmudic Law. The Jewish population preferred to continue to speak Yiddish and to preserve its separate Judeo-Germanic subculture based on Yiddish language and Jewish ethnic and religious tradition. Thus, modern Jewish legal, governmental, and educational system - as well as philosophical concepts and religious beliefs - evolved in Poland between the sixteenth and eighteenth centuries. Any Jew who chose to convert to Catholicism was free to join the noble estate of the *szlachta* (shlahkh-tah). The 16th century brought the final Polonization of the urban population of the Polish Commonwealth including immigrants from Germany, Armenia, Scotland, and other countries.

The political nation of *szlachta* included, besides the ethnic Poles of all denominations, ethnic Lithuanians, Ukrainians, and Belarussians, as well as Prussian and Baltic gentry of German descent. Frenchmen, Scotts, Swedes, Muslim Tartars, Armenians, and other foreigners were often granted the status of nobility as well, usually for military merit.

Disputation of Cardinal Hosjusz with Protestants, 16th - cent. etching.

THE FIRST POLISH REPUBLIC

(Late Renaissance Period)

Modern Ideas in 16th-Century Poland

The founding of the formal Polish Nobles' Republic took place in 1569 at the conclusion of the Union of Lublin. It was viewed as a necessary development in view of the approaching end of the heirless Jagiellonian Dynasty. The new republic was called Rzeczpospolita (zhech-pos-po-lee-tah), though it is now often referred to as the First Polish Republic (1569-1795).

The ideas introduced in the middle ground of Europe in the 16th century by citizens of the Polish Republic were modern even by the standards of the 20th century. They are fundamental to contemporary political theory:

*general elections by all citizens
*social contract between government and the citizens
*the principle of government by consent
*personal freedom
*individual civil rights
*freedom of religion
*the value of self-reliance
*the prevention of the growth of authoritarian power of the state
*the prevention of rule by any form of oligarchy

Making One out of Two States

The Union Act by the Seym of Lublin (1569) formally made Poland and Lithuania one country, which was to elect one head of state and chief executive with the title of the king crowned in Kraków. The supreme political power was to reside in one national parliament, the Seym Walny, meeting in Warsaw. The united country was to have one currency and one foreign policy; Poles, Ruthenians, and Lithuanians were to be free to settle anywhere in the Republic. However, identical but separate territorial offices, treasuries, and armies would remain. On July

1, 1569, the formal proclamation of the Union Act was made by the King Zygmunt August Jagiellończyk. The conclusion of the union represented a unique act on the European scene. It resulted in peaceful and voluntary federation, which made one out of two separate states. The role of the Seym's became that of a "guardian of freedom," supervising the actions of the King who was to be elected to serve as the chief executive of the Republic. The Seym was made up of three estates: the deputies representing the masses of the nobility and the major towns, the senate composed of the senators ex-officio, and the elected king.

Reaction of Ivan the Terrible

Muscovy Tsar Ivan IV "The Terrible" earned his nickname because of his reaction to the news of the founding of the Republic of Poland-Lithuania. In 1569 in Novgorod, the most civilized city in Russia, he ordered the torture of suspected sympathizers of the Polish Republic, and then systematically had them killed daily in batches of 500 to 1,000 men for five weeks. Ivan's atrocities also engulfed hundreds of Moscovites for the same reason. In one of his rages, he tortured and killed his own son. Ivan IV created his own terror apparatus out of a force of his own bodyguards. In the tradition of the Mongol Empire, he enforced the principle that all forms of property within his domain belonged to him, and therefore that any of it could be used unconditionally on state service. Even though the Muscovy Tsar Ivan IV was defeated by Poland in the war over Livonia, he was a candidate in the general elections for the King of Poland-Lithuania in 1573. No one in Poland took his candidacy seriously.

Religious Freedom, General Elections, the Social Contract

In the atmosphere of religious toleration, a Protestant Church of Poland was founded by Lutherans, Calvinists, and Czech Husite Brethern in 1570 in Sandomierz. However, the Anti-Trinitarians or Arians were excluded because of their rejection of the Holy Trinity. They published an anti-Trinitarian translation of the Bible in Polish called the *Bible of Nieświerz*.

While the Senate was to call for the Convocation Seym to

conduct the elections, emergency (hooded) Courts were founded in 1572 to maintain law and order during preparation of the elections.

The Convocation of Seym in Warsaw passed the constitutional amendment that established general elections called *viritim,* the first in Europe. Every member of the political nation of nearly one million citizens had the right not only to choose his head of state, but also to offer himself as a candidate for the crown. The title of a king was preserved, while the king's official function was that of a lifelong head of state and chief executive of the Polish Nobles' Republic.

The Primate Bishop of Poland was appointed as a temporary head of state for the period between the death of an elective king and the election of the next. The bishop was to call for the new session of the parliament; to preside over the Senate; to establish the candidates approved by the Seym for the next royal election; to name the king elect; and to perform the act of coronation. The formal public statement naming the King Elect was made by the Grand Marshal of the Crown. Warsaw was to be the election site, where each member of the political nation of free citizens could cast his vote. Elections were to be decided by a simple majority. The Social Contract between the royal candidates and the electorate was formulated in the Articles of Agreement,

Manor in Poddębice
(built in 1610-1617).

which was accompanied by the Articles of Impeachment. A "watchdog" senatorial committee was also confirmed. The General Election Law was accompanied by judicial reform. Elected judges were independent of the executive branch. Courts of Appeal were also established.

Foreign Candidates for the Polish Throne

The parliamentary motion of Chancellor Jan Zamoyski (1542-1605) to limit general elections to the native citizens of the Polish Commonwealth was, unfortunately, tabled and never acted upon. The acceptance of foreign candidates for the Polish throne eventually proved to be disastrous for the Polish-Lithuanian State. The Polish Commonwealth was the largest territory in Western Christianity. It faced the rest of Europe with the possibility of a sudden switch in military alliances, depending on the unpredictable outcome of Polish general elections. This possibility generated anxiety in some of the major powers of Europe. They feared an adverse change in the European balance of power. Soon government lawyers in such capitals as Berlin, Vienna, St. Petersburg, etc. had to become experts in Polish constitutional law in order to organize effective (and expensive) campaigns in Polish elections. This caused a penetration of the open government of Poland by foreign- financed subversion and corruption, and eventually led to the destruction of the First Polish Republic. The admission of foreign candidates legalized foreign contributions to their election expenses. This also had a demoralizing effect on those Polish citizens who wanted to run for an office, but who did not have enough money for the election campaign. Naturally some looked to foreigners for campaign contributions, which were given in exchange for support of the interest of foreign powers. (When the Founding Fathers restricted the office of the president to people born in United States they did not repeat the same mistake in America - perhaps because of the familiarity of some of them with the experience of the Polish Nobles' Republic. Poland, by the time they were writing the American constitution, was treacherously assaulted and dismembered by the greedy absolute monarchies that surrounded it.)

"The Republic of Good Will, Equals with Equal"

The transformation of the Polish-Lithuanian Commonwealth into a formal republic by the Union of Lublin was characterized as bringing *"The Republic of Good Will ... Free Men with Free. Equals with Equal ... ."* There was a pride in Polish citizenship throughout the new Republic among its political nation of free citizens (which soon would number one million people). After the incorporation of Lithuania, the republic had 815 sq. km and a population of 7.5 million in 1569.

The Seym was elected on a two year schedule. A law was passed abolishing nobility titles and giving equal rights to all the nobles, including the large number of citizen-soldiers who lived in fortified villages called *"zaścianki"* (zah-śhćhahn-kee). Throughout the huge territory of Poland-Lithuania, every Polish noble, no matter how small his holdings, was proclaimed equal to a provincial governor.

Among the founding fathers of the Polish Nobles' Republic was Jan Zamoyski (1542-1605), who served as the chancellor of Poland until 1578, as well as a defense minister (Grand Hetman). He was one of the most important and talented political leaders of Polish Renaissance. In 1595, he founded the famous Academy of Zamość.

Poland created a unique civilization, which was in many respects more advanced than medieval and early modern Europe. It became a major center of development of civil liberties and a pioneer of the representative form of government. The Polish Republic was by far more republican both in structure and in spirit than the constitutional monarchies of England and Sweden. She was the very opposite of the absolutist systems of Russia, France, Austria, and Spain.

The Toleration Act

During the Reformation, Poland was a "haven for heretics." The principle that no one could be persecuted for his religious belief had always been recognized in Poland as a basic civil right. It became a law when the Toleration Act of Warsaw was passed in 1573 by the Seym. The article on religious toleration represented an important element in the Polish political culture of the period. It was based on the belief that an honest agreement and mutual respect were fundamental for successful political action. The Seym continued to be the main forum for political dialogue in the Polish Republic. This dialogue included the confrontation of views between Catholics and Protestants. Unlike in western Europe, the law in Poland did not allow the landlords to force their own religion on their serfs. In this spirit, Polish diplomacy secured the Postulata Polonica, or concessions in favor of Protestants persecuted in France.

A New Republican Era and the Social Contract of 1573

Upon the death of King Zygmunt August in 1572, the Jagiellonian Dynasty came to an end. The 1573 election of Henryk de Valois, Duke of Anjou (1551-1598), as the king, head of state, and chief executive of the Republic started a new republican era. Under oath, he swore to uphold the Social Contract composed of the *Pacta Conventa* and *Henrician Articles,* guaranteeing the preservation and enforcement of the Polish Bill of Rights and Constitution. It was the first formal conclusion of a comprehensive Social Contract in Europe. The terms of the Social Contract were as follows: calling parliament into session every two years; maintaining a continuous supervisory council of sixteen senators as a "watchdog" commission over government activities; declaring of war only after approval by the Senate; and new taxation and mobilization for war only after approval by the Chamber of Deputies.

In case of a breach of the Social Contract by the king, the Impeachment Procedures were to be started with the release from civil obedience (*de non prestanda obediencia)* of the political nation of free citizens. Another part of the Social Contract called *Pacta Conventa* included specific agreements with each king elect; in the case of Henry de Valois these included an "eternal alliance with France," construction of the Polish navy on the Baltic, and payment of the debts of the previous administration. However, Henry de Valois secretly departed for Paris in 1574 to succeed the deceased King of France, Charles IX. Henri de Valois became Henri III, King of France (1574-1589), the last of house of the Valois Dynasty.

Elections and the Winged Cavalry

The general elections of 1575 were the first in Europe. King Stefan Batory (1522-86) of Transylvania was elected as the head of state and chief executive of the Polish Nobles' Republic. The Seym's ratification of the royal election was followed in 1576 by the act of renewal of the rights and laws of the Jews. The victory of counter-reformation in Poland was secured by the Catholic clergy's acceptance of the limitation of each priest's income to one source.

During Batory's reign, Polish *Husaria* (see cover) replaced heavily armed medieval mounted spear-men. The Poles adopted light laminated armor with an opened helmet, wings in the oriental style and decorations of the furs of tigers, leopards, and wolfs. Polish lances were up to sixteen foot long, hollow inside for lightness, and designed to be crushed upon impact. The lances were provided by the government in order to control their quality and length. The sabers were owned by each cavalryman and especially fitted to each owner's hand. The 17th-century Polish saber became the European and American standard until the Second World War.

Poles developed very successful cavalry tactics. Polish hussars attacked in full gallop moving up to 30 m.p.h. and, upon driving home the iron head of their spears, they immediately discarded the snapped shafts of their lances and continued the attack with sabers, estocs (koncerz or large thrusting sword up to five foot long), war hammers, and pistols. *Husaria* approached the enemy formation on a wide-spread arched front in order to minimize the effects of the gunfire, then immediately before impact they formed tight formation, "knee to knee." The crushing blow by the concentrated weight of horses, men, and weapons was devastating on the battle field to all European military formations including Swedes, Muscovites, Turks, and Tartars.

A rebellion in Gdańsk was put down by hetman Jan Zborowski in 1577, and a penalty of 200,000 zlotys was collected from the city. The same year, an Act of Seym created the peasant elite infantry, one man was selected per 823 acres. It was known as *Piechota Wybraniecka* (pye-kho-ta vi-bra-ńets-ka) and soon became renowned for its patriotism.

The Independent Judicial System

The Supreme Court of Appeals created by the Seym was independent from the executive branch of the government. Its freely-elected judges pronounced final decisions in civil and criminal cases previously tried in lower courts -- a unique development in generally absolutist Europe where a king was the supreme judge, whose authority could not be challenged. The act also served as an important step in the division of power in Poland into legislative, executive, and an independent judiciary powers. (This development in Poland preceded similar proposals in France and in the United States by 200 years.) The territorial branches of the Supreme Court of Appeals were established by the Seym in 1581. Lithuania's branch held sittings, at first in Nowogródek and Mińsk, and then in Wilno and Grodno. An additional branch of the Supreme Court of Appeals for Prussia was created in 1585. It was known as the Supreme Tribunal of Civil Law of Prussia.

The supreme parliamentary court of the Seym was convened for dealing with high treason. It was punishable by the deprivation of civil rights and honor, as well as exile from Poland. The new Jesuit University in Wilno helped train the needed lawyers.

The Last Years of the Golden Age

A Muscovy aggression against the Polish Fief of Inflanty (Latvia) was defeated by Poland with three Polish invasions of Russia - all under the leadership of the King Stefan Batory. After the loss of 300,000 soldiers from 1579 to 1581, Ivan the Terrible sued for peace. A ten year truce, favorable to Poland, was signed at Jam Zapolski. Unfortunately, King Batory's death marked the end of Poland's Golden Age in politics and at war. The era in which the influence of the of Polish middle nobility prevailed and produced striking cultural achievements was now drawing to a close.

Poland was, in every respect, far ahead of northern and eastern Europe and equaled the West not only in economic development and political power but also in scholarship, arts, and literature. The West simultaneously broadened its horizon by discovery of the New World and of Poland, a powerful and cultural country which contributed to European science with the splendid discoveries of Copernicus. Polish writers were among the leading European political ideologists. Jan Kochanowski (1530-1584), the greatest poet of the Polish Renaissance, is considered equal to Pierre de Ronsard, the father of lyric poetry in France. Kochanowski is recognized to be as good as the best poets of the Elizabethan period in England. Poland, the largest territory in the Western Christianity, was perceived as a powerful and cultured country, impressive in its wealth and size.

Adversities Brought by the Third General Elections

The next General Election in Warsaw was won in 1587 by King Zygmunt III Vasa (1566-1632), the Swedish candidate. He was sponsored by Chancellor Jan Zamoyski, who at first advocated election of a native Pole, but then supported the nephew of the last Jagiellonian king with the vain hope that a union with Sweden would be a voluntary one for peaceful cooperation and security. Instead Poland became entangled in the wars of Swedish succession. In fact, Poland became exposed to hit, rob, and run invasions by the Swedish opponents of the Polish Vasas. The Swedes could do extensive damage to Poland without exposing their own country to similar devastation. During the elections, the Church gave secret support to the Habsburgs, and successfully opposed Zamoyski's plans for the elimination of the Habsburgs as future candidates for the Polish throne in favor of native Poles or Slavs. Chancellor Zamoyski foresaw that an unrestricted access of foreign candidates would legalize foreign campaign contributions and turn the general elections into a vehicle of foreign subversion and corruption of the Polish Nobles' Republic. Ironically, the Chancellor fostered the very problems he was warning against.

The New Law of Seniority

Polish laws did not restrict the size of land ownership; though, the traditional Slavic custom of dividing the inheritance equally among all children resulted in the majority of landed property being of small or medium size. The nobles who owned these plots represented the equivalent of the modern "middle class" in the parliament. During the

Golden Age of Poland in the 16th century, this relatively moderate "middle class" was in control of Polish politics. There was a feeling of stability and security that upward mobility was encouraged in the Polish society.

A major blow to this state of affairs occurred when the political machines of land magnates succeeded in passing the Law of Entails, or the seniority succession law, in 1589. The Seym passed it under the excuse that it was needed to prevent disintegration of large estates that were to be inherited in full by the senior male; the Law of Entail was truly meant to preserve economic strength and military potential of the holdings of huge landowners, who unfortunately had the potential of turning the republic into an oligarchy. Fortress repair, the upkeep of garrisons, the winter quartering of troops, and the maintenance of a fixed quota of regiments in time of war were among the legal obligation of such landowners.

The dynamic growth of new land potentates was accompanied by the transformation of former knights who owned land into gentlemen-farmers who prospered on the grain trade. The new law weakened the stabilizing effects of Polish law of succession, according to which the family property was divided among sons and daughters alike. The new law did not provide safeguards against eventual damage to the democratic process by the political machines of huge land owners who, at times, accumulated more land than all of Great Britain, Belgium, Holland, or Ireland. While the 1510 Act of Seym prohibited bequests of property to the Church in last wills and testaments in order to limit the political and economical power of the clergy, no similar law was passed to limit the size of estates of land magnates. Political threats to the Polish democratic process by the political machines of huge estates, later known as latifundia, seriously increased with the passage of the Law of Entail. The new law helped to make the 17th century the "Golden Age" of land magnates.

In the meantime, democracy was practiced. The Representatives returning from a session of the National Seym were obligated to attend "report-back" meetings in their regional legislation in order to give their formal report on the achievements of the national parliament. The same sessions observed by the public, also served to shape opinions on current affairs in every constituency.

The Union of the Greek and Catholic Churches

The Synod of Brest of 1595-1596 created a union of the Catholic and Greek Churches. The Greek Uniates adhered to the Eastern rite and discipline but submitted to papal authority. Creation of the Uniate Church was an attempt to heal the schism, and bring equality to the Orthodox citizens of the Republic; but instead, it produced bitter controversy between Uniates and Dis-Uniates. However, it tied the Ukrainian people more closely to western civilization and the Polish political tradition based on the opposition to all forms of autocracy. The Union also gave roots to Ukrainian nationalism under the leadership of the Uniate clergy. Sustained and bitter railing and condemnation by the Moscow Patriarchate (created in 1586) soon resulted in violence. Ethnic cleansing in Ukraine resulted in the murders of some 200,000 Catholic and Jews in 1648. These atrocities were repeated on the same scale in 1768-72 during the Koliszczyzna uprising. (More recently, in 1942 in Volhynia, under the German occupation, the Uniate Fascists allied with the Nazis murdered about 100,000 unarmed Polish civilians in Volhynia.)

Political and Military Developments

In 1596, after King Zygmunt III, moved the capital of Poland from Krakòw to Warsaw, the Seym reformed the State Treasury and established a separate Royal Treasury for the upkeep of the royal court in Warsaw.

The war theater stayed busy. Vasa succession struggles brought a Swedish invasion of the Polish Fief of Inflanty (in Latvia) in 1600. The Poles invaded Valachia (Romania) in order to strengthen the southern border and establish a Polish fief there in competition with the Turkish Muslim Empire. The Seym passed taxes for the war with Sweden in 1601. Polish victories over Sweden occurred at Kochenhausen, and then at Biały Kamień in 1604. The following year, a Polish victory over the Swedes in the battle for Riga at Kircholm resulted in the complete recovery of Inflanty. Polish forces took the town of Parnawa, and

Polish Naval Victory over the Swedish Navy at Oliwa in 1627.

Hetman Jan Karol Chodkiewicz (1560-1621) defeated Swedes at Biały Kamień and Kicholm.

Poland's warships destroyed a squadron of Swedish Navy in the Baltic port of Salis.

Meanwhile Polish-Ukrainian magnates interfered in the Russian succession in 1604-1606, and conducted the first, short-lived Polish occupation of the Kremlin in Moscow. It ended in disaster and the proclamation by the boyars of Vasili Shuiski as Tsar of Russia.

Arguments about Reforms

The Seym issued the Act of General Amnesty for those who rose up to protest violations of the Social Contract and lack of reforms in 1610. They were led by the Governor of Kraków Mikołaj Zebrzydowski. Their government reform project included an increase and reorganization of the armed forces and a definite abandonment of the principle of unanimity in favor of majority rule; it also included a general confirmation of the civil rights of citizens and inviolability of the general elections. They justly complained that the principle of unanimity resulted in delays and the postponement of motions, which did not have the unanimous support of all representatives. However, no one had yet dared

Hetman Stanisław Koniecpolski
(1590-1646). Defeated Swedes at
Trzciana and Tartars at Rog.

Hetman Stanisław Żółkiewski
(1547-1620). Took Kremlin in
1610.

to singlehandedly veto any decision of the Seym Walny. Such action would have been considered irresponsible and verging on treason. There was a procedural rule that canceled any motion if its initiator was not present throughout the resulting debate. Thus, the very absence of the representative who would introduce a debated motion would cause such a motion to be declared null and void. Unfortunately, the opposition to reforms grew as the electorate feared that any strengthening of the machinery of the government would bring absolutism to Poland.

The Second Polish Occupation of the Kremlin

The second Polish occupation of the Kremlin (1610-1612) followed the Polish victory at Kłuszyn near Moscow. Polish commanders displayed tactical brilliance; using relatively small forces, they were successful on the battlefield. However, the funding of the army was inadequate because of the fear of the deputies that the armed forces could help the king to assume absolute power.

The Polish Crown Prince Władysław was accepted as the new Tsar of Russia in 1610 amidst objections by his father King Zygmunt III, who wanted the Russian crown for himself, and intended to convert Russia to Roman Catholicism. A Polish garrison subsequently occupied the Kremlin for two years, finally ending in surrender after a long siege. Mikhail Romanov was proclaimed the new Tsar of Russia, starting the Romanov Dynasty. The alliance between the Pope and the Hapsburgs took advantage of the Church's freedom in Poland to press for an alliance with Austria and for missionary expeditions against Russia.

Reacting to the ineptness of the King Vasa in Moscow, the Seym of 1611 further specified the conditions for impeachment and the legal refusal of obedience to the King's government; it also banned purchases of landed estates by the burghers. In 1613, the Seym established the Tax Court of the Treasury. The same year, Polish forces took the town of Smoleńsk after a siege. The Seym authorized an agreement with the Cossacks and ratified an armistice with Russia that ended Polish plans to conquer Russia. The territory of the Polish Nobles' Republic of 1,060.000 sq. km. (1618) included the fiefs of Livonia and Prussia. The peace treaty with Russia confirmed the new borders in 1634.

In spite of the protest by the Prussian population, an inept agreement was made by the King's government on the succession rights of the Berlin line of the Hohenzollerns to the Polish Fief of Prussia (in return for Brandenburgian neutrality during Polish conflicts with Sweden and Russia). This was the first step in the eventual achievement of Berlin's hegemony over the rest of Germany that, at the time, was fragmented into some 350 independent principalities; though the Berlin line of the Hohenzollerns continued to pay taxes and homages to Poland, while kneeling.

Adversities on the Turkish and Swedish Fronts

During the war with Turkey (1620-1621), Polish forces were defeated at Cecora and their commander Hetman Stanisław Żółkiewski was killed. The second wave of the Turkish invasion was successfully stopped by the Polish defense at the Castle of Chocim. The treaty with Turkey established a new border on the River Dniestr. The Seym reiterated military duties of the citizens of the Republic (1621). Troubles on the southern border led to the 1622 Armistice at Mitawa. The Swedes occupied Riga and Parnawa and controlled the rest of Inflanty. In 1623, the Seym promulgated the Ordinance for Commerce. New hostilities with Sweden broke out two years later over the control of the Vistula River Delta and the economic freedom of Poland.

Economic Strife and the Counter-Reformation

The expansion of manorial farms employing serf labor involved the curtailment of peasant holdings, while the landlords obligated the peasants to buy vodka and beer in bars owned by the manor. Southern Ukraine became sanctuary for peasants fleeing manorial oppression. However, the chance of a flight to the Ukrainian Cossacks helped to relieve the pressure on the peasant serfs who suffered most severe abuse on the huge Ukrainian estates. Peasants and towns suffered when conflicts between the land magnates sometimes resembled small civil wars. As a result, the impoverished peasants bought less from the urban craftsmen in small towns. Larger cities grew in importance as grain exports expanded. At the same time, private towns located on huge estates were subject to severe exploitation.

The economic crisis paralleled difficulties in social, political, and religious life, which was related to the progress of Counter-Reformation (enhanced since the arrival of the Jesuits in 1565). The acceptance of Catholicism marked the Polonization of Belarus and Ukrainian nobles. Catholic Poland faced Protestant Sweden, Orthodox Russia, and Islamic Turkey. The exponents of the Counter-Reformation demanded the reduction of serf labor, a stabilization of rents and taxes in kind, and the right of serfs to leave manorial land. Catholic lords were encouraged to compel their serfs to convert to Catholicism. Religious upheavals brought the destruction of many Protestant churches.

The Catholic party attempted to block the enforcement of the provisions on toleration established by the Confederation of Warsaw. A 1647 edict forbade the Anti-Trinitarian Polish Brethren to operate printing houses and schools. The enforcement of the edict was weak, but the Protestants were accused of high treason if they looked for assistance from Sweden or other Protestant countries. The traditional anticlericalism of Polish nobles, however, out-lived the efforts of the exponents of the Counter-Reformation. The citizens of the Republic at peace enjoyed their freedoms, privileges, and wealth while the Thirty Years' War was raging in fragmented Germany. The Poles did not attempt to regain Silesia and Pomerania, despite requests to do so by John Christian the Piast Duke of Silesia. The development of Ukraine with its huge landed estates was an important factor in drawing Poland to the east at the expense of efforts to regain ethnic Polish provinces in the west, then controlled by Germans.

New Laws and Gains of the Land Magnates

At the time of King Władysław IV Vasa's ascent to the throne in 1632, the Seym ratified a series of new laws, and passed instructions for the Custom Service as well as the Law on Taxation. The following year, the Seym took over control of the mint, increased the serfs' labor rent for land, and specified penalties for runaway serfs. The import, printing, and distribution of anti-Semitic literature was made illegal.

In 1637, however, the spirit of the Polish democratic process was violated by a Seym dominated by huge land owners in Ukraine. They enacted the "severe" (undemocratic) Cossack constitution that made serfs of the Cossacks ineligible for territorial defense; abolished command by the atamans; and nominated its own commissioner who was directly responsible to the grand hetman.

In 1638 the Seym banned the use of titles other than knighthood, with the exception of six Lithuano-Ruthenian princes' families, who could use their traditional titles stripped of all legal privileges.

In 1641, the Seym enlarged the Senatorial Watchdog Committee, regulated the issue of coinage, and established the Taxation Register for Prussia. The Seym specified maximum rates of interest on loans in 1643. The same year, the Elector of Brandenburg, Frederick William of Hohenzollern (1620-1688), paid Prussia's last homage to Poland.

In Ukraine the "golden decade" of peace (1638-1648) and economic expansion of landed estates blossomed. Numerous new towns and villages were founded using serf labor. The financing of pre-paid short time leases had a built-in incentive for severe exploitation. These leases were concluded between noble estate owners and Jewish financiers active among Polish Jewry - almost one million strong and undergoing an ever increasing differentiation.

The Kahals, responsible for Jewish debts, controlled the granting of credit and performed the function of banks. These banks were dominated by a wealthy elite in charge of considerable capital, deposited with them at interest by the gentry and clergy. Jewish concentration of usurious and commercial capital was large enough to reach beyond the borders of Poland. However, the majority of Polish Jews lived in extreme poverty in self-contained Jewish communities, where trade and sex outside of marriage were the only links with gentiles.

Struggle for Cossack Civil Rights

Plans and preparations were made in 1644-7 by the government of King Wladystaw IV to eliminate the Crimean Tartar "hornet's nest" of terrorism and to free Balkans Slavs from the Moslem yoke.

As the lower and middle nobility were in favor of winning the Cossacks a greater stake in the Republic as citizens, the Cossacks were promised full civil rights and a gradual inclusion in the political nation. Accordingly, the harsh exploitation by Jewish holders of short time leases was to be lessened by banning the collection of such payments as church fees for funerals, weddings, baptisms, etc. The capital punishment for disobedience to a lease holder was to be eliminated. The Cossacks furthermore opposed the Jesuits' pressure on the Orthodox to submit to the Rome's authority.

In 1648, however, the Seym, dominated by huge land owners, rejected crusade plans; Cossack demands for civil rights and for the eviction of Jesuits and Jews from southern Ukraine; and demands for a guarantee to nominate only Orthodox officials there. It was a major defeat for the government and the lower and middle nobility at the worst possible time.

The End of the Great Power Status of Poland

Cossack uprisings under Bohdan Chmelnyćkyj (*c.*1595-1657) occurred as the political strength and greed of land magnates increased. Simultaneously, the pauperization of lower and middle nobility widened. It was the beginning of a deluge of invasions that ended the great power status of Poland. Growing masses of landless nobles, known as *szlachta gołota* (shlakh-tah-go-wo-tah) or *hołota* (kho-wo-ta), soon meaning "mob" or "rubble," became corruptible by bribery and easily manipulated by the political machines of huge landowners. Foreign financing of Polish political campaigns was openly conducted by the Russian, French, Austrian, Swedish, and Brandenburgian "parties." The old saying that virtue was the basis of Polish parliamentary government was sarcastically changed to *Polska nierządem stoi*, meaning that Poland stands on anarchy and weakness so that no country feels threatened by it.

Sarmatism grew into an all-embracing xenophobic ideology of the *szlachta,* while it was still fashionable among the land magnates to claim descent from Greco-Roman heroes.

Chmelnyćkyj at the Point of No-Return

The Ukrainian Cossack uprising of 1648 was exploited by Muscovy Russia, Sweden, Brandenburg, and the Ottoman Empire. It marked the beginning of the political and military disintegration of the Polish Nobles' Republic during the next 147 years. As noted before, some 200,000 Catholics and Jews were murdered across Ukraine. The Uniates were forcibly converted to the Orthodoxy. In 1648, the beleaguered Poles of Lwów rejected Chmelnyćkyj's offer to lift the siege of the city on condition that all Jewish inhabitants be handed over to the Cossacks for slaughter.

In 1651, the Poles achieved a victory in the battle of Beresteczko against a Cossack army abandoned by Crimean Tartars. (The Tartars, apparently, were ordered by their Turkish masters to withdraw rather than further weaken Poland and bring about an outcome favorable to Russia.) The armistice signed at Biała Cerkiew was favorable to the Poles. On July 2-3 of the following year, however, the battle of Batoh was lost by Hetman Marcin Kalinowski. There, he surrendered some 5,000 elite troops to the Tartars with the promise that the captives could be exchanged for a ransom. Cossack Hetman Bohdan Chmelnyćkyj paid the ransom of 100,000 gold talars, and then he ordered the execution of the 5,000 prisoners.

The killing of the prisoners and the massacres of Catholics and Jews later prevented Chmelnyćkyj from backing out of the unification of Ukraine with Russia, when the Muscovy Tsar refused to recognize the same Cossack freedoms and elective system, which they had enjoyed for centuries within the Commonwealth. Thus, Cossack councils at Perejesław voted for the unification of Ukraine with Russia (1654). The Polish-Russian war of 1654-1656 ended when the Swedes invaded Poland. A two year armistice was signed with Russia without territorial changes. The Seym authorized devaluation of coinage, as Warsaw tried to repair the damage caused by the political machines of the Ukrainian magnates.

The recognition of Kievian Ukraine as an equal partner of Poland and Lithuania was spelled out by the Seym in 1659 in the ratification of the Treaty of Hadziacz signed with the Cossacks. It was a belated effort to make Poland a Republic of the Three Nations of the Poles, Ukrainians, and Lithuanians (who included the Belarussians).

The Constitutional Crisis of the Veto

A constitutional crisis broke out when the session of the 1652 Seym was declared null and void by a precedent-setting illegal admission of a single vote of protest known as the *Liberum Veto*. The first veto cast by Jan Siciński was formally registered shortly before Siciński fled the town. His early departure should have caused an immediate rejection of his motion. However, the speaker (Marshal) Andrzej Maximilian Fredro illegally accepted it, thus violating Polish parliamentary rule, which required the presence of the author of any motion during the resulting debate. The unusual event of disruption of the session appealed to Fredro who authored the *Paradoxical Philosophy of Anarchy.* Attempts to legally overturn Fredro's unfortunate decision were paralyzed by foreign subversion; his ruling was immediately supported by agents of Moscow and Berlin. Siciński acted on orders of Janusz Radziwill, one of the wealthiest magnates in Lithuania and a leader of dissidents, who later (in

1655) committed high treason and signed allegiance to the King of Sweden.

The Polish parliamentary principle of voluntary agreement deteriorated into a rigid and formal requirement of unanimity. For the next one hundred years, it virtually paralyzed the Seym (until 1764). The *Liberum Veto,* together with the misconceived *Golden Freedom* and the admission of foreign candidates for the royal elections, became the main tools for the subversion of the open Polish government by neighboring absolutist regimes.

The erosion of the Republic began when a deluge of invasions in the 17th century ruined the economy and shifted political power from the lower and middle gentry to the owners of rapidly expanding huge estates. This paralyzed the progress of reforms necessary for updating constitutional acts (of 1505 and later). Instead of broadening the democratic process, reverse trends were set into motion. The condition of the peasant serfs worsened. A number of rebellions broke out for diverse reasons, ranging from the civil rights of the Ukrainian Cossacks to the opposition to constitutional reforms.

The magnates, whose political machines were promoting their oligarchical control over the Republic, often became tools of foreign subversion. The Russian autocracy used them extensively.

The Loss of Prussia

The military and political successes of the Swedes ended at the sieges of Częstochowa and Gdańsk. The tide of war turned under the leadership of Hetman Stefan Czarnecki. However, in 1656, the Seym was notified that Frederick Wilhelm Hohenzollern of Berlin had offered himself as a vassal of Sweden out of the Polish Fief of Prussia. The next year, the Seym passed the Excise Tax Law and issued the authorization to use copper coinage. The Seym also ratified the Treaty of Bydgoszcz and Welawa, relinquishing the Polish Fief of Prussia in exchange for termination of the Hohenzollerns' association with Sweden.

A permanent representation of the burghers of Lwów was admitted to the Seym in 1658. Under pressure from the Catholic Church, at the same time, the Seym expelled the (anti-trinitarian) Arian Sect of the

Polish Unitarians. The official reason for this expulsion was the refusal by the sect to bear arms in defense of Poland; in fact, it was an act of intolerance breaking with the Polish tradition of toleration - a result of the political victory of the Counter-Reformation and the loss of political power by the middle gentry in favor of the land magnates.

As a result of the multiple wars fought in Poland, the population of Warsaw had dropped precipitously from 18,000 just a few years earlier to 6,000. Polish armed forces nonetheless entered Denmark to assist their Danish allies in the war against Sweden. The final terms of the peace treaty with Sweden in 1660 included King Jan Kazimierz Vasa's resignation of all rights to the Swedish throne, and the loss by Poland of Inflanty minus the Duneburg region. Thus ended Polish involvement in the political life of Sweden.

The country's battles with Muscovy Russia, however, raged on as fiercely as ever. Though Polish victories over Muscovy at Połonka and Cudnowo forced the Muscovite evacuation of Wilno and Lwów in 1661, Poland's independence was preserved by the self-sacrificing military effort of its population.

Rebellions and Gains by Muscovy

In 1662, the Seym prohibited royal elections *vivente rege* (or while the King was still alive). The soldiers, unpaid for years, rebelled and formed unions - the "Holy Alliance" and the "Pious Alliance"- trying to get the back pay. In 1665-1666, the Seym faced a rebellion by the Grand Marshall and Army Commander Jerzy Lubomirski (1616-1667), who claimed that he was upholding the Social Contract and the Constitution of the Republic. The rebellion degenerated into a high treason and weakened the Republic, making the necessary political and social reforms impossible. It also prevented the armed forces' recovery of Eastern Ukraine, which was lost to Russia after the Cossack uprising in 1648, and obstructed an effective defense against the Muscovites.

The 1666 fratricidal battle of Mątwy was won by Lubomirski against the loyal troops under Hetman John Sobieski. Some 2,000 Polish elite cavalrymen perished, which weakened the Republic's armed forces that were needed on the Russian frontier. The central government of

Poland was also weakened, while foreign interference and subversion, aimed at fostering anarchy in the Republic, grew in strength, especially after the Muscovites were able to seize control of Eastern Ukraine. The truce of Andruszów was signed in 1667, and with it, came the end of the Polish expansion eastward. It was in fact, the beginning of Russian expansion westward.

Poland still might have regained the upper hand. However, the exhausting war with Turkey drove Poland to give critical territorial concessions to Russia in 1688 in return for 146,000 rubles and a (questionable) alliance against the Turks and the Tartars.

The Seym ratified the truce concluded with Russia at Andruszów and accepted the loss of Eastern Ukraine to Russia, as well as Kiev for two years, when a ransom was to be paid. It was never paid, and Kiev was permanently lost. Thus, the ceded territories gave Muscovites a critical advantage over Poland. The land on the eastern bank of the Dnieper River represented the most important element in the transformation of Muscovy into the great Russian Empire. Moscow could thus proceed to fill the power vacuum created in northern and central Asia by the earlier disintegration of the Mongol Empire.

War with Turkey and Territorial Losses

The aforementioned war with Turkey was authorized by the Seym in 1667 because the Cossack Hetman Pyotr Doroshenko made Southern Ukraine a Turkish Fief. Despite a Polish victory under the leadership of Hetman Jan Sobieski over the Muslim forces at Podhajce, the territory of the Polish Nobles' Republic shrank to 774,000 sq. km. due to the loss of 286,000 sq. km of Eastern Ukraine to Russia and 20,000 sq. km. of eastern Prussia to Brandenburg. The population of the Republic thus decreased to some six million.

The Seym ratified the abdication of King John Casimir Vasa in 1668, clearing the way for a weak six-year reign of King Michał Korybut Wiśniowiecki. Under his reign the 1672 Treaty of Buczacz (boo-chach) was signed, which ceded Southern Ukraine to Doroshenko as a Turkish Fief - a fief that included Podolia and Kamieniec Podolski, as well as an annual tithe of 22,000 ducats. The treaty was considered a disgrace

King Jan III Sobieski (1629-1696)-
Victor in the Battles of Vienna
and Parkany in 1683.

Scale Armor of Hetman Stanisław
Jabłonowski (1637-1702). It was
used at Vienna and Parkany.

throughout the Republic, causing the Seym to immediately bolster the
defense budget.

The Victory over the Turks by King John III

John III Sobieski was elected and crowned in 1674, one year
after his victory over the Turks at Chocim (kho-cheem). He had the
support of campaign contributions from France. In 1675, the Treaty of
Jaworów (ya-vo-roof) was concluded between Poland and France against
Brandenburg and Austria. Its purpose was to reestablish Polish
overlordship over Prussia and to recover all of Silesia. The treaty was
thwarted in 1681, however, when the Seym was dominated by pro-
Austrian magnates. At the same time, the Pope was worried about
collapse of Austria and the resulting Turkish threat to Italy. Thus, the
Church also opposed the Treaty of Jaworów.

A Polish victory over Turkish forces at Lwów in 1676 resulted
in the Treaty of Żurawno. Turkey returned two-thirds of Ukraine, leaving
the other one-third under Doroshenko as a Turkish Fief. The matter of

Podolia was left open for further negotiations. The Seym ratified the treaty and revised the operations of the Treasury in order to have more money for the defense. In 1677, the Seym specified the rates of Church taxes to be paid to the Treasury. The same year, a secret agreement with Sweden was finalized in Gdańsk by King Jan Sobieski. It supported the 1675 Treaty of Jaworów, and was directed against the Hohenzollerns of Berlin. Diplomatic means were used one year later in an attempt to restore Kiev to Poland.

In 1681-3, the Seym ratified an anti-Turkish treaty with Austria that was meant to prevent Turkish advances along the southern border of Poland into Austria and to reduce the threat to the Vatican. Subsequent preparation were made for a life-and-death struggle with the Turks, who were at the zenith of their territorial expansion in Europe. King John III Sobieski was to be the Supreme Commander of the Allied Christian Armies. In this capacity, he won crucial battles of Vienna (Sept. 12, 1683) and at Parkany (Oct. 7-9, 1683), which effectively ended Turkish expansion into Europe.

The "Holy League" of Poland, Austria, Venice, and the Papal State was founded against Turkey in 1684; though only Poland and Austria continued the war against Turkey. Poland and Turkey exhausted each other and gradually became the "sick men" of Europe, while Muscovy power grew.

Poland was a bastion of Western Christianity during the struggle against its two enemies: the Turkish Moslem Empire and Orthodox Russia, especially after the strengthening of the Russian absolute monarchy by Peter I. Poland stopped Turkish expansion into Europe, but was not able to prevent Russian subversion, while Russia benefitted from the Polish victory over the Turkish Empire. In 1687, the Seym refused to ratify the Krzysztof Grzymułtowski Peace Treaty with Moscow, which offered to relinquish eastern Ukraine, Kiev, and Smoleńsk. It was a turning point. Muscovy Russia for the first time had an upper hand on Poland. The Seym had to recognize Russia's interest in the preservation of the Orthodox Church in Ukraine and Russian action against the Uniates. Thus, the Tsar was given a strategic opportunity for subversive activities against the Republic in her eastern borderlands.

Polish Science during the Baroque Period

After the "Golden Age" of the Polish Renaissance came the "Silver Age" of the Baroque, which was characterized by population losses; a fall in farm production, as arable land reverted to waste; livestock reduction; and a drop in yield per acre. The large estates expanded at the expense of middle nobility. The revenues of the treasury fell and a monetary crisis grew. Devaluation spread and towns declined economically. Many towns lost half of their population. Urban trades and crafts declined. Poland's foreign trade suffered as the center of international trade shifted to the Atlantic and the colonies.

Many Polish scientists thus emigrated to teach abroad, mainly in Germany. This "brain drain" indicated the Europeanization of Polish science and a period of weakening of Polish cultural life. Thus, for example, doctor Marcin Chmielecki and theologian Amandus Polonus taught at Basel; Hebraist Bartłomiej Keckermann at Heidelberg; Calvinist theologians Jan Makowski and Bartłomiej Arnold at Franeker; Wawrzyniec Bodoch, professor of rhetoric and president, at Rostock; Cartesianist Jan Kołaczek Placentinus, professor of mathematics and president, at Frankfurt an der Oder; and Celestyn Myślenta, professor of Hebrew and theologian, served as president of the University of Koenigsberg, where Jan Stanisław Kaliński and Szymon Żywicki lectured in the Law School.

In Poland, Adam Burski Bursius distinguished himself in Hellenic and Byzantine studies at the Academy of Zamość, where he wrote *Dialectica Ciceronis*, together with Grand Hetman and Chancellor Jan Zamoyski.

The Great Scientific Dictionary of Polish-Latin-Greek by Grzegorz Knapski, entitled *Thesaurus Polono-Latino-Graecus*, was published in 1621. It was an important work for Polish and Slavic lexicography. The first printing shop in Warsaw was established in 1624. Polish dictionaries, grammars, and other books were printed in Królewiec (Koenigsberg) in the Polish Fief of Prussia.

Important achievements of Polish mathematicians like Jan Brożek should be mentioned. He supported the Copernican theory and published a textbook, *Arithmetica Integrorum* (1620), and *Apologia pro Aristotele...* (1652). Brożek was the first historian of science in Poland. He taught mathematics, astronomy, and geodesy at the University of Kraków, where he served as president (rector) in 1652. He also wrote papers on the theory of music, on cartography, and on medicine. He wrote a satire on the Jesuits in 1625.

Armandy Kochański, mathematician and physicist, an associate of Leibniz, brought calculus to Poland. He was the author of *Analecta Mathematica sive Theoreses Mechanicae Novae* published in 1651. Another mathematician, Stanisław Solski, published the first Polish textbook on architecture entitled *Architekt Polski* in 1690.

Advances in astronomy were made by Jan Hevelius who discovered several constellations and named two of them after Polish kings, *Stellae Vladislaviane* and *Scutum Sobiescii*. The royal court in Warsaw supported the linguistic work of Franciszek Mesgnien-Meniński, who authored a dictionary of oriental languages and published a Polish grammar text entitled *Gramatica seu instituto Polonicae lingue* (1649).

Polish Unitarians friendly with the Bohemian Brethren established their gymnasium at Leszno near Poznań. After arriving in Poland from Bohemia in 1621, Jan Amos Komensky (or Comenius, 1592-1670) a famous Czech educator, taught there and, in 1631, published *Janua Linguarum Reserata,* which was an innovation in the teaching of languages. From 1636 on, he was a rector of the gymnasium and was elected bishop of the Unitas Fratrum in 1648. He left Poland in 1656 after he wrote *Orbis Sensualium Pictus*. He was the first to write a textbook with pictures for the teaching of children. Polish Brethren or Anti-Trinitarians or Arians founded their Academy in Raków, near Sandomierz. In the 1630s, it became a center of intellectual life with broad contacts with the West, and it remained so until the eviction of Polish Unitarians in 1656.

Polish rationalist philosophy (founded in 1562) was published in Amsterdam in the monumental *Biblioteca Fratrum Polonorum* (1661). This philosophy helped to form the basis of the world view of such philosophers as Baruch Spinoza (1632-1677) and John Locke (1632-1704).

Literature during the Baroque Period

Polish Baroque in the field of literature had three periods. From 1580 to 1620, the influence of the Renaissance still encouraged the creation of new literary forms. The mature period, in which Polish Baroque writings were influenced by the Counter-Reformation, lasted from 1620 to 1670. The decline of Polish Baroque literature occurred from 1670 to 1730. Valuable works were rarely printed then; instead, poetry and prose contained mostly religious motifs presented in a sumptuous and flowery style. Most of this decline was the result of the "Saxon Night" in Poland.

Polish Baroque literature contained a great variety of genres such as the historical epic, memoirs, journalism, religious writings, lyric poetry, poetry of "worldly pleasures," eulogies, historical writings, and voluminous plebeian or picaresque literature.

Metaphysical poetry was written by Mikołaj Sęp Szarzyński (c. 1550-1581). Entitled *Wiersze Polskie* (Polish verses), the verses were published in 1601 and characterized as "Christian pessimism" due to their treatment of the problems of life and death, evil and sin. They also encouraged the search for everlasting happiness in Heaven.

Hieronim Morsztyn (1580-1623) wrote a series of poems about country life entitled *Światowa Rozkosz* (*Worldly Pleasures*). He was the first to write fantastic fables in Polish. His poem "Kindhearted Bośnian Princes of Banialuka" gave Polish language the word "banialuki" which means "nonsense."

Love songs about Ukrainian beauties were written by Szymon Zimorowic (1608-1629). Published in 1654 under the title *Roxolanki,* these poems, written with an extraordinary artistry, were closely related to authentic folk songs and constitute one of the greatest achievements of early Polish Baroque love lyrics.

Andrzej Zbylitowski (c. 1565-1608) wrote a poem about the idyllic life of Polish country squire ("Żywot szlachcica we wsi"). His cousin Piotr opposed luxury and effeminacy among country squires, as well as new fashions. He also wrote satiric poems "A Rebuke to Overdressed Ladies" ("Przygana wymyślnym strojom białogłowskim," 1600); "A Conversation between a Polish Noble and a Foreigner" (1600);

and "Schadzka Ziemiańska" ("Get together of Country Squires") (1608). Burghers' poetry dealt with the Vistula River trade, the Wieliczka salt mines, and ironworks. Sebastian F. Klonowic wrote "Flis" ("A Boatman," 1595) recording boatmens' language and customs. Walenty Roździeński gave the first professional description of metal works in *Officina ferraria abo Huta i warsztat* (*Smelter and Workshop, 1612*). The poem included the history of metallurgy and miners' legends and tales.

From 1590 to 1655, anonymous plebeian literature had a satirical character. Written mostly by parochial school teachers, it dealt critically with current social problems and advocated disloyalty in an obscene language. Usually poorly printed - addressed to a mass audience - it was quickly included in the index of prohibited books.

Piotr Skarga Pawęski (1536-1612) - an outstanding preacher, theologian, and biographer - published Żywoty Świętych (*Lives of Saints*, 1579) and a political treatise entitled *Kazania Sejmowe* (*Sermons in the Parliament*, 1597), which condemned the main faults in Polish political and social life. He was also an exponent of the Counter-Reformation that had started with the Council of Trent in 1577.

The Polish translation and adaptation of Torquato Tasso's *Gerusaleme liberata* (1575) as *Jeruzalem wyzwolona* (*Jerusalem delivered*, 1618) by Piotr Kochanowski made Polish readers familiar with Italian literature for the first time.

By the end of the 16th century, diaries, memoirs, and itineraries, including impressions of foreign countries, became fashionable in Poland. Mikołaj Radziwiłł's *Peregrynacja do Ziemi Świętej (Peregrination to the Holy Land)* was written in 1582-1584. It gave an interesting description of adventures, nature, architecture, and ethnic and social groups. Marcin Borzymski wrote a poem "Morska nawigacyja do Lubeka" ("Sea Voyage to Lubeck, 1662). Numerous memoirs reflected the stormy political and social events of the mid-17th century.

Wacław Potocki (1621-1696) published a national epic, *The War of Khochim* (*Wojna Chocimska*, which was based on published diaries of Jakub Sobieski, father of King Jan III Sobieski). It was written in beautiful language with vividness and realism in battle scenes. This poetic chronicle was full of patriotism, chivalric spirit, and the glorification of past virtues. Potocki also wrote moralizing religious poetry, novels, short stories, and heraldic verses *Poczet herbów* (*The Gallaxy of Armorial Bearings*, 1696).

Wespazjan Kochowski (1633-1700) wrote a poetic rendition of Polish history in the messianic style under the title of *Psalmodia Polska*. Kochowski took part in the battle of Vienna in 1683 as a royal historiographer. He wrote *Dzieło Boskie, albo pieśni Wiednia wybawionego (God's Work, or a Song of Vienna Delivered*, 1684). Kochowski believed that Poland was a chosen nation capable of immortal deeds. He wrote the three-volume *Annalium Poloniae*, a valuable Latin work covering Polish history from 1683 to 1684.

Stanisław Herakliusz Lubomirski (1642-1702) was a perfect stylist. He wrote with equal ease in Polish and in Latin. Among his works was a prototype of a novel developed in form of a dialogue: *Rozmowy Artaksesa i Ewandra (Conversations Between Artaxes and Evander,*1683). In his Latin work, *De vanitate consiliorum* (1600), he criticized the political system in the 17th century Poland. A son of a rebel, he was known as an intriguer and a brawler despite the fact that he wrote love poems, moralizing stories, and biblical paraphrases. After his father played a destructive role in Polish politics, he wrote on politics in Latin in the spirit of humanism and Christianity. His work, entitled *De vnitate consiliorum,* was a vigorous criticism of the conditions of Polish politics in the 17th century. He did not offer a program for reforms and looked with pessimism on the future of his country, while his family helped to push Poland towards an oligarchy of land magnates.

In the vast memoir literature of the 17th century, the memoirs of Jan Chrisostom Pasek (1636-1701) are considered a masterpiece. They were written in 1691-1695 in the style of a historical novel, which included such events from 1656 to 1688 as battles with the Swedes in Poland and Denmark, and wars with Muscovy. He gives good descriptions of the mentality and lifestyle of the masses of Polish nobility in the second half of the 17th century, who farmed, debated, dueled, passionately sued one another, and forayed against each other's estates.

The slow decline in Polish literature started at the end of the 17th

Mansion in Radzyń Podlaski. Built by Jakub Fontana in 1740-1758.

century. It resulted from the political, social, and economic decline known as the *Saxon Night* Thus, by the turn of the century, mainly theological treatises on the divine grace and free will were published together with vast numbers of prayer books. Baroque writings were full of Latin borrowings and references to the Greek mythology. Heretical books were burned as the Counter-Reformation progressed.

The high level of college education declined as theology was gaining over the sciences after the "Deluge" of invasions. Young men preferred to study abroad. Learning became a domain of the urban middle class. The victory of Counter-Reformation broke contacts with the Protestant scholars and forbade everyone to read books placed on the Index of Forbidden Books. Contradictory trends developed in Poland - rationalism versus Sarmatian irrationalism, for example. During the "Saxon Night," the "Sarmatian Myth" excluded the lower classes from the legendary Sarmatian links. It served to justify social injustices.

Baroque Architecture in Poland

Early Polish Baroque was influenced by Italian architects who worked in Poland in the first half of the 17th century. The St. Peter and Paul Church was founded in Kraków by King Sigismund III Vasa; it was built (1597-1605) in late Mannerist style. In the same style, the St. Mary's Church was built in Bielany near Kraków. Sacral architecture in Poland in the first half of the 17th century often consisted of different combinations of late Gothic, Renaissance, Mannerism, and early Baroque. A Mannerist church built in Sieraków served as a mausoleum for the Opaliński family. The church in Klimontów, built by Lorrenzo Senes with stucco by Faconi, shows the influence of Polish Mannerism. The 14th-century basilica at Jasna Góra in Częstochowa was altered by the addition of a high tower in 1690. The Roman Baroque Church of the Holy Cross, built during the reign of King John III, is the most monumental in Warsaw. The University Church of St. Anne in Kraków, built between 1680 and 1705, is the best example of the mature Baroque in Poland. Rafał Leszczyński, the governor of Poznań, employed Pompeo Ferrari of Rome to build the late Baroque Church of St. Mary in Gostyń and to finish the palace in Rydzyna integrated with parks and gardens. The typical Baroque city planning had the church located at the end of a street.

The most beautiful examples of the late Polish Baroque are the churches built in the 17th and 18th centuries in Wilno and Lwów, now in Lithuania and Ukraine respectively (lost by Poland in the Second World War). Italian architects were hired by Poles to build the Jesuit Church of St. Casimir; the Church of St. Peter and Paul in the Antokol district in Wilno; the Church of St. Catherine; the Church of the Missionary Fathers; and the 15th-century Church of St. John the Baptist. Following their war time destruction, most of these churches were redecorated in the rich Rococo style.

The royal castles of Kraków, Warsaw, and Ujazdów, on the other hand, were redecorated in the secular Mannerist style. An example of a *palazzo in fortezza* is the castle of Wiśnicz rebuilt by Lubomirski in 1615. It is the work of Maciej Trapola. Elegant shapes were combined with exaggerated stucco decoration and an arcaded courtyard was added. Modern fortifications protected the castle. The Castle of Nieświerz, built

Palaca in Wilanów of King Jan III Sobieski. Painted by Canaletto in 1750.

in 1583-1720, has twelve great halls, seven gilt domes, and a peristyle of gilt columns. The defensive castle of Nieświerz - as well as the castles of Krzyżtopór, Ujazd, Łańcut, and Podhorce - are examples of Sarmatian megalomania when fortunes were spent on extravagance and display.

The royal palace in Wilanów was enlarged in the style of an Italian villa by King Jan III Sobieski. His victory at Vienna was commemorated by Queen Marie Casimire, who founded the church of Benedictine Sisters. It was built by Tylman of Gameren in Paladine Baroque style. Tylman built a commercial building in 1695, a shopping center with fifty-four stores under arcades on the ground floor and inns on the second floor. Tylman also designed and built the palace of Nieborów in 1690-1695 in the new French style called *entre cour et jardin*. Pompeo Ferrari of Rome built the late Baroque style Leszczyński palace in Rydzyna. It was integrated with parks and gardens, as was the palace built in Białystok by Hetman Jan Klemens Branicki. (It resembled the French royal palace in Versailles.) A grand hall was added to the royal castle in Warsaw facing the Vistula River. It was later used by the Polish parliament, and then the castle was referred to as the Castle of the Republic during the reign of King Stanisław II August Poniatowski.

In Radzyń Podlaski, Jakub Fontana built a mansion decorated outside and inside in the late Baroque style.

Baroque Sculpture

The mature Baroque sculptures are of open form, picturesque style, and accentuated expression executed in stucco with the rich use of gold and illusionist wall paintings. Giovanni Battista Flaconi worked in Poland from 1625-1660. He decorated St. Peter and Paul Church, the Camaldolese Church in Kraków, and the castle in Baranów, to mention a few. A pillared monument of King Sigismund III was erected on the Castle Square in Warsaw in picturesque Baroque. The socle was made in red marble and the figure in gilt bronze. Similarly executed were the figures of the Jagiellonian kings in the Cathedral of Wilno. New tomb designs consisted of a bust cast in bronze set against an ornate wall - a style used in the Kraków Cathedral on the tombs of bishops Marcin Szyszkowski (1631) and Piotr Gembicki (1654).

Baroque figures created by Balthasar Fontana in St. Anne's Church in Kraków are in agitated theatrical postures with strong expressions, richly swirled hair, and draped clothes. A more subdued style was used in the decoration of the Royal Castle in Wilanow by a Flemish sculptor, Andreas Schlueter. Warsaw sculptures created by Johann Persch are in expressive and dramatic poses in the Saxon Garden, in the Augustinian Church, and in the Cathedral of Warsaw. Rococo style, the last phase Baroque, was used to decorate palaces, public squares, and churches. "Christian Knights," made in the Rococo style, decorate the St. Gorge's Orthodox Church in Lwów. Palace and Church architecture flourished in ornate Rococo and Baroque style, often accompanied by elaborate landscape gardening. The number of Polish architects grew. Wood architecture was replaced by buildings in stone. High quality sculptures in wood were used for the decoration of the interiors. The magnates tried to imitate Versailles in their palaces. The splendor of religious services required an ornate art setting and proper musical accompaniment.

Baroque Painting

A gallery of paintings in the Wawel Castle in Kraków was made in a combined Baroque and Mannerist style by Tomaso Dolabella. He included features of the Sarmatian culture in dramatic expressions, exaggerated characteristics, and Slavic facial features. His portrait of young Stanisław Tęczyński of 1634 is typical. However, some church paintings reverted to medieval forms with subjects taken from the Bible. In Northern Poland, realist Dutch Mannerism prevailed.

The nearly fifty-foot roll painting entitled *The Entrance of Sigismund III to Kraków in 1605* was created by Abraham van Westerfelt, who also painted *The Entrance of Jerzy Ossoliński to Rome in 1633*, as well *Janusz Radziwiłł's Entrance to Kiev* - all important documents of the period.

Paul Peter Rubens influence Polish painters such as Franciszek Lekszycki, who in his Crucifixion in the Benedictine Church in Kraków painted Polish plebeian types. Portraits of Polish kings John Casimir and Michael Wiśniowiecki (1669) were painted by Daniel Schultz in Dutch style. His best portrait is that of Bishop Andrzej Trzebicki (1664).

Polish Sarmatian Baroque portraits of King John III Sobieski were painted by Jan Tritius or Tretko in 1692 and by Jerzy Siemiginowski. The latter painted the heroic king in the Battle of Vienna.

Italian painters were hired to decorate a number of Churches in Poland, such as St. Peter and Paul Church in Wilno, the Sacramentine Church in Warsaw, and St Casimir chapel in the Cathedral of Wilno. All of these buildings were decorated with illusionistic paintings both expressive and didactic. This style was also used in the monastery of Lubiąż and in many churches in Great Poland and in Silesia. A portrait of King Augustus III in Polish national costume was reminiscent of Sarmatian portraits of Polish noblemen. Portrait painting in the "low brow" Sarmatian style was used to show wealth and social standing. It was fashionable to have portraits of the deceased painted on coffins, many of which still exist today.

Szymon Czechowicz (1689-1775), graduate of the Academia di

San Luca in Rome, painted religious motifs in the idealistic and expressive manner of the Baroque. Tadeusz Kuntze Konicz, or Taddeo Polacco (1733-1793), studied in the French Academy in Rome. He painted in late Baroque and early Classicist style. He decorated churches in Poland and in Italy. He painted an excellent portrait of Bishop Załuski, his patron. He introduced Polish Sarmatian types in genre scenes in Villa Borghese in Italy.

Polish Theater in the 17th and 18th Centuries

The 17th-century Poles who traveled to the universities in Italy and France noticed the changes brought to the theater by the Renaissance. They observed how in Italy classic tragedy had turned into opera, and comedy into *commedia dell'arte*. The Italian stage first changed with the use of revolving panels, which permitted a rapid change of scenery and then modern wings. Meanwhile the English had discarded the medieval concept of simultaneous action. These changes were brought to Poland by traveling foreign theater companies. The first permanent auditorium, equipped with the latest stage facilities, was built at the royal court in Warsaw in 1638; it was the first theater outside of Italy equipped with such modern facilities. The summaries of the librettos of foreign plays were printed in Polish for the local audience.

Minstrel comedies were written and performed by poor parochial school teachers. Piotr Baryka wrote a comedy, *Z chłopa król (The Peasant King)*, that was popular in country manors. Most popular, however, was school theater. The Jesuits ran about sixty school theaters in Poland that staged some 4,000 performances. Eventually, school theaters gave way to a permanent Polish national theater that included many talented playwrights.

A new theater was built in Warsaw in 1748. It was called Operalnia; there, performances were put on two or three times a week. Admission was free and invitations were easy to acquire because the new theater had 500 seats and a large standing space. Branickis built magnificent theaters in Białystok and the Radziwiłłs in Nieświerz, Słuck, and Biała. Large auditoria were added to the royal courts in Ujazdów and in Kraków. There were also theatrical schools at Kraków and at large magnate courts where actors were courtiers. Some theater owners wrote plays in Polish for their own stages.

Music in Poland in the 17th and 18th Centuries

Mikołaj Zieleński published his compositions in concertante style in Venice in 1611; in them, musicians appeared to compete for the attention of the listeners. The conductors of the choir and music at the royal chapel in Warsaw, Bartłomiej Pękiel and Jacek Różycki, also composed in this style. So did Mikołaj Mielczewski, Damian Stachowicz, Stanisław S. Szarzyński, and Grzegorz Gerwazy Gorczycki - all choir conductors at the chapel of the Wawel Cathedral.

Instrumental music flourished in Poland in the 17th and 18th centuries. Polish composers wrote mostly chamber music for several instruments. Best known among Polish composers was Adam Jastrzębski (*c.* 1590-1648). He was a violinist, an architect, poet, violin maker, and politician. His compositions, *Canzoni et concerti* (1621), were played throughout Europe. Other well known Polish composers of canzoni, sonatas, and concerti were Mikołaj Zieleński, Marcin Mielczewski, and Sylwester Szarzyński.

The first operas consisted of dramatic performances with music and were staged in Poland in the 1620s by foreign singers, mainly Italians. The first opera house was opened to the public in 1724 in Warsaw. In theaters owned by land magnates, operas and musical comedies were staged in Polish in free translation often describing Polish topics. Usually the plot was a love story set in the country.

Polish Press in the 17th and 18th Centuries

On Jan. 3, 1661, the first newspaper was printed in Poland. Entitled *Merkuriusz Polski* (*Polish Mercurius bringing the history of the whole world to the common people*), it was edited in Kraków and opened the first period of Polish journalism, which ended in the 1740s. It followed a period of newsletters or "ephemeral letters," the distribution of which started in the 15th century. The newsmen of that time were called *novellatores* and were both lay and clerical. Their handwritten newsletters were delivered to the royal court, to palaces of princes and land magnates, to bishops and wealthy merchants. In 1525, for example, Hieronim Wietor distributed his newsletter to Bishop Krzycki. The distribution of handwritten newsletters did not stop with development of the regular press. They were commonly used throughout the Enlightenment and, in printed form, they continue to be in circulation at the present time.

In 16th-century Poland, the copying, distribution, and sale of newsletters was the domain of the Piarist monks, who charged subscribers as much as 100 ducats per year. These newsletters were popular because they were lively and informative and were not subject to censorship by the Church or anyone else.

The *Merkuriusz Polski* was published by the royal court from Jan. 3 to July 22, 1661. The paper's chief editor was the Marshal of the court, Łukasz Opaliński, who controlled the editorial policy. The newspaper was published because King John Casimir Vasa wanted to legalize the royal election of his successor while he was still alive - a *vivente rege* election. It was to counteract the participation of foreign candidates and foreign campaign financing, both of which were legal in Poland during the general election of a new king. The law on elections *rege vivente* failed to pass and the publication of *Merkuriusz Polski* stopped. During the 17th century eight periodicals, including five new editions, were published in Poland.

Sarmatian Crafts and Manufacturing

Polish Sarmatian culture was expressed in the huge production of artistic handicrafts in rich Baroque style. French influence can be seen in Polish Rococo style joinery and in the furnishing of churches and private residences.

A large Armenian community brought eastern influences to Poland. The Armenian Christians suffered persecution in form of "ethnic cleansing" by the Turks. Persian enemies of the Turks permitted Armenians to immigrate and prosper. Armenian tradesmen brought Persian objects of art, richly decorated weapons, precious vessels, clothing, furs, and textiles.

The Polish climate required warmer clothing than was fashionable in southern and western Europe. Thus, Poland was exposed to eastern influences. The Armenians introduced Persian-style clothes to Poland. On the other hand, centuries of wars with the Ottoman Empire exposed the Poles to Turkish clothes and decorations.

Dress fabrics of silk interwoven with gold or silver threads, based on Persian designs, were made. So were carpets that imitated the oriental designs. In Poland, the factory at Brody owned by the Koniecpolskis was best known for production of these items. Polish national patterns dominated the weaving of carpets, often combining Eastern and Western influences to create new Polish Rococo designs, or just continuing the traditional folk art. High quality Polish tapestries were produced in Nieświerz and in Słuck.

A casting technique developed in Gdańsk was used to manufacture sacral objects. Peter von den Rennen, for example, wrought the silver coffins of St. Adalbert for the Gniezno Cathedral and of St. Stanislaus for the Cathedral in Kraków; and Michał Weinhold wrought the bronze door for the Vasa Chapel at the Kraków Cathedral. High quality carpentry was used to produce such altars as that of St. Catherine Church in Kraków and to build grand wardrobes in the Gdańsk style.

Polish factories produced ceramics in the Dutch style of the city of Delft. A Polish factory at Biała Podlaska produced porcelain with Meissen motifs.

Early Polish Development of Rocketry

Kazimierz Siemienowicz (1600-1651?), an engineer serving as a Deputy Commander of Polish Artillery, published a standard textbook on rocketry, *Artis Magnae Artilleriae Pars Prima,* in 1650 in Amsterdam. He published, for the first in the world literature, the design for multistage solid fuel rocket engines, as well as for multiple warhead rockets with steering and stabilizing systems. His designs included fins, rotational stabilizers, as well as rocket launching guide rails. The rocketry handbook, with production specifications, as well as firing and steering instructions, was used in Europe for the next 200 years. (It was translated into French in 1651, into German in 1676, and into English in 1729. A copy of it can be read in NASA's files of the history of rocketry.)

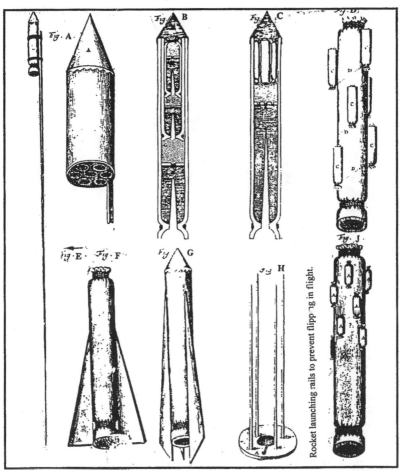

Multiple Stage and Multiple Warhead Polish Rockets of 1650.

115

Baroque Church of the Nuns of the Visitation in Warsaw.

CRISIS OF SOVEREIGNTY OF THE POLISH NOBLES' REPUBLIC

Late Baroque

The Destruction of the Polish Defense Establishment

Peter I of Russia understood that the republican system of government was a legal structure, which he could mortally wound if he could poison it at the top of the organization of the Polish state. In order to accomplish this aim, he "engineered" the "Saxon Night" that lasted from 1697 to 1763. Peter I disbursed ninety-six percent of state revenue on the army and mobilized his police-military complex to subvert and overthrow the representative government of Poland. In the process, he pioneered a "5th column" and disinformation methods. He had Russian lawyers schooled in Polish law and electoral procedures for subversion purposes. He used bribes to corrupt Polish politicians and manipulated special interest groups to cause confusion in the Polish parliament. After he subjugated the Russian Orthodox Church and made it a state-controlled propaganda machine under an Oberprocuror, he used it to foment trouble in the Ukrainian part of the Commonwealth. Peter I concluded the process of "nationalization" of all forms of property in his domain, including clerical holdings. Thus any use of land, buildings, or merchandise was the subject of *tiglo* (or taxation) in form of money, labor, or military service etc. He actually perfected the concept of the state terror apparatus much more effectively than did Ivan IV the Terrible.

The "Saxon Night" occurred during the personal union of Poland with Saxony. It started with the illegal crowning of August II Mocny (1697-1734) in Kraków, which was occupied by Russian and Saxon armies. August II had lost the elections in 1697. Thus, a deliberate violation of the law and the sovereignty of Polish Nobles' Republic was staged by Peter I. He subverted the Polish Nobles' Republic by imposing an illegal and unstable administration of a Saxon king, who became a Russian puppet. It was the beginning of twenty years of systematic destruction of Poland's defense establishment.

A private treaty (concluded in violation of the Constitution of the Polish Nobles' Republic) between Tsar Peter the Great and King Augustus II was signed at Rawa Ruska in 1698. It embroiled Poland in another war against Sweden. Russia's aim was to break the sea power of Sweden on the Baltic, while King Augustus II fraudulently tried to convert the Polish Fief of southern Livonia (then occupied by Sweden) into a Fief of Saxony. In 1699, the Seym ratified the Treaty of Karłowice signed by Poland and Austria with Turkey. Southwestern Ukraine including Kamieniec Podolski and up to the River Dnieper was recovered by Poland, as Russia now considered Turkey to be more dangerous opponent than the subverted Polish state.

The New Kingdom of Prussia

The 1701 proclamation of a new Kingdom of Prussia in Brandenburg, with its capital in Berlin, resulted in a new location and a new use of the name "Prussia." The proclamation was introduced to exploit the difficulties of the Polish Republic with Russia, while giving a chance to the Hohenzollerns to be Prussian kings of a territory formally outside the Roman Empire. This move shaped the cradle of the modern German militarism. The name "Prussia" symbolized the continuity of German militaristic tradition by recalling the 13th century conquest and genocide of the Balto-Slavic Prussians by the armed monks of the Teutonic Order.

Foreign Domination of the Polish Throne

Poland was still treated as an equal partner at the beginning of the Northern War (1700-1721), despite its subversion by Peter the Great. However, the situation changed when rogue Lithuanian magnates, the Sapiehas, caused a civil war in 1700 by tyrannizing the lower and middle nobility. Once defeated, the Sapiehas asked Charles XII for help and took his side in the war, which eventually involved Denmark, Saxony,

Poland, Russia, Prussia, and Hanover on one side, and Sweden on the other.

The occupation of Warsaw in 1702 by Charles XII, King of Sweden, was followed by the defeat of Augustus II in the battles at Kliszów and at Pułtusk in 1704. The Confederation Seym in Warsaw (1704) impeached King Augustus II and held general elections.

An ally of France and Sweden, Stanisław I Leszczyński, was elected King of Poland. King Augustus II officially abdicated in 1706. However, as a result of the defeat of

King Stanisław I Leszczyński (1677-1766).

Charles XII by the Russians in 1709 at Poltava, the Seym was forced by Russia to ratify Augustus II of Saxony as King of Poland in 1710. The defeated Swedes were dominated by Peter's terror apparatus after 1709. In 1713, the Seym formally protested the bringing of the Saxon Army to Poland.

The Russian Protectorate

The Confederation Seym of Tarnogrod (1715-1717) protested an attempt to abolish the Constitution and Social Contract of the Republic by Augustus II, when he used Saxon troops to establish himself as an absolute ruler in Poland. It was the last major effort by the citizens of the Nobles' Republic to reestablish legitimate and orderly democratic process. The fake "mediation" between the Seym and the Saxon administration by Peter the Great was, in reality, the first step in the imposition of the Russian protectorate on Poland. This was made possible by twenty years of systematic crippling of Polish defense establishment conducted by Russians with the help of the Saxons. This event led to the Seym session of 1717 being held under the guns of the Russian soldiers. This session of the Dumb Seym (Sejm Niemy), in which no deputy or senator was permitted to speak, was to legalize Polish submission to Russian "arbitration." Thus, Seymiks' taxing power and armed forces control was restricted; a tax to support only 24,000 troops was passed; the first budget was formulated and accepted; and the Tsar's guarantee of the status quo was accepted as the basis of Russian protectorate over Poland. Peter the Great turned Poland into a demilitarized and neutral zone. The Saxon army was evicted except for 1,200 bodyguards of Augustus II and six officers of the Saxon Chancery, while Russian troops remained. Under the Saxon rule, Poland had no permanent representatives abroad.

50 Years of Terrorism by Berlin and St. Petersburg

Thus began fifty years of Russian and Brandenburgian terrorism and the continued subversion of the Republic of Poland-Lithuania. This period could serve as a classic example of how an open republican government can be paralyzed by ruthless authoritarian opponents. A secret pact between Russia and Brandenburg-Prussia was concluded in 1720. It formulated detailed plans for further fostering anarchy in Poland and for interfering in general elections using military force and bribery. The Liberum Veto and "Golden Freedoms" were used to prevent reforms and the passage of defense appropriations. Russia acquired a free hand in Poland after peace treaties with Turkey (1720), Sweden (1724), and Austria (1726). In 1721, Peter I proclaimed himself the First Emperor of Russia. He did not want to partition Poland. His aim was to have a Russian protectorate over a passive, demilitarized, and neutralized country that would make Russia's western frontier safe.

On Sept. 12, 1733, a general election resulted in a war for the Polish throne. A majority elected King Stanisław I Leszczyński, who was backed by France and Sweden. During his campaign, Leszczyński wrote his political platform in a paper entitled *A Free Vote Insuring Freedom.* In it, he advocated personal freedom for the peasants, cash payments for land use by peasants, limits on the use of Liberum Veto, reforms of the sessions of the Seym, as well as reforms of taxation, and a permanent Army of the Republic of 100,000 men. One month later, an illegal second royal election was staged by Russia and Austria who supported the candidacy of Augustus III of Saxony. They staged the inauguration of their protege during the War for Polish Succession (which ended with the peace treaty of Vienna). The thirty-year reign of August III Wettin of Saxony (1696-1763) represented the last phase of the "Saxon Night" in Poland. Augustus III was a lazy man who was obedient to Russia. He delegated the business of governing to a former servant, the corrupt Heinrich Bruhl, to whom he gave the title of "count."

The Abdication of King Stanisław I

In 1726, the Seym established improvements in the procedures of the Supreme Court and ordered the new issue of currency (1732). Stanisław Konarski (1700-1773) published the *Volumina Legum,* or *Volumes of Polish Laws.* The year 1733 brought the definite victory of the Counter-Reformation as the Seym banned elections of non-Catholics for deputies and senators. In 1734, the Seym passed the voting ordnance for Kurland (Latvia) and the Ordinance for the Post Office.

King Stanisław I Leszczyński traveled to France, where his son-in-law, King Louis XV, gave him the Duchy of Lorraine for life. There he reigned as a titular king. King Stanisław I Leszczyński abdicated the Polish throne in 1736. The same year, the Seym passed an amnesty for the confederates of Dzików, the supporters of King Stanisław I and an alliance with France. The confederates were defeated by the Russian and Saxon forces.

The Press and Schools during the "Saxon Night"

Cultural stagnation prevailed during the "Saxon Night" in Poland until 1740. Demoralization and drunkenness were widespread. People were saying: *"Under the rule of the Saxon king loosen your belt, eat, and drink."* Warsaw decayed as the court resided in Dresden.

A weekly, *"Poczta Królewiecka,"* was published by Dawid Cenkier in 1718-1719 in Królewiec. It covered local news, the international economy, and currently published books. In 1729, the Piarists of Warsaw won a competition against the Jesuits and obtained the exclusive editorial rights for the press from the king. In 1729-1737, the Piarists published in Warsaw newspapers edited by Fr. Jan Naumański. The successive titles were: *Nowiny Polskie, Kurier Polski,* and *Gazeta Polska.* Piarist publications concluded the first period of Polish journalism (1661-1740).

In 1740, the Collegium Nobilium was founded in Warsaw by Stanisław Konarski (1700-1773?). It was a new type of an eight-year school for the elite, with Polish as the language of instruction, the teaching of foreign languages, philosophy (in the spirit of the Enlightenment), mathematical and physical sciences, geography, history, civic virtues, public speaking, military sciences, and horseback riding. The Jesuits, faced with new competition, soon similarly modernized their sixty-six colleges throughout Poland.

A 400,000 volume national public library was donated by the brothers Andrzej Stanisław Załuski (1695-1758) and Józef Andrzej Załuski (1702-1774), who were among the first Polish exponents of the Enlightenment. The library was opened in Warsaw in 1747. Despite the fact that the Załuski's and others advocated reforms, the low point in Polish education was reached in 1750. The program for raising standard of living of the peasants, entitled *The Anatomy of the Polish Republic* was published by Stefan Garczynski (1690-1755). A broad political program, - *On Effective Counsels* (1760), was published by Stanisław Konarski - an educator, political writer, playwright, poet, and publicist. He advocated the removal of anarchy by the abolition of Liberum Veto, a reform of the elections by banning the participation of foreign candidates, and a thorough reform of the Seym.

Threat to the Life of the Kingdom of Prussia

The Austro-Prussian war for Silesia (1740-1748) rendered Brandenburg-Prussia nearly broke as a price for acquiring Silesia. Berlin flooded Poland with bogus money and continued to act as an international parasite. So far on three occasions (in 1656, 1720, and 1733), Berlin had proposed schemes for the dismemberment of the Polish Republic. The Seym was disrupted by the Liberum Veto in 1744, and the project of treasury and army reform was killed as a result of Berlin's bribes.

The Kingdom of Prussia faced destruction during the Seven Year War (1758-1763). Berlin was twice occupied by conquering armies. The Austrians occupied it in 1757, and the Russians occupied and burned Berlin in 1760. Russian leadership saw the Hohenzollerns' expansion into

the former Prussian Fief of Poland and the annexation of the
ethnic Polish province of Silesia
as a threat. Russia decided to
destroy the new Kingdom of
Prussia, in order to prevent it
from acquiring the means to
unify the 350 independent
German principalities into a
united Germany with its capital
in Berlin.

The Russian plan, as
formulated by minister Alexis
Bestuzhev-Riumin (1693-1766),
included the recovery of the Fief
of Prussia by Poland and also of
the province of Silesia, in return

King of Prussia Frederic II
(1712-1786), the Initiator of the
Crime of the Partition of Poland.

for Podolia or Belarus. The Polish parliament did not want to accept the
Russian plan, because it would have strengthened the enforcement of
Russia's protectorate over the Polish Nobles' Republic. Also, Polish
citizens living in the eastern territories did not want to become subjects of
the Tsar. The Poles felt that any degree of Russian domination was a
disgrace and missed the window of opportunity to get rid of Poland's
more insidious German opponent. However, no democratic process could
cope with the situation in which Tsarist agents continued to deal with the
owners of huge landed estates and were able to preserve the Liberum
Veto.

Polish refusal to help in the destruction of the new Kingdom of
Prussia permitted the Hohenzollerns of Berlin to return to their schemes
for the partitioning of Poland after a new and weak-minded Tsar Peter III
(1728-1762) became very accommodating to Prussia. The situation
remained favorable to Berlin after Peter III was assassinated with the
connivance of his German wife, Catherine II (1729-1796), who usurped
the Russian throne by a coup d'etat on July 9, 1762. Thus, saved from
destruction, the Prussians were able to provoke a series of Polish-Russian

wars; each war gave Berlin a chance for robbery of Polish land by annexation.

Parasitic Activities of Berlin and the Problems of Reform

In 1761, the Seym had to pass a universal proclamation on coinage because of the perennial problems of fraud by the Berlin government, which was issuing fake Polish money to fill its coffers. Frederick II Hohenzollern conquered Saxony and got hold of the mint which coined Polish money. Now he could flood Poland with depreciated money. A sharp rise in prices caused chaos in the Polish economy.

The Czartoryski family formed a confederation for the reform and reconsolidation of the Republic. They proposed to replace the veto by a simple majority vote in the Seym. In 1763, they unsuccessfully attempted a coup d'etat against the Saxon king. They naively believed that they could get financial support and arms from "the enlightened Tsarina" Catherine II. It should be mentioned that a nephew of one of the Czartoryski's, Stanisław Poniatowski (1732-1798), had a three-year long affair with Catherine in 1755-1758 in Petersburg (he was 23 years old; she was 26 and married to the Grand Duke Peter). The affair did not help the Czartoryskis, and the absolute rulers in St. Petersburg, Berlin, and Vienna contrived to foster anarchy in Poland.

Stanisław Poniatowski (1676-1762), Castellan of Kraków.

On April 11, 1764, Petersburg and Berlin signed a treaty of alliance despite their differences about Poland's future. Berlin wanted to annex northwestern Polish provinces, while Petersburg intended to dominate all of Poland and have a free hand to act against Turkey and its territories on the Black Sea.

124

STRUGGLE FOR FULL SOVEREIGNTY OF POLAND THROUGH REFORMS

The Period of Enlightenment

Reforms and the Election of King Stanisław II

The Convocation Seym created treasury and army reform in Poland and Lithuania in 1764; abolished private tolls; established the majority of customs duties on the borders of the Republic; improved the parliamentary procedures; and established majority rule in the matters of treasury revenues. The same year, a National Treasury Commissions was established; the mint was transferred to executive control; and a proposal was made for the emancipation of the 750,000 Jews in Poland (without conversion to Christianity) and for the abolition of the Jewish Seym of the Four Lands. Jewish congregations, the Kakhals, refused and acted as little republics governed by the Talmudic Laws and elective presidents.

In 1764, an Election Seym conducted general elections on the Wola fields near Warsaw. Stanisław August Poniatowski (1732-98) was elected king on September 6, 1764 thanks to the support of the Czartoryski family and of Catherine II of Russia. The new king was highly educated. Besides highly sophisticated Polish, he spoke fluent French, German, Italian, English, and Russian. However, he was of weak and passive character. He wanted Poland to reclaim its sovereign status through a "revolution" in its government. He rejected qualities of "Sarmatism," believing them to be isolationist, backward, and anarchist. At the same time he was an intellectual with a streak of melancholy and fatalism. He was the opposite of his father Stanisław Poniatowski, Castellan of Kraków, about whom Voltaire wrote (in *Histoire de Charles*

King Stanisław II August Poniatowski (1712-1786).

XII, p.186)t: " *He was a man of extraordinary merit, a man who at every turn in his life and in every dangerous situation, where others can show at the very best only valor, always moved quickly, and well, and with success.* "

Before the elections, Poniatowski proposed to make Poland a constitutional monarchy ruled by a strongly centralized government. King Stanisław August felt that the republican system based on general elections and ruled by the chamber of deputies was so hopelessly subverted that it was not reformable, and therefore a step back to a constitutional monarchy was justified to provide stability. He went as far as to propose a return of the Saxon dynasty, since he was not married and did not have a heir.

The Coronation Seym signed the Social Contract (Pacta Conventa), the Bill of Rights, and appropriated money for the *Szkoła Rycerska,* or the Knights' School. The Seym promised political and educational reforms. The reign of King Stanisław August Poniatowski (1764-1795) started with the formation of a conference for close work by the king with well qualified government ministers. In parliamentary elections, the king worked with the middle nobility. The Senate dominated by land magnates and supported by Russia won supremacy over the Chamber of Deputies. The King commanded a majority in the lower house and had to deal with the oligarchical opposition united against any attempts to strengthen the central government. Both the king and the opposition were manipulated by the Russians, so much so that people talked about two "Muscovite parties" in Poland. Russian interference continued under the guise of toleration for dissidents and in support of the Liberum Veto. The Russians meddled in such domestic issues as the exclusion of Protestants from the jurisdiction of the Catholic Church.

Russian Meddling and Terrorism

Russian ambassador Nicolas V. Repnin organized the Radom Confederation in 1767 for the purpose of the abolition of the laws passed by the Convocation Seym of 1764. Repnin terrorized the Confederate Seym of 1767. He ordered it to give equal rights to dissidents and to confirm the "Cardinal Laws" of general election with the participation of foreign candidates, the Liberum Veto, the exclusive right of the nobility to hold positions in the administration of the country, and the unlimited power of the nobility over the serfs. Repnin ordered the kidnapping of senators

Royal Reception Chamber, Castle of the Republic, In Warsaw.

opposing Russian subversion and had them deported by Russians soldiers to Kaługa, inside Russia. The terrorized Seym adjourned until the following year.

Russians and Prussians insisted on five "eternal and invariable" principles so that "Poland is kept in lethargy":

1. Free general elections including foreign candidates.
2. The free veto power of each deputy in the Seym.
3. The right to refuse allegiance to the King.
4. Nobles' exclusive right to own land and hold office.
5. Landowners' dominion over the peasants in their estates.

127

BAR CONFEDERACY THE WAR OF THE FIRST PARTITION OF POLAND (1768-1772)

The Bar Confederacy fought a war against Russia for freedom and national independence. It was led by Roman Catholic conservatives; among its military leaders was the "Eagle of the Bar Confederacy," Kazimierz Pułaski, who later commanded the American Cavalry (as an American Brigadier General) under George Washington.

Repnin controlled the chief of Polish defense establishment, Hetman Ksawery Branicki and the troops under his command. During the struggle of Bar Confederacy the Russian government and the Orthodox clergy fomented the *Koliszczyzna* - a Cossack rebellion in the Polish part of Ukraine. It was a repetition of the events of 1648. The Cossack mass murders encompassed thousands of Catholics and Jews. Russian pacification brought about even greater loss of life. The fall of the Bar Confederacy led to the First Partition of Poland.

The Turkish Empire declared war on Russia on October 8, 1768. It demanded the withdrawal of the Russian army from Polish territory, and an end of Russian meddling in Polish affairs as Turkey feared the growth of the power of Russia.

The annexation of Spisz and three other Polish counties by Austria (1769-1770) was enforced during Austrian negotiations with Russia about the joint partition of Poland.

The Bar Confederacy proclaimed the impeachment of King Stanisław Augustus in 1770. The plight of the Bar confederacy stimulated the formulation of new opinions on national independence and civil liberty in the West.

A Russo-Prussian agreement on the partition of Poland was co-signed by Austria in 1772; the government of King Stanisław August protested throughout Europe against the illegality of the international crime of partition. The Poles were slandered by the hostile statements of Voltaire (1694-1778) and other exponents of Enlightenment who, paradoxically, became paid apologists for the partitioning powers, while ignorant of Polish history and values. It was the beginning of an unending process of the slandering of everything Polish on the international scene by propagandists of the despotic governments of Russia and Prussia (including their 19th and 20th- century successors).

Gen. Kazimierz Pułaski
(1747-1779).

Austria annexed 83,000 sq. km. with a population of 2,650,000; Prussia annexed 36,000 sq. km. with a population of 580,000; and Russia annexed 92,000 sq. km. with a population of 1,300,000 in the first partition of Poland. Poland thus lost about one-third of its population of about 12 million. The number of noble citizen-soldiers dropped to 8% of the population (as a result of war casualties), while the Jewish community grew to 10%. Peasants, both free and serfs, represented 72%, while Christian burghers accounted for 7%.

Poland was victimized by ruthless colonial policies. It was the beginning of the deportation of hundreds of thousands of Poles, including poor and landless nobility, to serve as slaves in the estates of Russian dignitaries who distinguished themselves in subverting and dismembering Poland. Thousands of young members of nobility, who took part in the Bar Confederation, were deported to Siberia. The Polish ethnic area was crippled by being cut off from the sea in the north and from the natural boundary of the mountains in the south. It was dangerously enclosed by the new frontiers of Prussia, which brutally imposed a system of an economic exploitation on Poland by means of outrageous custom duties. As a result, the exports from Poland decreased twofold while exports from Prussia flooded the Polish Republic.

Łazienki Palace of King Stanisław II August in Warsaw (1772-1792).
D. Merlini, Etching.

RESUMPTION OF THE STRUGGLE FOR THE SOVEREIGNTY OF POLAND (1772-1792)

Enlightenment in Poland

The Bar Confederacy, defeated by the Russian army, developed national consciousness and sensitivity to the issue of national freedom in the masses of nobility, the political nation of Poland-Lithuania. This experience started to shape modern Polish national identity and stimulated new thinking about civil liberty and national independence.

Despite the first partition and a loss of one-third of its population and one-third of its territory, Poland-Lithuania remained one of the largest states in Europe. The governing Permanent Council was composed of eighteen senators and eighteen deputies elected by the Seym for two years. The Hetman or defense minister was controlled by the Russians, used by them to oppose any measures strengthening the Republic. The oligarchy of land magnates opposed King's efforts to reform the government and the country.

Culture, Press, and the Economy

In 1765, the *Szkoła Rycerska*, or military academy, was opened in Warsaw at the initiative of King Stanisław II. It was the first state- owned and financed school in Poland. Its program of general education promoted civic virtues and patriotism. It was designed to prepare mainly landless nobles for civil and military service. Army officers taught military science and conducted field exercises. The curriculum included history, geography, law, economics, and modern languages. Many of the 650 graduates were among the leaders in the struggle for the freedom of Poland. The school was closed in 1794.

The second period of Polish journalism which lasted from 1740 to 1820 was strongly influenced by the political, cultural, and educational events. In 1740, the Piarists lost their exclusive right in favor of Jesuits, but were allowed to publish in Warsaw in both French and German: *Journal de Varsovie* (1756-1758), *Gazette dela Campaigne* (1758-1764), the *Warschauer Zeitung* (1757), and the *Wochenblatt* (1762). The Jesuit papers, the *Wiadomości Uprzywilejowane Warszawskie* and the *Kurier Warszawski,* soon deteriorated to gossip and sensational society news.

The Polish press became more stable in 1740-1764. The *Kurier Polski* and *Wiadomości Uprzywilejowane z Cudzych Krajów* were edited by a secular group until 1760. "Learned" magazines were appearing. The *Warschauer Bibliothek* started in 1753.

Moralistic journalism started in 1761 with the *Patriota Polski* edited in Toruń by T. Bauch, who followed bourgeois ideology. The Jesuit *Kurier Polski* was edited from 1761 to 1774. It merged with the *Wiadomości Uprzywilejowane Warszawskie* in 1765 under the title *Wiadomości Warszawskie,* soon absorbed by the *Gazeta Warszawska,* edited by Fr. Stefan Łuskina.

The Polish press flourished during the reign of King Stanisław II August Poniatowski. The press served as a medium of propaganda for the Enlightenment, modernization, and laicization. Flourishing of the press included scientific, cultural, and economic papers. Political parties used the press for their propaganda especially during the Four-Year Seym. The press benefitted from the dynamic political and cultural life when the people of Poland struggled against the dismemberment of their country.

The publication of the journal *Monitor* continued until 1785. It was published on the King's initiative and modeled on the English *Spectator.* It advocated tolerance and development of industry as well as reforms of agriculture and improvement in the situation of the peasants. Ignacy Krasicki and Franciszek Bohomolec wrote for the *Monitor* regularly. Adam Naruszewicz wrote for the *Zabawy Przyjemne i Pożyteczne (Useful and Pleasant Games).*

Elżbieta Drużbacka (*c.*1695-1765), the first outstanding Polish woman writer, wrote the first Polish descriptive poem, "A Description of the Four Season, " in 1752. She died the same year that Michał Kleofas Ogiński

(1765-1833) was born to become an outstanding diplomat, musician, and composer of famous Polones dance music. Puławy of the Czartoryskis competed with Warsaw as a political and cultural center. The competition involved cultural values, the will to serve the country, and the ideals of Enlightenment. The most prominent poets of the sentimentalist style, Franciszek Dionizy Kniaźnin and Franciszek Karpiński, resided in Puławy.

Wacław Rzewuski (1706-1779) wrote the first authentic Polish historical dramas, *Żółkiewski* (1758) and *Władysław pod Warną (Lasislaus at Varna,* 1760). Rzewuski also wrote the first classicist manifesto in Poland, a rhymed theoretical work, *O nauce wierszopiskiej (On writing Poetry,* 1762). It is the best poetic work of the early Polish Enlightenment.

The Seym of 1766 passed a currency stabilization reform, new coinage; and a revised Tax Law. Weights and measure were standardized; a General Post Office was established; and general custom duties were introduced. An economic revival was in progress. Agricultural production expanded. Work started on the Ogiński Canal connecting the Rivers Neman and Pripet, and the "Royal Canal" connecting the river Pripet with the Bug. These canals were to connect the Baltic with the Black Sea. A number of industrial enterprises owned by stock holders were organized with government's support in 1767. They failed because of lack of experts and the inefficiency of the poorly-paid serf labor. In 1776-1777, Poland's deficit in the trade with Prussia amounted to a huge sum of forty four million zlotys. Despite these difficulties, grain production increased and agricultural literature helped to make progress in farming techniques.

Architecture during the Reign of Stanisław II

In the second half of the 18th century, there was some return to the architectural forms of antiquity, while classicized French Rococo and Baroque were often used in alterations of existing buildings. French and Italian architects were contracted for these projects. The "Bath" of Warsaw was made into the Palace on the Water for King Stanisław II in the style of Classicism.

The first commercial buildings were built in Warsaw by Szymon Bogumił Zug (1733-1807) in a new "anti-Baroque" style, with shop windows on the ground floor for the first time. Zug worked for bankers, land aristocracy, and clergy. He designed the Lutheran Church in Warsaw in the French style. He extensively used the new neo-classical and pre-romantic style. Zug designed landscape architecture for the Romantic park in Arkadia of the Radziwiłłs'. Various garden pavilions were built in different styles. Zug, Fontana, Kamsetzer, and many others rebuilt palaces in the French style, some in pure Louis XVI.

A Polish version of the Italian neo-classical style became known as the style of Stanisław August. It included the splendor of the Baroque and flourished between 1780 and 1795, when the first phase of the neo-classical architectural style ended with the fall of the Polish state.

Stanisław Zawadzki (1748-1806), a graduate of the Roman Academia di San Luca, worked as military architect in Warsaw and, together with Feliks Radwański, built the Astronomical Observatory in Kraków in 1788. Wawrzyniec Gucewicz, educated in Rome and Paris, rebuilt the town hall of Wilno in a pure monumental style that he applied to the reconstruction of the city's cathedral in 1777.

The equestrian statue of King John III Sobieski in Łazienki Park was executed in 1765 in a classical style still influenced by the Baroque. Pre-Romantic, historical style was used in bronze busts of famous Poles in the Knights' Hall in the Royal Castle in Warsaw. Rococo style was used in executing sacral figures by Michał Filewicz in Chełmno and in Lwów in 1770. Sculptor Maciej Polejowski also worked in the courtly, sensualist style of Rococo.

King Stanisław II, a great protector and lover of art, created a school of great historical painting: the Royal Academy of Painting, where Marcello Bachiarelli (1731-1818) was the main professor. He combined the tradition of Baroque and the elegance of Rococo with elements of the new Classical style. Besides many official portraits, Bachiarelli painted historical scenes such as *The Union of Poland and Lithuania, John Sobieski's Victory at Vienna,* and *The Founding of the University of Kraków.* Bernardo Bellotto - Canaletto (*c.*1720-1780) became a painter of architecture and monuments in Warsaw. The great accuracy of his paintings were invaluable during the restoration work in Warsaw after the Second World War. A Frenchman, Jean Pierre Norblin de la Gourgaine (1745-1830), painted Polish national types in the Rococco style: peasants, burghers, and squires of the Sarmatian cultural tradition. Daniel Chodowiecki was an excellent illustrator of the life and people of Gdańsk. Stanisław Stroiński, born in Lwów, was an outstanding muralist who painted in the Baroque Illusionist style. Franciszek Smuglewicz, professor of the Academy of Wilno, contributed to the development of Polish historical painting. Polish portraitist, Aleksander Kucharski, painted the famous last portrait of Queen Marie Antoinette. An excellent portrait of General Kossakowski was painted by Kazimierz Wojniakowski, who created many allegorical compositions, religious paintings, and portraits with symbolic motifs - *Polonia in Shackles*, for example.

At the same time, modern industries were organized in Poland. Porcelain was produced in Korzec and at the Belvedere in Warsaw. Imitations of the famous Persian "sash" and western style designs were woven in Słuck and Grodno. Workshops of the Castle of Warsaw produced engraved hardware, vases, and ornaments as well as flooring blocks for the royal residencies. Kolbuszowa became the main center of furniture production. Many aristocrats industrialized their properties.

Polish Theater during the Enlightenment

The National Theater was opened in Warsaw in 1765. It consisted of three troupes: one Polish, one French, and one Italian. The building of the Operalnia was leased for performances that included Polish plays selected by a competition sponsored by King Stanisław II. In two years, eleven Polish plays were staged. The Russian embassy then intervened to close the theater because of the patriotic slogans and propaganda used on stage in reaction to the first partition of Poland in 1772. The first originally Polish opera was staged in 1788 *Nędza uszczęśliwiona*

Wojciech Bogusławski
(1757-1826).

Teatr Wielki, the Grand Theater of Warsaw. Engraving by F. Dietrich.

(Poverty Made Happy), a vaudeville based on a play by Franciszek Bohomolec with the music by Maciej Kamieński.

In 1779, the theater was reopened in a new building with 800 seats. Wojciech Bogusławski (1757-1829), an author, an actor, and a director became "the father of Polish national theater." The theater company of twenty people performed comedies, operas, tragedies, and dramas. It supported the Patriotic Party for the full independence of Poland and started its repertoire with *Powrót Posła (The Return of a Deputy)* by Julian Ursyn Niemcewicz and *Krakowiacy i Górale (Cracovians and Mountaineers)* by Wojciech Bogusławski. The music composed by Jan Stefani included many folk tunes. Polish national music was exemplified by works of Michał Kleofas Ogiński, who was an officer in the last battles before the third partition of Poland. Before he emigrated to Italy, he composed the famous Polonaise *Pożegnanie Ojczyzny (Farewell to the Fatherland).*

Permanent theaters were soon established in provincial capitals: in Lublin in 1778, in Lwów in 1780, in Kraków in 1781, and in Poznań in 1783. Popular support kept Polish theater alive through the century of partitions. It helped the continuity of Polish language and culture up until the restoration of the independence of Poland in 1918.

The First Ministry of Public Education in Europe

The Seym voted in the hearth tax and equalized custom duties in 1773. The same year, it established the Ministry of Public Education, the first in Europe. It put education under state control to a much greater extent than it was in other countries of Europe.

The reorganization of the school system was financed (despite protests of the Papal Nuncio) with funds appropriated from the liquidation of the Jesuit Order by Pope Clemens XIV.

Two school provinces were created. The Crown territory included Polish and Ukrainian ethnic areas, while Lithuania included Lithuanian and Belarus ethnic areas. The Universities of Kraków and Wilno served as Principal Schools,

Hugo Kołłątaj, (1730-1812). Reformer of Polish Education.

one for the Crown and one for Lithuiania. Below the universities were divisional schools or higher secondary schools, which were above the sub divisional schools or lower secondary schools. Parish schools for boys and private schools for girls were supervised by the lower secondary schools. Hugo Kołłątaj made a modern university out of the Kraków Academy by changing the teaching staff and appointing lay professors educated in leading European universities. They included Jan Śniadecki (1756-1830) - a talented organizer and an outstanding mathematician, linguist, and astronomer - who published *The Theory of Adaptation of Algebraic Expressions to Curved Lines*; Jan Jaśkiewicz, professor of natural history and the founder of the Botanical Garden; Dr. Rafał Czerwiakowski, anatomist and surgeon; Dr. Jędrzej Badurski, pathologist and clinician; Antoni Popławski, physiocrat and professor of natural, civil, criminal, and international law; and Feliks Radwański, lecturer on mechanics and hydraulics.

The ex-Jesuit professor of astronomy, Marcin Poczobut (1728-1809), modernized the Wilno Academy. These universities had regular teaching programs and, in addition, served as learned societies, teachers' colleges, and education offices. They performed an "educational revolution," in which Polish was the language of instruction. Mathematics and natural sciences dominated the teaching program, which also included agricultural sciences, Polish history, civic virtues, and paramilitary training. Due to organizational difficulties and lack of funds, the number of students dropped to about 17,000 students (they attended 74 schools) in 1781-1790. The students were supplied with Polish textbooks of a high standard by the "Society for Elementary Books." King Stanisław II August served as the "patron" of the Commission, which was presided over by King's brother, the Primate Bishop of Poland, Archbishop of Gniezno Michał Jerzy Poniatowski. Polish Enlightenment became known as the Enlightenment in Stanislaus' Style in recognition of the cultural merits of King Stanisław II.

Language of the Early Polish Enlightenment

"The refinement of language helps in the process of public enlightenment" was the motto of Jan Śniadecki who wrote *On the Polish*

Stanisław Staszic, Political Writer, (1755-1626).

Language and *On the Native Language in Mathematics.* He helped to introduce Polish terminology to mathematics, physics, astronomy, and grammar. Other treatises on Polish language were published by S. Konarski, *On The Improvement of Eloquence*; by O. Kopczyński, *On the Spirit of the Polish Language;* and by F. Bohomolec, *A Discourse on the Polish Language.* They were written in the spirit of the Enlightenment or "the age of reason." The early Enlightenment in Poland started in about 1730 and ended in 1764. After the Saxon Night it was the beginning of Polish cultural revival imbued with patriotism and a renewed sense of civic duty.

Culture and Technology during the Late Enlightenment

The late Polish Enlghtenment lasted from 1765 to 1795, when improvements occurred in culture, economy, and politics under the moral and material leadership of King Stanisłw II August Poniatowski.

Political writings by Stanisław Staszic reflect his belief that the liberum veto and royal succession must be abolished; the army must be reorganized and strengthened; and the work of the Seym should be made more efficient. He was the first to publicly accuse the few richest land magnates for causing the decline of Poland. He demanded equal right for the burghers and substitution of land-use rents for the serf labor. This program was published by Staszic in *Uwagi nad życiem Jana Zamoyskiego (Remarks on the life of Jan Zamoyski, 1787)* and in *Przestrogi dla Polski (Warnings for Poland, 1790)*.

In 1788, Hugo Kollataj published a program for the abolition of serfdom, the introduction of free hiring, and the complete equality of townspeople and nobility. He advocated modern government led by a strong executive under a modern constitution, and proposed an efficient legislative procedure. He organized *"Kuźnica" (the Smithy)*, a center for political propaganda, to shape public opinion by means of political poems, lampoons, and position papers by many writers. Kołłątaj published *Do Stanisława Małachowskiego (To Stanisław Małachowski, 1788-1789), Prawo polityczne narodu Polskiego (The Political Rights of the Polish Nation, 1790), and Rozbiór krytyczny zasad historii o początkach rodu ludzkiego (A Critical Analysis of the Principles of History on the Beginnings of Human Society, 1842)*. In his last book, he pioneered the concept of the evolutionary development of humanity. Piotr Switkowski published the *Scientific Record of History, Politics, and Economics*. It was one of the best scientific publications in Europe.

Among the large number of Polish writers and poets of the late Enlightenment was Adam Naruszewicz, translator of classical Roman authors, poet, and the initiator of the modern Polish historiography in his *Historia narodu polskiego (The History of the Polish Nation, 1780-1786, and 1824)*. He condemned the faults of humanity in general, and Sarmatian

Archbishop Ignacy Krasicki,
Poet and Novelist, (1735-1801).

features of Polish culture in particular. He believed that dynastic succession to the throne was more practical than were the Polish general elections the included foreign candidates and allowed foreign campaign contributions.

Another outstanding and very prolific poet and man of letters of Polish Enlightenment was Archbishop Ignacy Krasicki, a friend of King Stanisław II. His satiric poetry criticizes uneducated monks addicted to alcohol and idleness, as well as Sarmatian fashions and obscurantism combined with moral and educational poverty. His novel, *Mikołaja Doświadczyńskiego przypadki (The Adventures of Mikołaj Doświadczyński, 1776)*, was the first in Polish literature that combined adventures, morals, and utopian notions with the structure of a popular romance. It included many topics he used in his articles in the *Monitor*. Krasicki's humorous presentation of his sharp criticism of his contemporaries was not offensive and became acceptable. He also published an encyclopedic work entitled *Zbiór potrzebniejszych wiadomości (Compilation of Useful Information, 1781-1783)*.

Excellent descriptive, political, and philosophical poems were created by the highly educated and talented Stanisław Trembecki (*c.*1739-1812). Representative examples of his work are *Do moich współziomków (To my compatriots)* and *Sofiówka* (1806), both written with unparalleled narrative artistry and rich vocabulary constituting a valuable contribution to the late Polish Enlightenment. A mock-historic work full of vigor and irony, as well as a comic satire on the clergy, *Organy (Organ, 1784)* was written by the free-thinker Tomasz Kajetan Węgierski (1756-1787). *Organy* predated similar criticism by Krasicki.

Playwright, poet, translator, author of historical novels, memoirs, and political pamphlets, Jan Ursyn Niemcewicz (1758-1841) wrote basically in Poland where he became very popular. He stayed in America from 1796 to 1807.

Leading Polish Jacobin poet, Jakub Jasiński (1761-1794), openly propagated prohibited Jacobin slogans and called for unity when the crimes of partition were committed against the Polish state. He wrote *To Polish Exiles about Faithfulness* in 1793 and, one year later, *Do Narodu (To the Nation)*, which was a call to arms addressed to all social classes to fight for the independence of Poland.

The Press and Engineering Feats

In 1786, Tadeusz Podlecki published the *Commercial Daily* in Warsaw. *National and Foreign Gazette* and a magazine, *Warsaw Correspondent,* were both published in 1791-1792 in Warsaw. National consciousness increased with the spread of literacy. The Polish language was modernized and entered a period of remarkable development. Traditional Polish civil liberties were expressed in the language of the Enlightenment. Criticism took form of satirical literature. The national costume, the *"kontusz,"* started competing with French frock as a sign of return to national customs.

In 1784, Polish engineers completed the canals that connected the Baltic Sea with the Black Sea through the Niemen and Vistula River Basins to the Dnieper River.

The Four-Year Seym or The Great Seym (1788-1792)

In 1776, five permanent departments of the government were founded: the Department of Defense (limiting the power of the Grand Hetman); the Department of Foreign Affairs; the Department of the Interior; the Department of Justice; and the Department of the Treasury.

In 1788, the Seym set the Army complement at 100,000. The following year, the Seym set the tax rate at ten percent for nobility and twenty percent for clergy.

In 1790, the Seym ratified the Treaty of Alliance with Prussia, while desperately trying to strengthen Poland's position vis-à-vis Russia. It fell for the provocation by the Kingdom of Prussia, which was only interested in fomenting Polish-Russian war as an opportunity for further annexation of Polish lands. However, during the Turkish-Russian war of 1787-1791, Poles were able to make more progress in reforming their country.

The Seym of 1791 revised the electoral Ordinance for the Seymiks. It also passed representation of the burghers.

A new Polish constitution was passed on May 3, 1791. It was modern, the first formal constitution in Europe. The Constitution was the first to voluntarily grant the extension of civil rights held by the political nation of the noble class to the townspeople and, in a more diluted form, to the peasantry. Polish politicians had much in common with their contemporaries in America, such as Thomas Jefferson, George Washington and the other founding fathers of the United States. Poland was the only major country that was a republic (1569-1795) until the founding of the United States of America.

The Constitution of May 3, 1791 also created conditions for the rebirth of Poland; and it was perceived as a "death blow" to the Prussian monarchy by E.F. Hertzberg (1726-1795), the Prussian minister, who wrote that it was better than the English and would permit Poland to regain the lands lost in the first partition.

In Jan. 1792, when Russia concluded its war with Turkey and turned her attention to Poland, Prussia was able to safely return to its parasitic activities against Poland and its plans of further partitions.

On Apr. 2, 1792 in St. Petersburg, an act of Confederation was falsely dated and signed as of May 14, 1792, at Targowica. It condemned the "democratic revolution of May 3." It was signed by a group of land magnates who were Russia's henchmen.

Without a significant capacity to produce weapons, Poland was no match for Russia. When on May 22, 1792 the Seym increased the army to 100,000, Poland was unable to buy arms abroad because of a new Prussian blockade. The Poles were able to put only 37,000 man army to face 97,000 Russian veterans of the Turkish campaign.

Opposite Page: Seym Working on the Constitution of the 3rd May, 1791. Painting by Kazimierz Wojniakowski.

WAR OF
THE SECOND PARTITION
OF POLAND IN 1792

War in defense of the Constitution of May 3, 1791 was fought from May to August of 1792. On May 14, 1792, Catherine II ordered her army, under Alexander Suvorov, into Poland. The Polish defensive battles of Zielence, Dubienka, Krzemień, and Brześć could not halt the continued retreat. The robbery of Polish territory cemented the alliance of Prussia and Russia.

On June 17, 1793, the Seym (dominated by Russia) repealed the Constitution of 1791; ratified the Treaties of the Second Partition; passed a Conservative Constitution; and re-established general elections for the King as the head of state and chief executive of the Republic.

Prussia subsequently annexed 51,000 sq. km. with a population of 1,000,000 people; while Russia annexed 250,000 sq, km. with a population of 3,000,000.

WAR OF
THE THIRD PARTITION
OF POLAND (1794-1795)
THE KOŚCIUSZKO
INSURRECTION

The Act of Insurrection was proclaimed in Kraków on March 24, 1794 by Gen. Tadeusz Kościuszko, the Commander-in-Chief. A former American general, the architect of West Point and other river fortifications to block British barge movements, he had saved the American Revolution by engineering the American victory at Saratoga-an event without which the French had refused to join the war against Great Britain.

Gen. Kościuszko issued the Act of Połaniec (May 7, 1794), known as the Manifesto of Połaniec. In it he provided the first through reform of the status of the serfs in the Nobles' Republic; freed the peasants who joined the national uprising from serfdom; upheld the Constitution of May 3, 1791 and the Social Contract; and called for regaining independence from Austria, Prussia, and Russia. Poland's first banknotes were printed. Of the 60 million printed, 8 million went into circulation.

The Prussian government subsequently convinced Russia that Kościuszko's reforms threatened central Europe with "the epidemic of Jacobinism" and offered to take part in the invasion of Poland.

The size of the Polish army swelled to 70,000 men. Through its ranks passed 140,000. Among them was the first small Jewish regiment (all-volunteer), formed by Berek Joselewicz to help in the struggle for Polish independence. Jewish volunteers fought for the preservation of the unique Jewish liberties in Poland and against the anti-Semitic policies of Austria, Prussia, and Russia. The Jacobin Club of Warsaw pressured the criminal court there to sentence to death by hanging several collaborators who had signed the Confederation of Targowica. Similar executions were conducted in Wilno.

In the Act of Kraków (1794), the Commander-in-Chief proclaimed the Supreme National Council. Land grants were offered to the soldiers fighting in the uprising and to their families. The Polish military campaign faced the combined forces of the Germans and Russians. The Poles won the first battle at Racławice and had successes in defense of Warsaw. The greatest Polish

An American General,
Tadeusz Kościuszko (1746-1817).

achievements were the battles near Warsaw, as well as the fortification and defense of the city, while an insurrection broke out in areas of Poznań and Pomerania annexed by the Berlin government. Thus, the Prussians were driven out of the main theater of war. On October 10, 1794, Kościuszko's corps of 7,000 was destroyed by the Russians in the hard fought battle of Maciejowice; the Commander-in-Chief was wounded and taken prisoner. At the end, Russian troops carried out a massacre of the civilian population of Praga, a suburb of Warsaw on the east bank of the Vistula River. The massacre of Praga was to be a terrifying example. The war of the third partition ended in November 1794. King Stanisław II August Poniatowski, the last head of state and chief executive of the First Polish Republic, abdicated on Nov. 25, 1795. The Third Partition of Poland and the commitment of Austria, Prussia, and Russia to eradicate the name of Poland and the Polish presence from the history of Europe was recorded on January 26, 1797. It was the final obliteration of the First Polish Republic.

Ruthless colonialist policies were applied to Poland. A total of about 500,000 Poles were subsequently deported to Russia as serfs.

Józef Wybicki (1747-1822), Poet, Politician, Freedom Fighter, and the Author of the Modern Polish National Anthem.

Together with vast landed estates, the prisoners were given by the Tsarist government of Russia to the officers and diplomats distinguished in the obliteration of the Polish Nobles' Republic.

Austria annexed 47,000 sq. km. with a population of 500,000.; Prussia annexed 48,000 sq. km. with a population of 1,000,000; and Russia annexed 120,000 sq. km. with a population of 1,200,000.

Prussia was the big winner, quadrupling its territory and becoming by far, the largest of the 350 independent German principalities. It was on its way to acquiring a hegemony over Germany, despite the fact that over 60% of Prussia's population was ethnic Polish and did not speak German.

The territory of 1,060,000 sq. km. held by the Polish Nobles' Republic in 1618 was partitioned in the three partitions as follows: the Austrian Empire annexed 130,000 sq. km. or 12.2%; the Kingdom of Prussia annexed 155,000 sq. km. or 14.5%; and the Russian Empire annexed 775,000 sq. km. or 73.3%.

The Polish national catastrophe of partition came by the end of the 18th century. Paradoxically it happened at the time of national rebirth and constitutional reforms. In 1795, Poland disappeared from the map of Europe.

The international crime of the partition and complete destruction of Poland-Lithuania resulted from the fear of Prussia, Austria, and Russia that the Old Republic was on its way to rebuilding its strength and reclaiming its earlier losses.

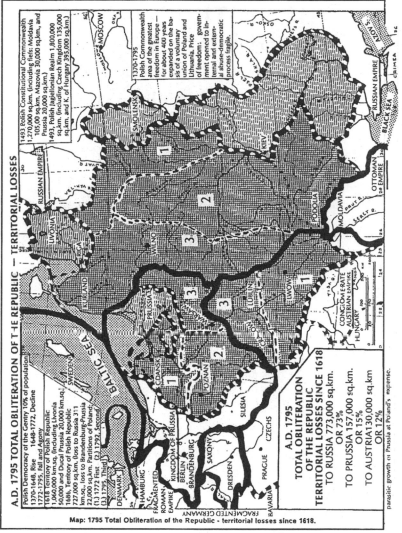

Map: 1795 Total Obliteration of the Republic - territorial losses since 1618.

Obliteration of the Republic in 1795 - Territorial Losses since 1618.

THE DESTRUCTION OF THE POLISH STATE (1795) THE GRAND DUCHY OF WARSAW (1807-1815)

(Neo-Classicism and Romanticism)

Polish Cultural Efforts 1795-1815

The extinction of the largest country in Western Christianity changed the European balance of power and violated the very principle of legitimacy for which the guardians of the old regime were fighting. From then on the "Polish Question" became an embarrassing internal problem for Austria, Prussia, and Russia, as well as an explosive international issue.

Polish culture entered a transitional phase between the fall of Poland in 1795 and the Congress of Vienna in 1815. The towns declined, while the masses of Polish nobles plunged into a fervent activity. Puławy of the Czartoryski's became an important center of Polish spiritual and artistic life. The universal romantic trend developed strong patriotic and national features under the patronage of Princess Isabella Czartoryska (1746-1835), who also initiated a collection of national art treasures, that were later exhibited in the Czartoryski Museum in Kraków. The first museum was housed in two romantic structures built in the park of the Puławy palace.

The first scientific society was formed in 1800 in Warsaw thanks to the efforts of Stanisław Staszic (1755-1826). Polish scientists continued working. The Polish University of Wilno was opened (1802) by Adam Czartoryski, who befriended the Tsar Alexander I and was appointed Deputy Foreign Minister and the Curator of Wilno Educational District. There, in 1804-1811, Jędrzej Sniadecki (1768-1838), natural scientist, physician, and a philosopher developed the theory of organisms; while his brother, Jan Śniadecki, chaired the department of mathematics. The University of Wilno sponsored a network of 400 secondary schools in Lithuania, Belarus, and Ukraine. In Krzemieniec, Tadeusz Czacki, a distinguished historian of the law, founded an excellent secondary school - a Lyceum that employed teachers recently released from Russian prisons, such as Hugo Kołłątaj and others.

Jan Śniadecki (1756-1830).

The New Polish State

In 1807, the Governing Commission appointed by Napoleon in Warsaw was presided over by the former Speaker of the House of Representatives, Stanisław Małachowski (1736-1809). He was one of the founding fathers of the Constitution of the 3rd of May. Stanisław Kostka Potocki (1752-1851) served as the President of the State Council and Minister of Education. He was a writer and a critic, as well as the first known Polish archeologist very interested in the architecture of antiquity, especially the Palladian style.

The Napoleonic Constitution was given to the Grand Duchy of Warsaw. It called for a strong central executive - a position filled by the King of Saxony. In practice, however, the executive functions were in hands of a prime minister. The Seym, a bicameral legislature, was in charge of the budget and the judiciary only. The privileged classes were abolished, and legal equality was recognized for all. The Seymiks remained as electoral assemblies for the gentry; communal assemblies were added for burghers and peasants. The peasants were to be free tenants without any right to the land. The Senate was composed of eighteen appointed senators. The chamber of 100 deputies included sixty nobles and forty professionals, burghers, and peasants. The territory of the Grand Duchy of Warsaw was 104,000 sq. km. with a population of 2,600,000 in six departments: Warsaw, Poznań, Kalisz, Bydgoszcz, Połck, and Łomża. Each department contained ten districts. The territory was made up of the annexations by Brandenburg-Prussia in the second and third partitions of Poland, minus the Białystok region that was ceded to Russia by Napoleon at the Treaty of Tilsit (Tylza July 7, 1807).

Treaty of Vienna (1809) recognized the territory of the Grand Duchy of Warsaw to include the additional four departments of Kraków, Radom, Lublin, and Siedlce - a total of 142,000 sq. km. with a population of 4,300,000 in 72 districts; the Chamber of Deputies added 66 deputies.

Napoleon's Duplicity

Napoleon proposed a joint domination of Europe to the Tsar, in order to have a free hand in his struggle against England. He even proposed to give the Tsar the Polish throne. The Tsar declined for fear of antagonizing his Prussian allies. Then Napoleon wanted the Polish State to serve as an eastern rampart of the French Empire, but not as a bone of contention in relations with Russia. Thus, he gave false promises to the

Poles about the rebuilding of Poland, while assuring the Tsar in a letter of January 1810 that the Kingdom of Poland would never be resurrected - and that its very name would disappear forever.

Napoleon chose King Frederic August of Saxony (1763-1827) to became the Grand Duke of Warsaw. He issued the decree freeing serfs and giving equality of peasants with burgers. The nephew of King Stanisław II August Poniatowski, Prince Józef Poniatowski, reluctantly became the minister of defense.

Polish Light Cavalry Charge at Samosierra - opening the Road to Madrid for Napoleon in 1808. Painting by J. Suchodolski.

In 1812, Napoleon appealed to the Poles to join him in the second "Polish War" against Russia. On the eve of the French invasion of Russia, the Seym constituted itself into a Grand Confederation of Poland for the revival of the Polish-Lithuanian Commonwealth. The Polish army of 100,000 became a part of the Grand Army of 500,000 that invaded Russia. During the march, the Grand Army lived off the land and devastated seventy-mile wide strip of the country along the road to Moscow. Polish forces entered Smoleńsk in a hard-fought battle after suffering heavy casualties. After the battle of Borodino, Napoleon entered Moscow, devastated by fire. During the retreat from Moscow, Poles fought in the rear guard and rescued Napoleon from imminent disaster during the crossing of the Berezyna River. Polish losses in the campaign reached 70% in killed, wounded, and prisoners; however, they rescued all their banners and guns. In all of Napoleon's campaigns, including the Polish Legions in Italy under General Jan Henryk Dąbrowski, nearly a quarter of a million Poles served with a hope that they were rebuilding an independent Poland.

Napoleon Bonaparte and Józef
Poniatowski at Liepzig in 1813.

Józef Poniatowski (1763-1813),
Polish General, Marshal of France.

CONSTITUTIONAL KINGDOM OF POLAND WITHIN RUSSIAN ABSOLUTIST EMPIRE (1815-1831)

(Period of Romanticism)

The Congress of Vienna (1814-1815) resulted in a new partition of Polish lands of the Grand Duchy of Warsaw. At first, Tsar Alexander I intended to create a unified kingdom of Poland joined in a personal union with the Russian Empire. He abandoned this idea in face of English protests and mobilization, as well as a joint threat of war by England, Austria, and Prussia. Thanks to the efforts of Adam Czartoryski, the outcome of the Congress was not similar to the destruction of the Polish State in 1795. Lobbied heavily by Adam Czartoryski, the Congress established the "free, independent, and strictly neutral" City Republic of Kraków as a joint protectorate of Austria, Prussia, and Russia. Prussia annexed Toruń and the departments of Bydgoszcz and Poznań as the Grand Duchy of Poznań; while Austria annexed the Tarnopol region, and the highlands south of Kraków, including the Wieliczka salt mines.

On December 24, 1815, Tsar Alexander I, acting as a crowned King of Poland, proclaimed the Constitution of the Kingdom of Poland. It was more liberal than the French constitution. It was the only constitutional experiment within the Russian Empire. The governmental functions were to be conducted by the Administrative Council. The Tsar would make the decisions on war and peace and retain all executive and many legislative powers. A guarantee of basic civil rights was promised. The bicameral Seym had no right to initiate new laws and was subject to the royal veto. Independent courts were promised. The army of the Kingdom of Poland was not to be used outside Europe. It was to be under the command of Grand

Duke Konstantin, known for his brutality and physical abuse of his soldiers. In practice, the Grand Duke became more important than the government. Russian senator Nikolai Novosiltzow acted as the unofficial supervisor of the Polish government. He was a member of the Administrative Council and an "imperial commissioner." Both these men were opposed to the freedoms promised to the Polish people by the constitution.

Thanks to efforts of Prince Adam Czartoryski (1770-1861), the Polish bicameral parliament was elected on the broadest social basis in all of Europe. While France was eight times larger, it had smaller number of voters than the truncated Kingdom of Poland. The Kingdom of Poland under the Tsar had an area of 127,000 sq. km. with a population of 3,300,000.

Culture in the Lands of Divided Poland

Polish scientific publications continued. In 1807-1814, *Polish Statistics* was published by Stanisław Staszyc (1755-1826). The first complete dictionary of recent Polish was published in six volumes in 1807-1814 by Samuel Bogumił Linde (1771-1847), a lexicographer who worked at the Załuski Library. At that point, the Polish language was as equally developed as the German and more advanced than the Russian; it was one of major European languages possessing a rich literature and a vocabulary of arts and sciences. The character of Linde's dictionary was historical and not normative. It included 60,000 entries.

In 1808, the decree on the founding of the Law School of Warsaw was issued. Izba Edukacyjna or the Department of Education added 500 new elementary schools. The Jewish population chose to continue their education in Judeo-Germanic tradition in Talmudic schools (unchanged for the last three hundred years).

In 1810, the Board of Directors of the Theater was formed at the suggestion of Wojciech Bogusławski. The theater received a subsidy for its upkeep, for its School of Drama, and a retirement fund for actors. The performances of dramas were most eagerly attended by the public. The structure and popularity of dramas helped evolve Polish romantic theater.

Maria Szymanowska (1789-1831) was a concert pianist and a composer of simple and short mazurkas, preludes, waltzes, polonaises, and etudes - forms later perfected and made world famous by Fryderyk Chopin

(1810-1849). The best Polish violinist ot the time was Feliks Janiewicz (1762-1842), a composer of concertos, sonatas, and music for the violin. He played in London in 1792 and settled in Scotland in Edinburgh in 1815. He was one of the founders of the Philharmonic Society of London and was concert master of its orchestra.

Neo-Classicism and Romanticism in Poland were, in a way, a continuation of the Enlightenment. Scientific work was perceived by many Polish scientists as a patriotic duty to preserve and develop Polish culture. The University of Warsaw grew in importance, training lawyers, teachers, and physicians. The Warsaw Institute of Agronomy and Forestry had a university level learning program, as did the School of Mines founded in Kielce. The Polytechnic of Warsaw opened in 1829.

The Ossoliński Library was founded in southern Poland in the city of Lwów. Polish patriotic student societies of the Filomats and Filarets were secretly founded in Wilno. Until 1830, Warsaw and Wilno were the most important Polish cultural centers. In the 1840s Poznań was most active, followed by Warsaw in early 1860s, and Kraków and Lwów until the end of the 19th century.

Cultural and Economic Oppression by Prussia

The year 1815 saw renewed colonialist efforts by the Berlin government to eradicate the Polish language and culture in Silesia. As a result, forty Polish villages went on strike in 1817 near Ostróda and Nidzica in Mazuria, East Prussia. The Germans immediately arrested the strikers.

In 1817-1823, clandestine Polish students' organizations in Wrocław (Breslau) proclaimed that Polish national territory covered all areas where Polish was the main language. There were 416 Polish grade schools in the Grand Duchy of Poznań in 1819. Józef Lompa (1797-1862) published the *History of Silesia* in 1821, reminding the readers that Silesia was and always had been Polish.

The year 1823 saw the beginning of agrarian reform in the Grand Duchy of Poznań. One year later, King Frederick Wilhelm III von Hohenzollern proclaimed the Constitution of the Grand Duchy of Poznań: the executive branch was to be headed by the King; the actual administration was to be conducted by the provincial president; the unicameral Seym was to be ruled by a two-thirds majority; elective rights were given to Christian males only; appointed judges were to enforce the laws decreed by the King; and the right to demand protection of person and property was granted.

In 1824, an Act of Incorporation of the Gdańsk region of Pomerania into a Prussian province with its capital in Koenigsberg (Królewiec) was issued; the rest of Pomerania was formed into a province with its capital in Stettin (Szczecin). The purpose of the new provincial boundaries was to enforce the Germanization program of the Berlin government.

The Berlin government ordered a massive expropriation of Polish landholders, and an increase in the Germanization pressure on the 416 Polish elementary schools in the Grand Duchy of Poznań. From 1824-1826, 230 Polish landed estates were taken over by new German owners in Poznań area. Protest marches were organized against the imposition of German language in church services in Silesia. The arrests of protesters followed.

In 1827, the Polish Seym of the Grand Duchy of Poznań successfully petitioned the government in Berlin to extend political rights and obligations to the Jews; this created favorable conditions for upper class Jews and led to their eventual assimilation in Germany, after the eviction of the Jewish proletariat to the Polish Kingdom under Russia. The successful assimilation of the wealthy Jews who remained in Germany was facilitated by their subculture based on Yiddish, a Germanic language. Jews were among the patriotic supporters of the policies of Berlin government and made an important contribution to the German culture; thus, in politics they often supported the anti-Polish policies of the Berlin government. In 1827, the Seym of Poznań protested the political discrimination against the Poles.

The Most Exploited Provinces of the Austrian Empire

During 1772-1867, Polish provinces annexed by Austria became the most exploited and most cruelly treated parts of the Austrian Empire. Austrian officials organized peasant mutinies against Polish landowners and fomented mutual hatred between Ukrainians, Poles, and Jews. Mass starvation periodically reached catastrophic proportions, claiming up to 50,000 dead during the worst years of Austrian colonial rule over southern Polish provinces.

Southern or Lesser Poland was renamed by the Austrians in 1772 as

Galicia and Lodomeria -- names of Ruthenian-Ukrainian provinces at the eastern end of the lands annexed by Austria. This was consistent with Austrian policy to eradicate everything Polish and to extend Ukrainian ethnic claims all the way to Kraków. A strict censorship was imposed. A huge Austrian imperial bureaucracy staffed with Germans pestered the population with complicated and intricate bureaucratic formalities.

In 1817, the Austrians revived the provincial Seym of Estates in Lwów, which functioned in 1782-1788 and would function again in 1817-1845. The Emperor Frances I of Austria ruled by decree. He appointed to the Seym of Estates wealthy landowners with aristocratic Austrian titles, two deputies from the city of Lwów, and the Chancellor of the University of Lwów. The Seym was not a representative body, it was entitled to petitions only.

The Economy in the New Kingdom of Poland

The new Kingdom of Poland was the most culturally and scientifically advanced territory within the Russian colonial empire. Poland's economy reflected this fact. Thus, the Finance Minister, Ksawery Drucki-Lubecki (1778-1846), was able to reorganize the economy of the new Kingdom of Poland. In 1819, he obtained the appropriation of funds for the first 1,000 km. of paved roads. In 1821, the Finance Minister balanced the budget of the Kingdom of Poland. When criticized that he did not insist enough on the independence of Poland, he answered: *"Poland needs money, schools, plants capable of manufacturing modern weapons."* Lubecki founded the Bank Polski in 1828. His policies produced a budget surplus of over fifty million zlotys in 1830, the largest since the times of Casimir the Great in the 14th century.

The textile industry was booming. Łódź became the most important textile center in Poland. Ksawery Lubecki included the mining administration in his Commission of Incomes and Finances and boosted zinc production. The metallurgical industry expanded after the development of pig iron, producing mainly agricultural implements and distillery equipment. Industries in Warsaw included silver plating and the production of precision instruments. The capital of Poland had some 40,000 industrial workers. The mining industry started organizing old-age pensions and sick benefits financed out of payroll deductions.

Science, Literature, and Music in the New Kingdom of Poland

In 1822, Jan Śniadecki published *The Philosophy of the Human Mind* on the theory of knowledge and perception, as well as logic. Romanticist Józef Gołuchowski (1797-1858) taught philosophy at the University of Wilno. He rejected the Enlightenment idea of the supremecy of human reasoning and stressed the value of intuition. Gołuchowski opposed the 18th-century materialistic philosophy and emphasized the imagination and emotions. Gotfryd Groddedck, professor of Greek and Latin philology at the University of Wilno, published the first synthetic textbook in Europe in 1811: a history of classical Greek literature. At that time, even a popular science magazine was published in Warsaw.

Frederic Chopin (1810-1849), Sketch by George Sand (1804-1876).

Frederic Chopin first became known in Warsaw as a child prodigy, and then as a composer who was able to make the extraordinary wealth of Polish folk music into world masterpieces.

Clandestine Patriotic Activity in the Spirit of Romanticism

In 1820, as the spirit of Romanticism spread throughout Poland, a clandestine Polish patriotic society was founded in Warsaw. The session of the Seym protested against censorship. Tsar Alexander reacted by closing the Seym for five years and ordering the sessions to be permanently closed to the public.

The National Masonic Lodge of Poland under Walerian Łukasiński (1786-1868) changed its name to Polish Patriotic Society and demanded the unification and restoration of Poland's pre-partition frontiers. The Tsarist authorities responded to it with a law prohibiting clandestine organizations. Walery Łukasiński was arrested and sentenced by a military court to ten years, which sentence was eventually changed to life imprisonment in the Shlisselburg fortress, where he spent 46 years and died in 1868. His military trial was in violation of the Constitution of the Kingdom of Poland, which specified parliamentary trial in such a case.

The next year, Russian secret police, under Nowosilcow, investigated the patriotic societies in Wilno. Some members of these societies were deported to Russia, where they established contact with clandestine Russian democratic societies. Nowosilcew released only those who paid heavy bribes. He turned the investigation of Polish conspirators into a source of considerable income, which he used for gambling, drinking parties, and debauchery. After a number of provocations, Nowosilcew replaced Prince Adam Czartoryski as curator of the educational system in Wilno. A number of students were exiled to the interior of Russia, among them the poet, Adam Mickiewicz, who wrote patriotic poems in the Romanticist style. He wrote the *Crimean Sonets* (1826) and *Konrad Wallenrod* (1828), in which he described the life of a nation in captivity.

Political discontent was spreading. From 1824-1830, unrest engulfed the Polish textile industry. Tsar Nicolas I ordered two Polish divisions to join Russian forces in the war against Turkey in 1828. The Grand Duke Constantine refused. By now married to Joanna Grudzińska, the Princess of Łowicz (1820), Constantine gradually evolved towards Polish patriotism. No one noticed the change.

In 1828, a clandestine patriotic organization was formed in officer's school in Warsaw under Lt. Piotr Wysocki. The organization spread in the Polish

Adam Mickiewicz (1798-1855).

armed forces, and was joined by Maurycy Mochnacki (1803-1834), who became one of its intellectual leaders. He wrote in his book on Polish literature that Romanticism's main task was to awaken the national consciousness at any price. Another leader in the struggle for the independence of Poland, Joachim Lelewel (1786-1861), a professor at the University of Wilno, published a book in 1829 entitled *Poland's Past.* Lelewel defined the Slavic pre-historic tribal democratic process. He called it *gminowładztwo,* or community self-government.

The Emperor of Russia Nicolas I (1796-1855) was crowned in Warsaw cathedral in 1829 as the King of Poland. He spoke fluent Polish and thought about using the Polish Army against Austria and Prussia. Instead he led the Russian army against the Turks, and defeated them at Warna. After this victory, Nicholas I said that he, the present King of Poland, had avenged King Władysław III, the Polish King who had been killed during a battle at Warna in 1444.

Polish-Russian War of 1830-1831

The news of the July (1830) Revolution in France caused a revolutionary fever in Poland, as an economic crisis was deepening and unemployment was widespread. The Polish uprising started on Nov. 29, 1830. Warsaw Arsenal Buildings were taken over by the revolutionaries. The uprising soon spread throughout the Kingdom of Poland. The Administrative Council became The Provisional Government of Poland. The Seym proclaimed a national uprising for the independence of Poland. Gen. Józef Chłopicki as-sumed dictatorial powers.

The uprising broke out in protest against the planned use of the Polish army against revolutionary movements in Western Europe, while Poland was to be occupied with Russian forces. Declaration of the independence of Poland followed.

Gen. Józef Chłopicki (1798-1845).

Gen. Ignacy Prądzyński
(1792-1850).

Polish forces included, besides the regular well-trained army of 40,000, a National Guard (Gwardia Narodowa) in which a separate battalion of 850 Jewish volunteers served. Regimental banners displayed a Polish and Russian inscription, "For our freedom and yours."

The Seym proclaimed the dethronement of the Tsar of Russia as King of Poland. A Polish Government was formed by Adam Czartoryski. Joachim Lelewel led the opposition in the Seym. Gen. Chłopicki's dictatorship collapsed, and the Seym passed the law on duties of a Supreme Commander. Prince Michał Radziwiłł (1778-1850) was nominated as the Commander-in-Chief.

In 1831, a Russian army of 115,000 marched into Poland. It was led by Gen. Iwan Dybicz (1785-1831). In the battle at Stoczek, the Polish cavalry of Gen. Józef Dwernicki (1779-1857) defeated the Russian Division of Gen. Gejsmar. Then, in a five hour battle at Dobre, Col. Jan Skrzynecki delayed the army corp of Russian Gen. Rosen. The hard-fought battle of Wawer followed. In it, Gen. Jan Żymirski and Gen. Piotr Szembek led Polish forces against the Russian forces of Gen. Pahlen and Gen. Rosen. Gen. Chłopicki was wounded in the battle of Grochów near Warsaw. Peace feelers by Gen. Skrzynecki were unproductive. The Army Corp of Gen. Dwernicki entered Lublin and Zamość. Russian forces regrouped in order to attack Warsaw from the south. Polish forces destroyed Gen. Geismar's regiment near Wawer and the corp of Gen. Rosen near Dąb Wielki.

In 1831, the Seym issued a Proclamation of Independence and Dethronement of the Tsar of Russia as King of Poland. It invoked the Polish Social Contract of the First Polish Republic and passed a law to compensate wounded soldiers and their families.

The battle of Iganie was won by Gen. Ignacy Prądzyński (1792-1850); however, the late arrival of Gen. Skrzynecki's forces did not permit it to take full advantage of the victory and to destroy Russian elite forces concentrated near Śniadów.

Fifty-eight questions were addressed to Gen. Skrzynecki about the failure of his leadership; the Seym dismissed him. Had the Seym replaced Skrzynecki much earlier with Gen. Prądzyński, the Poles would have had a better chance in the war.

Adam Czartoryski (1770-1861).

Revolution broke out in the streets of Warsaw. A mob lynched several men accused of treason. The government of Adam Czartoryski resigned. Gen. Jan Krukowiecki (1772-1850) started negotiations on the terms of surrender.

Russian forces of 77,000 attacked Warsaw, defended by 38,000 Poles. The battle lasted two days and, despite Polish heroic resistance, the Russian forces entered Warsaw. Polish defenders crossed the Vistula River to Praga and retreated to Modlin.

The last Commander-in-Chief of the uprising, Gen. Maciej Rybiński, crossed the Prussian border near Brodnica on October 5, 1831 with 20,000 men. The fall of the fortresses of Modlin and Zamość followed.

In late 1831, the Seym decided to go into exile rather than submit to the Tsar. It was the beginning of the Great Emigration of some 9,000 members of the insurrection; two-thirds of them went to France and the rest to England, Switzerland, Belgium, United States, and Canada. Emigrants' properties were soon confiscated. The Polish-Russian war enhanced revolutionary movements in Europe, and Polish professional soldiers helped revolutionaries everywhere.

KINGDOM OF POLAND WITHIN THE RUSSIAN ABSOLUTIST EMPIRE (1831-1917)

(From Romanticism to Positivism)

The Tsar Nicolas I declared the Constitution of the Kingdom of Poland null and void. He abolished the Polish Seym and the Polish army, and he incorporated the Polish Kingdom into the Russian Empire. However, he did not remove the customs, which were actually increased in order to economically exploit Polish provinces. The Tsar imposed martial law (it was to last till 1858) and imposed high taxes to finance the building of Russian fortresses in Poland. The Tsar proclaimed an amnesty for the participants of the uprising except the initial conspirators, the members of Polish parliament, and the Polish Government of Adam Czartoryski.

In 1832, the Highest Criminal Tribunal was established in Warsaw. It immediately tried 254 Polish leaders and sentenced most of them either to death or to deportation to Siberia. However, most of the tried people managed to go into exile. The leaders of the uprising, Piotr Wysocki and Wincenty Niemojewski, were apprehended and sentenced to death. Their death sentence was soon changed to life in prison.

Polish soldiers were assigned to the Russian Army for 25-year tours of duty. The new Organic Statute guaranteed a separate legal system in the Kingdom of Poland and the use of Polish as the official language of the Kingdom.

Tsar Nicolas I ordered and enforced the resettlement of 50,000 Polish noble families - some 250,000 people - east of the Volga River, to Siberia, and about 10% of them to the Caucasus. The deportees were from Podolia, Volhynia, and Lithuania, the areas where Polish independence activities were strong. Russian victory brought the confiscation of over 5,400 manors (1 in 10) in Poland and Lithuania. Two million rubles were collected in punitive taxes. The Holy Alliance was strengthened and, in 1832, the Pope accordingly condemned the uprising. There was a colonialist solidarity. The British did not protest against the treatment of the Poles, in order to be consistent with their denial of home rule in Ireland.

The Universities of Warsaw and Wilno were closed and university libraries were shipped to Russia.

The program of "organic work" was to be used as a legal activity in defense of Polish national culture and land ownership. Poles worked for the eradication of illiteracy and for an increase of national consciousness, especially in the Grand Duchy of Poznań, Silesia, Pomerania, Mazuria, and Warmia under Prussia, as well as in the Kingdom of Poland under Russia, and in Lesser Poland (Galicia) under Austria.

King of Prussia Frederic Wilhelm III, Austrian Emperor Frantz, and Tsar Nicolas I met in 1833 to coordinate anti-revolutionary activities, especially in Polish provinces.

The construction of the citadel in Warsaw was started. In 1839, executions of revolutionaries such as Artur Zawisza, Andrzej Wołłowicz, Szymon Konarski, the emissary of "Young Poland," and others were conducted on the grounds of the citadel, in which thousands of Polish patriots were imprisoned. Polish resistance movements spread through the area of the three partitions and continued with varying intensity.

Prussian efforts to unify the 350 independent German principalities brought a marked coolness in Berlin's relations with Russia. This brought the relaxation of censorship in Poznań.

Activities of the Great Emigration

Poles arrived to Paris as "knights of liberty." The French government granted them a modest allowance and placed them under police surveillance. Some 75% of the exiles were of noble stock, but most of them had no substantial means of support. The name, Great Emigration, was given to them in later years in order to distinguish them from the next waves of political refugees from Poland.

By the end of 1831, the Left Wing formed the Polish National Committee in Paris. Its leader was Johim Lelewel. More radical politicians formed the Polish Democratic Society in 1832 for an independent and reformed Poland free of serfdom.

Adam Czartoryski purchased a palace called Hotel Lambert on the beautiful river island of St. Louis in Paris. He attempted to solve the Polish question by diplomacy; in 1834, he was supported by the Association for National Unity. Lelewel, expelled from France, settled in Belgium and took over the leadership of the "Young Poland" in 1834.

Transition from Classicism to the Romantic Neo-Gothic

The last palaces and the first monumental buildings were built in neo-classical style. Typical is the main building on the campus of the University of Warsaw, which was rebuilt in 1815-1824 in neoclassical style with an arcaded portico on the ground floor. (Originally it was a Baroque Palace of King John Casimir). St. Alexander Church in Warsaw was built in the style of the Roman Pantheon. The monumental building of the Polish Academy of Sciences was built in the new style of Polish classical architecture. The Palace of the Commission of Treasury and Revenue, the Palace of the Minister of Treasury, and the Bank of Poland were built by Antonio Corazzi. Bankowy Square was an example of contemporary urban planning. The Bank of Poland covered the cost of restoration and preservation of many architectural treasures in Poland, like the 14th- century medieval castle of Będzin. The most brilliant design of Corazzi was the Grand Theater of Warsaw, which became the center of artistic and social life in Poland. It included a stage and auditorium, reception rooms, and ballrooms.

Neo-Gothic architecture started in Puławy in 1788-1810. Henryk Marconi (1792-1862) designed the Central Railway Station in Warsaw as an imitation of Palazzo Pitti in Florence. The Europejski Hotel in Warsaw was designed in the Neo-Renaissance style. The Golden Chapel in the Cathedral of Poznań was built in Neo-Gothic style in 1836-1840.

Busts of prominent Poles, scientists, and university professors were sculpted in Wilno by Kazimierz Jelski. Jakub Tatarkiewicz made beautiful sculptures in the antique allegorical style. Romanticism became dominant in Polish sculpture after 1830. Władysław Oleszczyński worked in Paris, Poznań, and Kraków, where he executed allegorical monuments. Oskar Sosnowski worked in Warsaw and in Kraków. Among other works, he is the author of the figure of the famous preacher, Piotr Skarga, and of the monument of

Queen Jadwiga and King Jagiełło in Planty Park in Kraków.

The international crime of the obliteration of the Polish State generated an increased demand for historical paintings, most of them in the Romantic style. Allegorical and historical scenes were painted by Józef Peszka and Aleksander Orłowski. Michał Płoński sketched Polish nobleman and peasants, while Franciszek Lampi painted romantic landscapes and portraits of wealthy landowners and burghers. Neo-Classical paintings such as works by Antoni Brodowski included theatrical compositions and exaggerated gestures. An ultra-romantic portrait of Mickiewicz was painted by Walenty Wańkowicz.

A country squire from the Kraków region, Piotr Michałowski (1800-1855) was one of the greatest Polish painters. Highly educated and talented, he was an excellent portraitist. He loved to paint horses, and did so in pre-Impressionist style. His most expressive work shows the charge of Polish cavalry in Samosierra, Spain.

Views of Poland, its architecture, landscapes, and people were painted with a patriotic accent on porcelain and shown in women's embroidery. The structurally simple Biedermeier became predominant in furniture and in porcelain designs by 1820. Polish porcelain factories were located in Korzec, Baranówka, and Nieborów. Polish sashes continued to be fashionable, as were woven tapestries. Warsaw produced silver-plated cutlery.

Romanticism in Polish Literature

Poles wrote in the Romantic style and many of their great works were written and published in Paris and other cities where Polish exiles lived. *The History of the Uprising of the Polish Nation in 1830-1831* was published by Maurycy Mochnacki, the most prominent critic of early Romanticism. The Polish national epic poem *Pan Tadeusz* was written and published (1834). It was the last work published by Adam Mickiewicz, who became the most renowned Polish poet since Jan Kochanowski. Mickiewicz also published a magazine, *The Polish Pilgrim,* and *The Book of the Polish Nation and its Pilgrimage*. The drama *Kordian* was written by Juliusz Słowacki in

Juliusz Słowacki (1809-1849).

Paris in 1834. One year later, he wrote the drama *Holsztyński*. Słowacki was the most prominent Polish playwright and a great innovator in Polish poetry. The vastness and diversity of Słowacki's talent can be appreciated in his many plays and such works as the philosophical, historical, and fantastic poem entitled "Król Duch" ("King Spirit", 1847). This work has no equal in European Romanticist literature and it inspired many modernist writers.

The third of the great Romantic bards of Poland was Zygmunt Krasiński (1812-1859), a philosopher of history who hesitated between catastrophism and optimism, as well as between tradition and progress. Krasiński wrote a national drama, the *Nie-Boska Komedia* (*The Undivine Comedy*, 1835). In it, he wanders through the nightmare of a revolution similar to Dante's wandering though hell in the *Divina Comedia*. Using his mastery of Polish poetic prose, Krasiński wrote a mythical symbolic drama, *Irydion* (*Iridion*, 1836), in which he describes the struggle of conquered nation with its invaders in a setting of the 3rd century Rome.

Aleksander Fredro (1793-1876) was the greatest playwright of Polish folkloric comedies that dealt with rich variety of Polish country squires and their peculiarities. Fredro served as Napoleon's bodyguard in 1812 and was very contemptuous of Napoleon as a person. Fredro's works still belong to the basic classical repertoire of Polish theater.

The first modern literary historian, Kazimierz Brodziński (1791-1835), published *O klasyczności i romantyczności* (*On Classicism and Romanticism*). He advocated the creation of an original national literature based on native tradition, in order to show the individual character of the Polish nation and its spirit. He believed in the "romantic school" and criticized the classical theory, which demanded the same pattern of literature to be followed by all nations.

The most prominent member of the "Ukrainian School" of Romantic poetry was Antoni Malczewski (1793-1826). He and other writers used Ukrainian themes and folklore. They lived and worked in Warsaw and presented a pessimistic view of life by describing tragic lives of typical Polish Romantic heroes who rebelled and could not free themselves as they drowned in conflicts and contradictions.

The *Great Manifesto* or the *"Poitiers Manifesto"* of the Polish Democratic Society was published in 1836. Its motto was *"Everything for the people, everything by the people."* It advocated the struggle for independence based on a democratic program of equality of all, freedom from serfdom, and conversion of the land held in tenure into ownership by the peasants. In 1836, Wacław Aleksander Maciejowski published *A Comparative History of Slavonic Legislations*. The history of the Polish culture was documented with archeological investigations carried out by the Learned Society of Kraków, the Wilno Archeological Commission, and many individual collectors. Polish Romanticism expressed an upsurge in national and patriotic feelings and the perception of martyred Poland as a future savior in European history.

Polish Theater under Foreign Censorship

In a typically colonialist-imperialist approach, Germans, Russians, and Austrians intended to denationalize the Polish people. They enforced an extensive censorship: certain plays, topics, and even words were forbidden on the stage. That included the Romantic dramas of Mickiewicz, Słowacki, Krasiński, and Norwid - all written in exile. Thus, the priority of the theater was the preservation of Polish language, customs, and traditional clothing. The Germanization programs were enforced from the beginning of the Prussian occupation. Severe Russian censorship was introduced in 1819. The capital of Lesser Poland, called Galicia by the Austrians, was moved from Kraków to Lwów. In both of these cities, Polish theaters played an important role in the preservation of Polish culture. In Warsaw, the Grand Theater was built in 1830-1833. On its large stage, opera and ballet troupes performed. Its smaller stage was named Variety Theater and was used by the drama troupe.

Jan Nepomuce Kamiński, playwright and translator of Shakespeare and Schiller, managed and directed the theater in Lwów from 1809 to 1848. The year 1834 saw the first staging of the comedy *Zemsta* (*The Revenge*), written by Aleksander Fredro, who helped the actors during the staging of his plays in which he emphasized verbal and situational humor. Fredro wrote in a vigorous verse, flexible and comical. He beautifully presented Polish tradition on stage and helped to achieve the splendid staging.

Germans did not permit a permanent Polish theater to exist in Poznań. Thus, with only three Polish theaters in the territories of the Old Polish Nobles' Republic, the Poles developed traveling theaters, which remained busy giving guest performances.

Polish National Music by Romantic Composers

Polish composers expressed their national identity through music. A Polish national style was crystallized by Frederic Chopin in his mazurkas and polonaises. He fully used the sound qualities of the piano and rendered his highly nationalistic compositions in an original and creative manner.

Composers Józef Elsner and Karol Kurpiński wrote music to texts based on Polish history.

Stanisław Moniuszko (1819-1872) created some 360 Polish romantic songs published in 12 volumes. He was also the most distinguished composer of Polish operas. Moniuszko's *Halka* was first staged in 1848 and his *Straszny Dwór* (*The Hounted Manor*) in 1864. All of Moniuszko's operas have a patriotic character, and their action takes place in the typically Polish environment of country squires. Their music is based on Polish national dances such as mazurkas and polonaises. His songs are swift harmonic, rhythmical, and easily accompanied by piano, and became well known throughout Polish lands.

An outstanding violin virtuoso and conductor of the orchestra of the Dresden Opera, Karol Lipiński (1790-1861) composed violin music and an opera. He was a master of violin technique, and played in a violin competition against Nicolo Paganini in Warsaw.

Oskar Kolberg (1814-1890), ethnographer and composer of Polish national dances, collected 13,000 songs with words and music from various regions of Poland. His collection - *Pieśni ludu polskiego* (*Polish Folk Songs*) - was published in 1857, and immediately hailed as a monument to the vitality of Polish folk culture.

The Beginning of the Industrial Revolution in Poland

Andrzej Zamoyski introduced cash payments instead of serf work in private industrial plants. Soon followed the considerable growth of linen factories in Żyrardów and large textile works in Łódź based on steam power. In 1840-1847, the railroad from Warsaw to Vienna was built.

The year 1850 is considered to be the beginning of industrial revolution in Polish lands. The first steamships sailed on the Vistula River.

In 1851, customs between the Kingdom of Poland and Russia were abolished. In 1856, the first gas street lamps were installed in Warsaw, where one year later, the Medical Academy was established and became a center of patriotic activities.

The Russian defeat in the Crimean War (1854-1856) at the hands of England, France, Turkey, and others brought the beginning of reforms by Tsar Alexander II. He allowed economic progress based on the "organic work," but staunchly opposed Polish independence. In 1858, however, the martial law was lifted in Poland; censorship was eased; and amnesty for emigrants was proclaimed. As an additional concession, the Polish language was permitted in the postal system.

Unrest and the Rule of Wielkopolski

In June of 1860, a patriotic demonstration took place during the funeral of the widow of Gen. Józef Sowiński (1777-1831), a hero of the battle of Warsaw in 1831. The people of Warsaw commemorated the uprising of 1830 on November 29 with protest marches. Among the posters carried some called for the free unification of Italy, which was currently in the news. Five demonstrators were killed by Russian soldiers. Renewed protest marches resulted in 100 people killed. In 1861, martial law was reestablished in Warsaw. The same year, the learned circles of Wilno published *Słownik języka polskiego (A Dictionary of the Polish Language)*, sometimes called *The Wilno Dictionary*. It included many regional words from north-eastern parts of Poland and is proof of a strong cultural connection between the Wilno region and the rest of ethnic Poland.

The Agrarian Association proposed cash rent for land use, instead of peasant labor. Margrave Aleksander Wielopolski (1803-1887), the head of civil government in the Kingdom of Poland, proposed a Land Reform and an act on Jewish Emancipation. However, Wielopolski banned political demonstrations; mass arrests followed, as well as the deportation of activists including Catholic and Jewish clergymen. Polish-Jewish solidarity blossomed. It was the high point of the trend towards Jewish assimilation in Warsaw.

Cyprian K. Norwid (1821-1883).

The Town's Resistance Committee (the Reds) was founded by Apollo Korzeniowski (father of Józef Teodor Konrad Korzeniowski, who wrote in English under the pen name of Joseph Conrad). Leopold Kronenberg founded the conservative Direction of Whites. At that time, Jarosław Dąbrowski, a Russian army officer and Polish revolutionary, arrived in Warsaw and joined the Reds.

In the years 1862-1863, several decrees were prepared by Aleksander Wielopolski. They pertained to contracts on the individual land use by the peasants and on the reformation of Polish-language school system, including Szkoła Główna, as the University of Warsaw was renamed. Wielopolski issued the decree on complete emancipation of the Jews in Poland. The decree primarily benefitted educated professionals who assimilated into Polish culture. The Yiddish-speaking Jewish masses remained within their traditional subculture, based on Jewish religious and ethnic tradition and the use of the Yiddish language. The University of Warsaw, the Medical School, and the Law School reopened.

The End of Romanticism in Poland

Polish Romanticist poetry did not end with the failure of the European revolutions of 1848. Cyprian Kamil Norwid was one of the greatest creators and innovators of Polish poetry. His *Vade mecum* contains a manifesto of innovative poetry. He wrote dramas such as *Kleopatra* (*Cleopatra*, 1872), and criticized the lack of humanitarianism among contemporary industrialists and bankers. He wrote about the love of work as well as of the feeling of tragic loneliness and individualism.

The best and most prominent Polish novelist, Józef Ignacy Kraszewski (1812-1887), wrote some 400 works - mostly historical novels but also including social, moral, and folk novels. Kraszewski wrote a series of novelized chronicles covering the entire history of Poland starting with *Stara Baśń (An Ancient Tale*, 1876) and ending with the "Saxon Night" or *Saskie ostatki* (*Saxon Shrovetide*,1889). In 1841-1851, Kraszewski accomplished great editorial work in the periodical *The Athenaeum* (1841-1901), which in 1876-1901 acquired an encyclopedic character.

Eclecticism in Polish Architecture

Eclecticism was prevalent in architecture of this time, combining neo-Renaissance and neo-Baroque, as well as utilizing early Romanesque, neo-Gothic, and neo-classical styles throughout the country.

Early Romanesque was used in St. Charles Borromeo Church in Warsaw, where the utilization of metal permitted inexpensive repetition of identical decorative motifs. More precious material like marble was used in the Bristol Hotel in Warsaw

Positivism and industrialization demanded industrial buildings for factories and the housing of workers. Neo-Gothic style was used on the campus of the University of Kraków and in Collegium Novum by Feliks Księżarski, as well as in the rebuilding of a monastery that served as the first Polish museum, the Czartoryski Collection.

The neo-Renaissance was used by Filip Pokutyński in the building of the House of the Academy of Learning; and by Tomasz Pryliński in the rebuilding of the medieval Cloth Hall in Kraków. Pryliński used the Florentine style in building the headquarters of the Florianka Insurance Company. The Savings Bank of Szpitalna Street was built in the same style by Maksymilian Nitsch and Karol Zaremba. Jan Zawiejski modeled the Municipal Theater of Kraków after the Paris Opera.

Designs in the style of Dutch Mannerism of bricks with metal ornaments were used by such architects as Władysław Ekielski and Teodor Talowski.

Sculpture and Painting by the End of the 19th Century

Sculptures of erotic and mythological subjects were made by Wiktor Brodzki in post-classical style, sometimes combining classical figures with neo-Gothic buildings. Many of the very talented Polish sculptors participated in styles common throughout Europe.

Realism dominated Polish painting during the second half of the 19th century. It was the style of Antoni Teofil Kwiatkowski, Franciszek Kostrzewski, Józef Szermentowski, and Aleksander Kostis, who painted Polish subjects including the Tatra Mountains and portraits.

Polish historical paintings have shown battle scenes by January Suchodolski , and sentimental historiographies by Antoni Piotrowski and Henryk Siemiradzki. Great portraitists and historical painters were Józef Simmer and Henryk Rodakowski. Juliusz Kossak painted 17th- century battles. Kossak's student, Artur Grottger, illustrated patriotic themes of the Insurrection of 1863 in the realistic style. Huge historical paintings by Jan Matejko taught Poles about important and glorious moments of their past with visionary reconstructions painted in a realistic style. Historical paintings by Józef Brandt were rendered in a very dynamic style. An excellent teacher of a generation of painters was Wojciech Gerson (1841-1901), who himself was a painter of historical themes. His most outstanding student was Maximilian Gierymski, who painted with photographic accuracy. Aleksander Gierymski was a realistic painter under the influence of Impressionism. Slavic folk tales were painted in realistic style by Witold Pruszkowski.

Stanisław Witkiewicz (1851-1915) rebelled against the realistic school and stated that formal and artistic values should be the most important rather than the

Jan Matejko (1841-1893).

content of a painting.

Along with painting and sculpture, artistic weaving flourished in Poland despite industrialization and mass production.

The Patriotic Role of the Polish Theater

During the second half of the 19th century, Polish theater worked under different conditions of censorship in the three zones of partitions. The leading actress of the Warsaw theater was Helena Modrzejewska-Modjeska who arrived from Kraków and brought about a revival of Shakespearian plays. The Warsaw theater was a theater of stars without a unifying directorial policy.

From 1866-1885, the theater of Kraków was managed by Stanisław Koźmian, who brought a new approach of working with actors and new staging techniques. He eliminated extravagances and insisted on truth on the stage, with the goal of making the performance as a whole excellent, rather than permitting strong individual displays. The actors were forbidden to acknowledge applause during the scenes. Koźmian staged eighteen Shakespearian plays translated directly from the English original. Besides a large repertoire of Polish plays by Kochanowski, Zabłocki, Bogusławski and Mickiewicz, as well as Fredro's comedies and Słowacki's tragedies, he staged French, Spanish, and Russian dramas. The main role of Koźmin's theater was the preservation of Polish language and literature throughout the three partition zones.

The Lwów theater used plots from national history and staged specific Polish variants of melodrama. It also had an opera auditorium where the operas by Władysław Żeleński (1837-1921) were first staged.

The Polish theater of Poznań

Helena Modrzejewska-Modjeska (Opid, 1821-1883), Actress.

was not allowed by the Prussians to acquire a building until 1870. Earlier it had to depend on guest performances only. Once reestablished, the Poznań theater gave guest performances in Gdańsk, Wrocław, and other cities in the Prussian zone of partition.

By the end of the 19th century, additional Polish theaters were built in Kraków (1893), Lwów (1900), Łódź, Kalisz, and Lublin. Polish theaters in the eastern part of the Old Republic were closed down by the Russians after the January Insurrection of 1864.

There were some fifty traveling Polish theater companies that gave summer open-air garden performances in Warsaw and other cities, as well as in numerous health resorts.

A popular and exuberant amateur theater movement developed in all Polish territories. It included members of farming community, industrial workers, and students.

Polish Music at the End of the 19th Century

Polish composers wrote mainly operas and songs, as well as chamber music and pieces for the piano and violin.

Henryk Wieniawski was a virtuoso violinist who also composed concertos and short pieces for the violin.

Eugieniusz Pankiewicz and Aleksander Zarzycki were the leading song composers. The best known piano composers were Antoni Stolpe, Antoni Rutkowski, and Juliusz Zarębski.

Polish singers often performed abroad. Marcelina Sembrich-Kochańska, an operatic soprano, was a prima donna in the best European opera houses and eventually became a permanent singer in the New York Metropolitan Opera. Polish musicians playing abroad included Polish pieces in order to popularize their national music.

The chairman of the Warsaw Music Society, Zygmunt Noskowski (1846-1909), composed four symphonies, orchestral works, piano music, and many songs. He was an excellent teacher of musical composition. Władysław Żeleński (1837-1921) conducted an orchestra in Warsaw, organized the Warsaw Music Society, and taught in the Musical Institute. He later became the director of a school of music at the Musical Society of Kraków.

Press in the Kingdom of Poland

Some 160 new Polish periodicals were on the market from 1849-1860, and about 120 from 1861-1864. Daily news was in demand. In 1868, 16 out of the 100 periodicals were dailies. Periodicals were specialized as political, economic, commercial, cultural-literary, technical, and scientific. Entitled *Rozrywki dla dzieci* (*Children's Entertainment*), newspapers for children were started in 1824 by Klemantyna Tańska-Hoffmanowa. Seventeen women's magazines were published in 1818-1835.

Henryk Rzewuski founded The *Dziennik Warszawski* (*Warsaw Daily*) in 1851 with 2,300 subscribers. The *Gazeta Warszawska* (*Warsaw Gazette)* in 1859-1861 had 7,000 subscribers. The *Gazeta Codzienna* (*Daily Gazette*) had 7,500 subscribers in 1861. The *Kurier Warszawski* sold 4,000 copies in 1863, and 20,000 in 1883. It installed the first rotary press in 1878.

A Warsaw periodical, the *Wędrowiec* (*The Wanderer*), printed the first photographic illustration in 1882. The greatest masters of Polish literature stimulated the development of Polish journalism by having their works printed in installments. From 1866 on, ideological presses of various political and social groups emerged. It grew rapidly. Many of political periodicals were published abroad. Attempts were made to reach the masses. The development of modern printing techniques helped the expansion of illustrated periodicals. The invention of photographic techniques brought the development of illustrated magazine. In 1860, photography was introduced in the *Tygodnik Ilustrowany* (*Illustrated Weekly*). It consisted of engraved pictures. Pictures produced by the photochemical carbon process of autotypy were introduced in 1881.

The Uprising of 1863-1864

An attempt was made on life of the Grand Duke Constantine, the viceroy in charge of the Kingdom of Poland. Jarosław Dąbrowski was arrested. Contacts between Polish and Russian revolutionaries increased. Weapons were imported in preparation of an armed struggle for the independence of Poland. The Russian Revolutionary Committee of "Zemlya i Volya" (Land and Liberty) promised to help the Poles. Wielopolski tried to torpedo the planned insurrection by ordering the conscription of members of Polish patriotic organizations into the Russia Army.

On January 22, 1863, the Central Committee of the leftist Reds, acting as the Temporary National Government, issued the Manifesto for the Insurrection. It called the Polish Nation to arms. The proclamation of the Provisional Government of Poland in Warsaw called for the abolition of serfdom; the recognition of arable land as the property of the tenants; and all inhabitants to be declared free and equal citizens of Poland. The proclamation also included the request for help from Poles in Austria and Prussia, without armed insurrection there, in order not to unite the three partitioning powers of Austria, Germany, and Russia against Poland. The Proclamation ended with an appeal to the Russian Nation to join the Poles in an effort to abolish tsarist tyranny.

During the night of Jan. 22, 1863, the first engagements between insurrectionists and the Russian units took place. The rail and telephone connections with Warsaw were cut. Russian garrisons of 100,000 men were attacked in some twenty locations. Insurrection spread from ethnic Poland to Lithuania, Byelorussia (Belarus), and Ukraine. The English, French, and Austrian governments demanded the revival of the constitution of the Kingdom of Poland of 1815. Prussia offered military assistance to the Tsar.

Romuald Traugutt (1826-1864), the last dictator of the uprising, did not hope for any significant help from western countries. Instead he had to rely on the peasants for a mass-levy and on closer relations with revolutionary movements abroad.

A manifesto was issued by the Tsar Aleksander II (1818-1881). In it, he promised amnesty to the insurrectionists if they lay down their arms within a month. The British, French, and Austrian governments sent diplomatic notes to Russia demanding a change in Russian policies in the Kingdom of Poland.

The fighting throughout Poland, Belarus, and Ukraine intensified. The leader of the uprising in Płock and Kalisz, Zygmunt Padlewski was executed. The payroll of Russian Army in Poland was captured by the units of Aleksander Waszkowski.

Polish casualties were heavy in the unequal struggle. Mikhail Muraviev (1795-1866), the Governor General in Wilno, was called the "Hangman" after he put down the uprising in Lithuania by mass reprisals and executions. Muraviev coerced the Kahals to cooperate against the insurrection, which in sixteen months fought in 1,229 engagements against the Russian Army (956 in the Polish Kingdom, 237 in Lithuania, and 36 in Ukraine and Belorus).

In 1864, martial law was imposed in Galicia as the Austrian, Prussian, and Russian governments cooperated against the insurrection. The leaders of the revolution were executed in the Citadel of Warsaw: Romuald Traugutt; Rafał Krajewski (1834-1864); Roman Żuliński (1833-1864); Józef Toczyski (1826-1664); and Jan Jeziorański (1834-1864).

Romuald Traugutt (1826-1864) Leader of the Uprising for Freedom and End of Serfdom was Executed in the Citadel of Warsaw.

The insurrection was started by revolutionary nobles. It was joined by young workers and craftsmen. The last to leave the struggle were peasant volunteers.

Russian Reprisals and the Economy

The Tsar proclaimed the abolition of serfdom, and a prohibition on land purchases by the Poles. They also were forbidden to build and repair Catholic churches in Lithuania, Byelorussia, and Ukraine. The Tsar ordered the enforcement of an intense Russification program.

The administrative system of the Kingdom of Poland was integrated with the rest of the Russian Empire in 1864. While the Tsar ordered the abolition of serfdom in the Kingdom of Poland, he left it in force in the rest of the tsarist lands. In 1867, an imperial order subjugated the Catholic clergy of the Kingdom of Poland to the St. Petersburg Roman Catholic College.

In 1869, the Russian language was imposed on the University of Warsaw and it became a Russian University. Thus, the only two remaining Polish Universities were located in Kraków and Lwów.

Strikes were prohibited. In 1870, Russian military courts acquired jurisdiction over civilian Poles. The harsh new rules increased Polish emigration to the United States of America and to Canada. Poles took part in the French revolution of 1871. Jarosław Dąbrowski was nominated Commander-in-Chief of the French revolutionary forces on May 5, shortly before his death in combat on May 23. Many other Polish veterans of the 1863 uprising took part in the revolution in Paris.

Warsaw's population reached 223,000. By 1880, the number of industrial workers increased to 150,000 in the Kingdom of Poland under Russia. The value of industrial production rose to 200 million rubles. The network of railroad lines increased to 2,100 kilometres in the truncated Kingdom of Poland. It was the beginning of rapid population growth due to industrialization and the integration of the Kingdom of Poland into the Russian economy. The Polish currency was eliminated. There was an increase in landless rural population and in ever-smaller farms.

Positivism in Polish Culture and Science

The failure of the insurrection of 1863 brought demands for "organic work" in order to raise the economic and intellectual potential of Polish people. The Main School (or the university) in Warsaw produced important scientific achievements in biology, chemistry, and linguistics until the Russians closed it in 1869.

In 1875, the Museum of Agriculture and Industry was opened, which, under the cover of economic activity, conducted editorial work, set up courses at a university level, and maintained research laboratories. Maria Skłodowska (-Curie) worked in physics laboratory (1890-1891), and Stanisław Kalinowski measured terrestrial magnetism in 1902. In 1881, the Mianowski Fund was organized for the support of research and publishing activity. It published university textbooks - such monographical publications as the Mathematical and Physical Library, Mathematical and Physical Works and Dissertations, Philosophical Library, Philological Works, and the Library of Legal Knowledge. The Mianowski Fund helped to finance scientific journals, to grant foreign scholarships, and to guide the development of scholarship in the Kingdom of Poland. In 1885, a clandestine Polish university was organized in Warsaw. Its faculty included prominent scholars, who were not permitted to teach in Polish.

In 1897, publication of *Poradnik dla samouków* (*Teach Yourself*) started. It was the only publication of its kind in Europe, presenting high-

178

quality material meant for students who could not attend foreign universities. The self-teaching textbooks were prepared by outstanding scholars in cytology, anatomy, theory of evolution, philosophy, psychology, tele-communications, theory of relativistic empiricism, chemistry (including the organic synthesis of urea), sociology, anthropology, economics, and the theory of pedagogy based on experimental psychology.

The *Monumenta Poloniae Historica* was published by August Bielowski, an eminent historian. New publications were designed to combat rural illiteracy and to popularize the natural sciences. Collective pub-lications such as the *Polish Geographic Dictionary*, the *Dictionary of the Polish Language*, and the *Great Illustrated Encyclopedia* were written by eminent scholars.

Poles continued to resist Russification. In 1875, Kondrad Pró-szyński, the publisher of *Gazeta Świąteczna (Holiday Gazette)*, designed for wide readership, also published the first modern text of elementary Polish language. Its yearly editions reached 1,200,000 by 1916.

National ideas were cultivated by learned periodicals to the point that there were nearly no local differences in all the zones of divided Poland. The monthly *Biblioteka Warszawska* discussed science, arts, and industry and favored ideas of Positivism. It strengthened the editorial movement in the Kingdom of Poland. *Biblioteka Warszawska* served as an important scientific directory. All aspects of Polish national culture were registered by Oskar Kolberg in 23 volumes of his publication *Lud (The Common People)* published in 1865-1890.

In 1880, *Poland's Internal History* was published by Tadeusz Kurzon of the "optimist school." Aleksander Świętochowski (1849-1938) published the Polish positivist weekly *Prawda*. He demanded social reforms, such as the emancipation of women and Jews.

The world first condensation of oxygen and nitrogen was achieved by Zygmunt Wróblewski and Karol Olszewski. Marian Smoluchowski discovered the laws governing the Brownian movement and advanced the kinetic-molecular theory of matter. Emil Godlewski worked on photosynthesis, respiration, and water movement in plants. Napoleon Cybulski separated the first hormone and created the basis for encephalography. In 1874, Tadeusz Browicz, an anatomo-pathologist, discovered the germ of the typhoid fever. Ludwik Teichmann discovered the hemin salt crystals. Karol Estreicher (1827-1908) created the monumental *Bibliografia Polska* (*The Polish Bibligraphy*), working in the Jagellonian Library in Kraków.

The Legal Society, founded in Lwów, published *Przegląd Prawa i Administracji* (*Law and Administration Review*) in 1870. The same year, Władysław Plater founded the Polish National Museum at Rapperswil in Switzerland.

In 1871, the Technical Academy was reorganized as the Polytechnic of Lwów under Maksymilian Thullie, a co-inventor of reinforced concrete structures. He added research in mining, metallurgy, agriculture, and forestry. Professor Ignacy Mościcki invented methods for extracting nitric acid from air.

World class scientists worked in Lwów. From 1856 on, Antoni Małecki lectured on Polish literature and language at the University of Lwów. Professor Ludwik Finkel published the *Bibliography of Polish History*. Tadeusz Wojciechowski taught medieval history, and professor Szymon Askenazy specialized in the modern history of Poland. Władysław Abraham taught the history of law. Polish philology was taught by Roman Pilat. Kazimierz Twardowski founded the Lwów philosophical school, the beginning of the Warsaw-Lwów philosophical school.

In 1874, the *Copernicus Society of Naturalists* was founded in Lwów and published a periodical, *The Cosmos*. In 1886, the Historical Society of Lwów started publishing the *Historical Quarterly;* the University Teachers Association published a journal, the *Museum;* and The Medical Society of Lwów published the *Archives of Biological and Medical Sciences.* The Philological Society inaugurated the periodical the *Eos* in 1893. Two years later, the Ethnographic Society of Lwów started publishing *Lud* (*the People*). Most of these publications were financed by the Association for the Support of Polish Learning in Lwów founded by Oswald Balzer, professor of the history of law. Funds for the preservation of monuments and archives in Lwów were provided by the Ossoliński Institution, which continued to publish and serve as a center of historical research.

Economic and Cultural Persecution by Germany

In 1874, the Berlin government ordered the arrest and two-year imprisonment of the Archbishop of Gniezno-Poznań, Mieczysław

Ledóchowski. One hundred parish priests were removed, and the Catholic Seminary in Poznań was closed by the blocking of Church funds. German was imposed as the official language in all Polish provinces under the Berlin government in 1876. One year later, the German language was imposed in the Seym of the Grand Duchy of Poznań, which was packed with Germans. In 1878 came the closing of the Polish Society for Rural Education on orders of the Prussian government.

Poles defended themselves by founding the Polish Association of Rural Libraries in 1880 in Poznań, which soon had 1,000 libraries in Poznania and Silesia.

In 1881, Wojciech Kętrzyński founded the Polish Aid Committee for Silesia, Mazuria, and Pomerania. The teaching of the Catholic religion in German language schools was prohibited by the Berlin government in 1883.

The imperial government of Germany issued a decree in 1886 that founded the German Colonization Commission with an initial capital of 100,000,000 marks for the purchase of land held by Poles, and for its resale to ethnic Germans as a form of economic "ethnic cleansing." It was also the Berlin government's response to the economic success of Polish banks in Poznań and in provinces. The Poles defended themselves by founding a Polish cultural and educational newspaper, the *Olsztyn Gazette,* the same year.

A new German decree came in 1887. It ordered the removal of the Polish language from all schools in Poznania, Pomerania, Silesia, Warmia, and Mazuria. In 1889, the Polish Miners' Union of Self-Help in Upper Silesia conducted a ten day general strike to protest against German colonial exploitation and the Germanization program. In 1893, the Polish Socialist Party of Greater Poland in Poznania was founded with the purpose of rebuilding an independent Polish state. Its program was proclaimed in 1897.

The anti-Polish extremist lobby formed the *Deutscher Ostmarkenverein,* or *Hakata* in 1894. It used political slogans that would be echoed by Hitler's *Lebensraum.* The Berlin government promoted glorification of German Brethren known as Teutonic Knights, perpetrators of medieval mass murders including genocide of the Balto-Slavic Prussians. There was a further intensification of anti-Polish measures.

German Emperor Wilhelm II von Hohenzollern (1859-1941) delivered an anti-Polish speech in Toruń. The wide-spread Polish response was summarized in the slogan: "No Kashubia without Poland." The Poles responded with a massive Polish national revival. In 1895, the Polish People's Bank was founded in Bytom, Silesia. It was followed by the similar formation of savings and loans banks throughout Upper Silesia: in Opole in 1897, in Siemianowice in 1898, in Katowice in1898, and in Racibórz in 1900. In 1896, the People's Party of Mazuria (southern East Prussia), was founded, with a newspaper called *People's Gazette.*

Anti-Polish Emergency Laws in Prussia were passed in Berlin in 1898. The funds of the German Colonization Commission in Polish provinces were increased to 995,000,000 marks. There was a noticeable growth of a German sense of insecurity in the East. "Ostflucht" was the name given to the German flight from Polish lands in the German-Prussian Empire. The *"Ostflucht"* was a sign of Polish successes in the struggle for the land. There also was the growth of west German industry, which was financed by the plunder of France in the war of 1870-1871 and resulted in a demand for labor in West Germany.

The Berlin government prohibited Poles from settling in new Polish villages without a special permit. This, and other similar measures, resulted in the growth of membership in the Polish National League for Self-Defense, as well as in protest marches in Poznań against the treatment of Poles as second class citizens in 1900.

In 1901, a schools strike in Wrzśsnia was held against changing school prayer from Polish to German. The German police conducted public flogging of children and jailed the protesting parents. Some parents spent up to two years in jail.

The Polish response effected the 1903 defeat of a German political machine in the race for a seat in the Berlin parliament. Instead, Wojciech Korfanty (1873-1939) won the election in Katowice-Zabrze. Incensed at this outcome, the Germans responded with an anti-Polish law on land settlements in 1904.

A two-year wave of strikes followed in protest of the persecution of the Poles in Silesia, in all of Poznania, in Pomeria, as well as in East-Prussian Warmia, and in Mazuria. In 1906, a strike of 100,000 school children in Pomerania and Poznania demanded religious education in Polish.

The following year, the Poles won an election victory in Upper Silesia. Five Polish deputies were sent to the Berlin Parliament, where they joined the Polish Circle of Deputies. The Polish Socialist Party of Prussia demanded the independence of Poland.

In 1908, the government in Berlin proclaimed the Law of Compulsory Expropriation of Polish owners lands and the resale of these properties to Germans. The new law was accompanied by a decree on the elimination of Polish from public meetings. Poles called it the "muzzle law." These German measures led to the 1909 creation of the National Democratic Party in Greater Poland and to the 1910 founding of the Mazurian People's Bank in Szczytno by the Mazurian People's Party. The Polish Christian Democratic Party of Silesia was also founded and published its own newspaper, the *Goniec Wielkopolski* (*Greater Poland's Messenger*). It soon reported on the population census in Prussia. A Polish Christian Democratic Party was founded in Silesia by Wojciech Korfanty. It was followed in 1912 by the founding of the Polish-Catholic People's Party in Grudziądz.

Fair in Lwów Shows a Gloomy Reality under Austria

The first national fair and exhibition in Lwów (Targi Wschodnie) was opened in 1874. It showed Galicia as the least industrialized and poorest province in Europe, with the highest birth and death rates. The exhibition ridiculed the "Austrian colonial program," which set 3 percent of Germans to oppress 45 percent of Poles, who were to oppress 41 percent of Ruthenians and Ukrainians, who in turn were to oppress 11 percent of Yiddish speaking Jews. The Jews, by virtue of their "strangle hold" on the economy, were to oppress everybody. The exhibition showed that only 400 families had enough land to be considered wealthy.

Galicia, the largest and poorest province of the Austrian Empire still paid the highest rate of income taxes in Europe and, as a result, two million people emigrated from Galicia by 1914 mostly to the United States. Mass starvation periodically reached catastrophic proportions claiming up to 50,000 dead during the worst years. The losses would have been greater if emigration had not occurred.

Economic and Political Life under Austria

In 1877-1913, the Seym of Lwów was controlled by a Polish majority and the Austrians were able to foment and exploit the friction between Poles and the large Ukrainian minority.

The Galician crude oil production rose from 92 to 1,488,000 tons from 1890-1911. In Cieszyn, Silesia, coal mining increased from 3,400,000 to 7,600,000 tons, or about half of the entire Austro-Hungarian production from 1890-1913.

In 1892, the Social-Democratic Party of Galicia was founded, along with its own newspapers. It demanded a ten or eight hour work day, better working conditions, and cheaper housing.

In 1895, Roman Dmowski (1864-1939) of the National League founded the *All-Polish Review (Przeglad Wszechpolski)* in Lwów. The National League became the National Democratic Party in 1897.

In 1903, the political program of National Democracy was published in Dmowski's book, *Thoughts of a Modern Pole;* it included the idea that Germany had been and was the main enemy of the Polish people and that Poland could be rebuilt only in alliance with Russia. Dmowski believed that there was no hope to integrate Yiddish-speaking Jewish masses and started to formulate anti-Semitic and anti-German political programs.

Stanisław Kutrzeba published the *History of Polish Government in Outline* in 1905. It was the first of the many well-documented 20th century works on Polish historical topics.

Polish Scientific Activity in the Early 20th Century

Education in Polish language was forbidden under the Russian colonial rule. Thus the Polish University at Warsaw had to be clandestine. It was renamed the Society for Scientific Courses. Its Division I taught linguistics and literature; Division II taught anthropology, social sciences, history, and philosophy; and Division III taught mathematics and natural sciences. In 1905-1918, the Society for Scientific Courses consisted of 300 scholars and 25,000 students, of whom 15,000 were women. In 1915, under the German occupation of Warsaw, the Polish University and Polytechnic was organized. After 1905, the activities of the Mianowski Fund intensified as it became "the ministry of Polish science in disguise." It financed, with vast public contributions, the Warsaw Learned Society and numerous laboratories.

Warsaw Learned Society was founded in 1907, after the Friends of Learning Society was organized in Wilno in 1906. However, since the Polonization of the universities in Kraków (1870) and Lwów (1871) and the founding of the Academy of Learning in Kraków in 1873, southern Polish provinces under Austria were the leaders of Polish intellectual life and acquired a European standard.

The Academy of Learning of Kraków held a leading position in scholarship among Polish learned societies until 1918. Two of its three departments were dedicated to humanities, and one to the mathematical and natural sciences. In the years 1873-1918, it produced about one hundred serial historical publications, plus 52 volumes of Reports of the Physiographic Commission.

The Kraków historical school at Jagiellonian University was led by Józef Szujski and Michał Bobrzyński, who analyzed the political and legal background of the downfall of Poland. Comparative Slavic linguistic studies were conducted by Lucjan Malinowski, Jan Rozwadowski, and Jan Łoś. Classical philology was taught by Kazimierz Morawski from Poznań, and Byzantine studies were organized by Leon Sternbach. Ludwik Gumplowicz influenced German and Anglo-Saxon sociology. A high standard was achieved at the Law School in teaching Roman law by Fryderyk Zoll, criminal law by Edmund Krzymuski, and canon law by Bolesław Ulanowski.

Maria Skłodowska-Curie, (1867-1934).

Among the emigrant Polish scientists was Maria Skłodowska-Currie, who twice won the Noble Prize (1903 and 1911) for her discoveries of polonium and radium and their respective compounds. A Polish patriot, she named the first element discovered by her polonium. She initiated the establishing of the Radium Institute in Paris (1912) and the Radiological Laboratory and Radium Institute in Warsaw in 1932.

Many Polish world-class scientists taught abroad. To name a few examples: mathematician Stanisław Leśniewski; Feliks Jasiński and Stanisław Kierbedź were specialists in structural analysis, bridge building, etc.; Wojciech Świętosławski pioneered thermo-chemistry, and later served as the Minister of Education in Poland in 1935-1939; Gabriel Narutowicz, a hydro-power engineer, taught at the Polytechnic in Zurich, and later became the President of Poland; physio-chemist Marceli Nencki ; organic chemist Stanisław Kostanecki; physicist Józef Wierusz-Kowalski; chemist Tadeusz Estreicher; classical philologist Tadeusz Zieliński; and Slavist, historian of culture, language, and literaure Aleksander Brukner. Most of them taught in Poland after the First World War.

Language and Literature in the Early 20th Century
The reform of the orthography of the Polish language was completed in 1891. Following its inauguration of *Prace Filologiczne (The Philological Studies)* in 1885, the Kraków Academy of Learning begun to issue two other publications: *Poradnik Językowy (The Language Handbook)*in 1901, and *Język Polski (The Polish Language)* in 1913. In addition, the Academy of learning published *Słownik Gwar Polskich (Dictionary of Polish Dialects)* from 1900 to 1911; and in 1915, *Język Polski i jego historia (The Polish Language and Its History)* - two volumes of the *Encyklopedia Polska.*

Another reform of Polish orthography was carried out in 1918.

Polish literature blossomed. Adam Asnyk wrote poetry linking the Romanticist traditions with social problems viewed in a Positivist manner. Adolf Dygasiński wrote excellent naturalist novels about animals. Eliza Orzeszkowa, writer and journalist, wrote tendentious positivist literature; her best and most famous novel was *Nad Niemnem (On the Shores of Niemen,* 1887). Bolesław Prus (Aleksander Głowacki, 1847-1912) was a writer and columnist of the period of realism. In *Lalka (The Doll,* 1890), he described the "last Romanticists" and the defeat of the positivist "dreamers." Henryk Sienkiewicz (1846-1916) wrote Polish historical novels. His novel, *Quo Vadis*, about early Christians in Nero's Rome won him a Noble Prize (1905) and was by far the greatest bestseller worldwide at the time.

In 1898, Arthur Górski was the first to use the term of the "Young Poland." The Young Poland literary style (1890–1914) of the *fin de siecle* was influenced by western European style. It included entire literary works written in regional dialect. The dialect of the Podhale mountain region in Southern Poland was used in some works by Stanisław Witkiewicz and Kazimierz Przerwa-Tetmajer; the dialect of the Kielce region was used by Stefan Żeromski; and the Łowicz dialect was used by Władysław Reymont, who was awarded the Nobel prize in 1926 for his epic novel *Chłopi (The Peasants)*.

Henryk Sienkiewicz (1846-1916).

A "demonic prophet of Polish modernism" of the Young Poland, Stanisław Przybyszewski (1868-1927) wrote, among other essays, *Chopin and Nietzsche* in 1895; a prose poem "De Profundis" (1900); and a cycle of plays in 1901-1903. Przybyszewski propagated the cult of the "naked soul" and "lust," which created around him an atmosphere of scandal. He wrote expressionist poetry after the World War One.

From 1905 on, the Green Baloon, a satirical cabaret in Kraków, was a center of artistic life. The Young Poland style was a rebellion against the utilitarian literature of the Positivist period. There was some pessimism in its frequent attacks on "dreamy Romanticism" expressed by the leading writers and literary critics, Stanisław Brzozowski, and Karol Irzykowski.

A professor of comparative literature and a symbolic, visionary poet, Jan Kasprowicz was also an outstanding translator of Greek, English, German, French, and Scandinavian literature.

The novelist, Stefan Żeromski, was called "the conscience of the nation." His novels cover Polish themes from the time of Napoleonic campaigns to the early post-World War One period.

Architecture and Sculpture at the Turn of the Century

Public buildings were still built in the palacial style. Franciszek Mączyński built the Palace of the Society of the Friends of Arts in Kraków, where also he built the Old Theater in the *art nouveau* style. He further designed the new Jesuit Church in combined Vistula-Gothic and the *art nouveau* style with sculpted decorations by Xavery Dunikowski, the most outstanding sculptor in the style of Young Poland.

Sławomir Odrzywolski built the Technical Society Building with a white ceramic front elevation adorned with sculptures by Jan Raszka. Odrzywolski also constructed brick apartment houses with metal decorative motifs in Tatra Mountain style in 1909, as well as, the Agricultural Society Building in Kraków with symbolic decorations sculpted by Jan Szczepkowski.

Józef Czajkowski designed the Museum of Technology and Industry in Kraków in early Functionalist style, which was also used in the Warsaw construction of the art gallery Zachęta and in the Philharmonic Hall.

Modern buildings included the Bristol Hotel, Savoy Hotel (1906), Under the Eagles Bank, and the Polish Theater (1912).

Modernism dominated in Polish architecture and sculpture. Konstanty Laszczka, influenced by Francois Rodin, sculpted nudes and portrait heads.

Xavery Dunikowski produced sculptures in his own individual style. He created symbolic sculptures such as Love, Concentration, and Motherhood.

Sculptor Henryk Kuna evolved through Impressionism and Modernism to Classicism.

Polish Painting at the Turn of the Century

The painters of Young Poland believed in an objective truth and felt the native landscape gave them the best means of expression.

A landscape painter, Józef Chełmoński painted with realism and felt that his perception of his native country was not compatible with French Impressionism.

Władysław Podkowiński was at first an Impressionist painter, then later changed to Symbolism. His famous *Ecstasy* is a romantic symbolic composition showing an ecstatic nude riding a black stallion.

Leon Wyczółkowski started painting in symbolist style; but about 1880, he changed to Impressionism in his many landscapes of Ukraine and Polesie.

Julian Fałat specialized in watercolor winter landscapes, which he painted in a transition style from Impressionism to the *art nouveau.*

Jan Stanisławski specialized in small size landscapes, which he painted on canvas and on cardboard in modernistic style.

Stanisław Wyspiański (1846-1916), self-portrait.

One of the most talented Polish painters was Józef Pankiewicz. He propagated the Impressionist style. His works such as the *Sand-Diggers* were perfect in design and color.

Olga Boznańska was a portrait painter with good psychological characterization of her subjects. She painted first in the Impressionist style, then evolved into Modernism.

Stanisław Wyspiański (1869-1907) was a poet, dramatist, stage designer, painter, and stained glass designer who gave a romantic interpretation to the modern European style. He saw the Cathedral of the Castle of Kraków as the Acropolis of Poland. He liked to use pastels. His portraits of children are especially beautiful. He created a Polish style in handicrafts.

Jacek Malczewski (1854-1929) was a symbolist painter fascinated with the history of Poland. He painted death as an angel rather than the usual

Painting, Jacek Malczewski,1905.

189

skeleton.

Ferdynand Ruszczyc (1870-1936) was a neo-Romanticist and a symbolist who liked Japanese landscape painting. He clearly outlined the objects painted.

Pre-World War One Polish Theater

Polish theaters in Kraków under director Józef Kotarbiński and in Lwów under Tadeusz Pawlikowski were the most important in the prewar period. They trained brilliant actors and staged splendid performances of Polish romanticist and modern plays. *The Wedding* by Wyspiański was first staged in Kraków in 1901. It was praised for its originality, precise structure, original verse, and dramatic atmosphere created by music and lighting with the help of the author. Kotarbinski was followed by Ludwik Solski, an experienced actor and director.

The theater in Warsaw was under heavy censorship and was prohibited from staging Wyspiański's dramas until the revolution in 1905. However, operetta and farce flourished. Polish soloists of world fame were invited to the best music theaters in Europe and in America. After the *Theater Polski* opened in 1913 in Warsaw, it became the leading stage in all Polish lands because of its repertoire, modern staging, and excellent scenography, which was painted using perspective representation. By the end of Modernism of the Young Poland in 1914, ten permanent professional Polish language theaters were in operation, besides many traveling theater companies performing throughout Polish lands.

Early Polish Film

Polish inventors started to experiment and publically display their cinematographic equipment in the early 1890s. Piotr Lebiedziński (1860-1934) completed the construction of his motion picture camera in 1893, two years before the Lumiere brothers unveiled their camera in public. Pleograph for writing words on a film was designed by Kazimierz Prószczyński. Jan Szczepaniak invented color film, and patented it in England in 1899 under patent number 7727. His invention was used in 1932 in the United States by Kodak in the Kodak-color film system. Thus, Szczepaniak was one of the forerunners of the modern cinematography.

The first Polish situation comedy was shown in 1908. It was

entitled *His First Visit to Warsaw.*

The first film that was an adaptation of a Polish novel was shown in Kraków in 1911. Its tile was *Meir Ezofowicz,* and it was based on the novel of the same title by Eliza Orzeszkowa.

Polish actress Pola Negri (Apolonia Chałupiec 1899-1987) became a star of silent film in Poland in 1914 and in America in 1923. She made her debut in Polish film *Niewolnica zmysłów (The Sex Slave).* The picture *Żona (The Wife)* brought her international fame. She starred in such pictures as *Carmen, The Spanish Dancer*, etc.

Music of the Young Poland

The symphonic music of Young Poland was best represented by Mieczysław Karłowicz. He composed six symphonic poems, and wrote music for poems written by some of the best poets of the Young Poland period. He composed powerful and expressive music in his own original style, typically changing from melancholy, sadness, and bitterness to resignation.

Polish virtuoso pianist, composer, and statesman, Ignacy Jan Paderewski played his first piano concert in 1887. He composed concertos, operas, and piano pieces, including a well known minuet. He wrote a *Symphony*, a *Piano Concerto*, and a *Polish Fantasia*. During the war in 1914-1918, he toured the United States raising funds for Polish relief. He donated his music book collection to the University of Kraków.

Karol Szymanowski (1883-1937), who composed operas, symphonies, orchestral works, chamber music, and songs made his debut at the turn of the century, though he became famous only in the 1920s.

In 1901, a philharmonic orchestra was founded in Warsaw. Its first conductor was the composer Emil Młynarski, who concentrated on symphonic music.

Ignacy Paderewski (1860-1941).

Its second conductor, Grzegorz Fitelberg, was a champion of Polish modern national music. He composed a symphony, symbolic poems, Polish rhapsody songs, and chamber music.

The Formation of Polish Legions

In 1908, Kazimierz Sosnkowski and Władysław Sikorski founded the Union for Active Resistance in Lwów with funds hijacked from Russian treasury shipment at Bezdany, Lithuania by *Bojówka* ("fighting team"), led by Józef Piłsudski. The new military association was co-organized by Władysław Sikorski.

In 1910, Piłsudski founded the Riflemen Association for conventional military training in Lwów, Galicia. He upgraded the guerrilla training of the Union for Active Resistance under the guise of training Austrian Army reservists. Thus, a small part-time Polish army was organized by 1911, with branches in France, Belgium, Switzerland and the United States contributing money.

In 1914, Piłsudski expected the outbreak of war and converted the Riflemen's Association into a small army of Polish Legions composed of Polish patriots, including a small number of Jewish Poles. The percentage of college graduates and students among them was relatively high.

Outbreak of the First World War

On June 28, 1914, the Serb national Gawriło Princip shot the Archduke and the Archduchess of Austria to death in the streets of Sarajevo. In response to the assassination, Austria issued a 48-hour ultimatum to Serbia on July 24. The following day Russia ordered military mobilization on behalf of the Serbs. Austria waited three more days for the Serbs to comply with its demands, before it declared war on the country and bombed Belgrade. On July 30, France declared its support for Russia and soon was joined by Great Britain, which had become increasingly wary of the of the buildup of Germany's navy and Berlin's colonial ambitions. The German declaration of war occurred on Aug. 1, after Wilhelm II Hohezollern's issued a 12-hour ultimatum for Russian demobilization expired without any response from Russia.

Germany adopted the Schlieffen plan of a two front war, which was to start with a quick destruction of France and then proceed with the task of defeating Russia.

When Germany declared war on Russia on Aug. 1, 1914 and World War I broke out, the Riflemen's Association (*Związek Strzelecki*) was converted into Polish Legions. The Legions entered the Kingdom of Poland with the Austrian Army. Piłsudski founded the Polish Military Organization in the Kingdom of Poland (*Polska Organizacja Wojskowa, POW*) as a nucleus of an independent Polish armed force.

Meanwhile in Warsaw, Roman Dmowski had formed a pro-Russian Polish National Committee and the Puławski Legion, a division of the Polish Riflemen that, in 1917, became a part of the First Polish Corps under Gen. Józef Dowbór-Muśnicki. This corps would be repeatedly attacked by Bolshevik forces, which Germany subsidized.

Elimination of the Eastern Front

On March 9, 1915, the government in Berlin received a basic plan for the elimination of the eastern front by crucial German support of a revolution in Russia. The author was an arms dealer and influence peddler named Alexander Helphand (1867-1924), born in the Pale of Jewish Settlement east of Wilno. (Eventually, he died the richest man in Germany.) Helphand proposed to convert a clique of conspirators into a Russian revolutionary power. He obtained virtually unlimited German funds (equivalent to about ten tons of gold) to carry out the plan to liquidate the Russian front, first by spreading defeatist propaganda in the Russian armed forces, and then, at an opportune time, by taking over the Russian government with Lenin, who agreed to capitulate to Germany.

In February, 1917, Nicolai Lenin was shipped by the German authorities from Switzerland, through Germany and Sweden, to arrive behind the Russian lines in April of 1917.

On July 18, 1917, the Russian Ministry of Justice under Prime Minister A.F. Kerenski declared Lenin and the Bolshevik leadership guilty of high treason and produced evidence that the Bolsheviks had received huge funds from the Imperial German Government.

German Sponsored Regency in Warsaw

Together with Austria, the German Government in 1916 proclaimed the Kingdom of Poland under a Regency in Warsaw. The Tsarist government protested the proclamation. The formation of Regency Council in Warsaw by Germany and Austria followed. A Provisional Council of State in the Kingdom of Poland (*Tymczasowa Rada Stanu*) included Józef Piłsudski.

In 1917, Berlin attempted to subordinate the Polish Legions to Germany and to create a Polnische Wehrmacht. Piłsudski refused and resigned in protest from the Provisional Council of State. The Germans responded with the arrest and deportation of General Piłsudski and Colonel Sosnkowski to the German fortress of Madgeburg.

Support for Poland and the Capitulation of Russia

A formal declaration by President Woodrow Wilson stated U.S. support for an independent Poland, reunited and with free access to the Baltic Sea. This declaration was restated and accepted in Versaille by the Entente of the United States, Great Britain, France, Russia, and others on June 4, 1917.

After the abdication of the Tsar, the Provisional Government of Russia established a commission to liquidate the Russian presence in the Kingdom of Poland and to recognize the independence of Poland in a military union with Russia. However, the Bolsheviks took over the Russian government in October of 1917, in St. Petersburg.

On March 3, 1918, in Brest-Litovsk, a town occupied by the Germans, the Bolshevik Government of Lenin signed a humiliating capitulation.

Towards the Independence of Poland

The disintegration of Russia and the defeat of Germany and Austria in World War I made possible the reunification of Poland as a sovereign country. Many Polish officers and soldiers, who served in the armies of the partitioning powers, acquired experience, which they later used in the defense of Poland.

A total of two million Poles were mobilized by Russia, Prussia, and Austria in 1914-1918; of these 220,000 were killed while serving in the Austrian Army; 110,000 in the German Army; and 55,000 in the Russian Army. Polish material losses represented the equivalent of ten billion dollars (of 1918), including half of all the bridges, two-thirds of the railroad yards and stations, and two million buildings - mostly rural.

Mass meetings were organized in 1918 in the Polish lands occupied by Germany (Poznania, Silesia, Pomeria, Kashubia, Ermland-Warmia, and Mazuria), and by the Poles in the German army and in the coal mines of Westphalia. These meetings were held in order to elect deputies to the Seym of Poznań for the purpose of joining an independent Poland.

Roman Dmowski (1864-1939).

The German and Austrian governments proclaimed the Regency Council in Warsaw the supreme authority in the Kingdom of Poland, replacing German military rule. The School System in the Kingdom of Poland was placed under Polish administration.

France and other Western Allies recognized the Polish National Committee under Roman Dmowski as representing the Polish Nation.

The American Government permitted the recruitment of volunteers to the Polish Army on United States territory.

The Government in Warsaw was formed by the Regency Council.

Elections were held for the Polish Council of State on the lands occupied by Germany and Austria in 1918.

Great Britain, France, and Italy declared support for Poland; unfortunately, all international Jewish organizations opposed Poland's independence.

On Aug. 29, 1918, the treaties of partition of Poland were annulled by the Bolsheviks, who hoped to convert Poland into a Soviet Republic.

The Liquidation Commission replaced Austrian authorities. It was formed by the Poles in Kraków in 1918. On Nov. 3, the Austrian government transferred its political control and its arsenal of weapons in Lwów to the Ukrainian Committee. This Austrian action started a war between the Poles and Ukrainians in Lwów and eastern Galicia.

The Jurisprudence was taken over by the Poles in the Kingdom of Poland from German occupational authorities. The German judiciary apparatus surrendered to Polish administration on Sept. 1, 1918. The next day marked the beginning of the disarmament of the German army of occupation by Polish military units of the *Polska Organizacja Wojskowa (POW)* in the regions of Lublin, Radom, Kielce, and Zagłębie Dąbrowskie.

On Oct. 7, 1918, the Regency Council issued rules for parliamentary elections in Poland. The government of Jan Kucharzewski, as well as the Council of State were dissolved.

The protectorate of Germany and Austria was abolished in Poland.

On Oct. 11, 1918, Polish deputies to the Berlin parliament demanded reunification of an independent Poland in accordance with the declaration by President Woodrow Wilson.

A Polish-Czech agreement to divide Cieszyn Silesia along ethnic lines was signed by elected representatives on Nov. 5, 1918.

The Provisional Government of the Polish Republic was organized in Lublin on Nov. 7, 1918. Ignacy Daszyński served as a prime minister, while Edward Rydz-Śmigły served as the minister of defense .

On Nov. 11, 1918, the Regency Council in Warsaw dissolved itself upon the collapse of Germany; it transferred its powers to Józef Piłsudski, the Commander of Polish Legions, as he was returning from the internment in Germany (in the Magdeburg fortress).

Jan Kucharzewski (1876-1952), historian and politician, author of *From the White to the Red Tsarate - The Origin of Modern Russia.*

Ignacy Daszyński (1866-1936), Leader of Socialist-Democratic Party, Prime Minister, Speaker, the House of Representatives.

THE SECOND REPUBLIC (1918-1945)

(Period of Modernism)

Declaration of the Independence of Poland

In Nov. 11, 1918, the Declaration of Independence of Poland was proclaimed by the Regency Council in Warsaw. The Regency Council in Warsaw then dissolved itself, upon the collapse of Germany and transferred its powers to Józef Piłsudski. Piłsudski immediately became the Commander-in-Chief and on Nov. 14, 1918, the Head of State.

Thus, the Poles declared their independence, but had to win six borderland wars. By far the most important was the Russian threat. It is described on page 15 and 18. Lord Edgar d'Abernon wrote that the battle of Warsaw in 1920 was one of the 18 most important battles in the history. The Poles turned the Communist tide in Europe for twenty-five years.

A new Polish government was formed on Nov. 18, 1918, with Jedrzej Moraczewski as prime minister. He formed a center-left cabinet and issued a decree on general elections (by men and women) to the Constitutional Seym. The new government decreed on Nov. 22, 1918 that Poland was a republic, and that Józef Piłsudski was the provisional head of state and Commander-in-Chief.

The Polish Army gained control in Lwów on Nov. 24, 1918, and created a Provisional Governing Committee.

On Nov. 30, 1918, Poland was admitted as a party to the peace negotiations by France and Great Britain.

Marshal Józef Piłsudski (1867-1935).

197

The Provincial Seym of Poznań met from Dec. 3 to 5. It included 1,403 deputies from Gdańsk-Pomeria, Warmia, Mazuria, Silesia, Poznania, and west German areas populated by Poles. The Seym appointed a Supreme People's Council and demanded that the Western Allies incorporate into Poland all of the lands annexed by Prussia in the partitions.

On Dec. 26, 1918, Ignacy Paderewski arrived in Poznań; and the German garrison was expelled by a popular uprising. The next day, as the Supreme People's Council took power in Poznań, with Germany broke out over the provinces of Greater Poland and Pomerania.

The Polish administration of the Lesser Poland (called "Galicia" by the Austrians) and Cieszyn was reorganized on Jan. 10, 1919. On Jan. 17, the government of Prime Minister Ignacy Paderewski was formed in Warsaw. Paderewski also served as the minister of foreign affairs holding office until Nov. 27, 1919.

The General Elections for Constitutional Seym were held on Jan. 26, 1919. Two hundred thirty deputies stood in for the Kingdom of Poland and Podlasie; 72 for western Lesser Poland; 26 for central Lesser Poland; and 20 German annexed lands in Poland. By March 24, 1922, with elections held in other districts, the total number of deputies would reach 432. (Many of the deputies were previously elected to the German and Austrian parliaments respectively.)

On Feb. 3, 1919, the Polish-Czech border agreement was signed in Paris on the basis of the ethnic delineation agreed upon by local representatives on Nov. 5, 1918.

Bolshevik "Target Vistula" and Piłsudski's Federation

The government in Warsaw issued a decree on Feb. 7, 1919 on the military draft to face the Bolshevik "Target Vistula" offensive. The first regular combat between the Red Army and Polish forces took place at Bereza Kartuska on Feb. 12, 1919. It was the beginning of the war between Poland and the Bolshevik Russia.

In Feb. of 1919, Piłsudski undertook a diplomatic mission to form a federation of nations led by Poland and including Finland, Estonia, Latvia, Lithuania, Byelorussia, Ukraine, Don Cossacks, Kuban Cossacks, Georgia, Azerbaijan, and Armenia. The purpose of the proposed federation was to achieve security and political independence of the participating countries. The plan failed primarily because of the British opposition out of fear that the new federation would be an ally of France; the British went on destroying the surrendered German arsenals rather than sending them to Poland (as France proposed). Meanwhile the Polish State was faced with a life-and-death struggle against Bolshevik Russia.

The French were willing to transfer surrendered German arsenals to Poland, which weapons were sufficient to secure the federation proposed by Piłsudski. Thus, the British refusal to transfer to Poland German weapons killed the federation plan. In artillery alone, the Poles were outgunned by the Soviets three to one. Great Britain underestimated the Soviet threat, and worried that France would have a strong ally in Poland. Thus, the British had a notion "to kill Communism with kindness," and proclaimed a policy of "hands off Russia."

The hope of George Clemenceau that Poland would be "a barrier against Russia and a check on Germany" was destroyed by David Lloyd George, whose lame excuse was that he would "rather see Russia Bolshevik, than Britain bankrupt."

On Feb. 20, 1919, the Seym passed the Provisional (Small) Constitution. It spelled out the powers of the Seym, the government, and the head of state.

Poland signed an agreement with France and Germany on Apr. 4, 1919 on the transfer of the Polish Army from France.

On June 28, 1919 the Peace Treaty at Versailles was signed; Roman Dmowski and Ignacy Paderewski signed the treaty for Poland.

The Allies decided on Feb. 9, 1920 that Gdańsk would be converted into a free city. It was the result of British pressure over French and Polish objections. At that point, the Marshal of France, Ferdinand Foch, predicted that the free city of Gdańsk would be the location where the next world war would start.

On Oct. 12, 1920 the Polish-Soviet Peace Treaty was signed in Riga. Allied Ambassadors created the Free City of Gdańsk - a decree they confirmed on Oct. 27th. On the fifteenth of November, Gdańsk established a constitutional government, which almost immediately signed a treaty with Poland. It was guaranteed by the League of Nations.

The Polish-Soviet Repatriation Agreement was signed in Riga on Feb. 24, 1921. It officially permitted over 700,000 Jews to enter Poland from the Soviet Union. Actually, about 800,000 Jewish refugees from USSR entered Poland - all of whom were given Polish citizenship.

Democratic Constitution of March 17, 1921

On March 17, 1921, the Seym voted in the Constitution of the Polish Republic. It provided for a bicameral parliament composed of the Seym and the Senate; the supreme political power was to reside in the legislative branch. This meant that at any time when the parliament failed to rally a majority to support the government in power, a new government had to be formed. Regional self-government was guaranteed, as well as an independent judiciary. The basic civil rights and the private ownership of property was guaranteed, as was the freedom of speech, the secrecy of correspondence, and the freedom of religion. Equal voting rights of both sexes were guaranteed - Poland was one of the first countries to guarantee women's rights to vote. The Seym was left to cope with an unworkable constitution, similar to that of France.

On June 22, 1920, the League of Nations gave Poland the responsibility to defend Gdańsk as a Free City and to represent it internationally. Railroads of the Free City of Gdansk subsequently became a part of the Polish transportation system.

The League of Nations assigned to Poland the peninsula of Westerplatte in Gdańsk on March 14, 1924, for the purpose of handling Polish defense materials there. On October 2nd, Poland signed the Charter of the League of Nations. Poland signed the 180 million dollar war debt agreement with the United States on Nov. 15, 1924; this act was followed the following year (Feb. 10) by a commercial agreement between the two nations. At approximately the same time, the Concordat with the Vatican was signed, marking an increase of Church's influence in Poland.

On March 24, 1925 Lloyd George proposed in the Commons a revision of Polish-German border in favor of Germany. Poland was viewed as an ally of France, and Lloyd George thought that Great Britain needed Germany on its side to achieve a favorable balance of power in Europe. This British attitude led in October to the Conference of Locarno, where Germany questioned the borders of Poland and made a secret agreement with the Soviet Union in violation of the Treaty of Versailles. France and Poland signed an agreement to counteract possible German aggression. In Dec. of 1925, the League of Nations authorized the stationing of a Polish garrison in Gdańsk on the Westerplatte.

Reforms and Coup d'Etat of 1926

The Seym passed the Social Security Law for the white collar workers on Oct. 28, 1925. Exactly two month later, the Seym voted the Agrarian Reform, which until Sept. 1939, distributed some six million acres or 19 percent of land held in large estate.

Marshal Józef Piłsudsk took over the government of Poland in May 12-14, 1926 and installed an authoritarian regime. His military takeover of the government was conducted in the name of stability and international security, after fifteen government crises since the formation of the Second Polish Republic in 1918. President Stanisław Wojciechowski and the government resigned after an armed struggle in Warsaw. The casualties were about 200 dead and 1,000 wounded. On May 31, 1926, Józef Piłsudski was elected President of Poland, however, he declined to serve as the head of state. On June 1, the election of President Ignacy Mościcki (1867-1946) took place; on Aug. 2, the Constitution of Poland of 1921 was amended. Presidential powers were increased to include the right to dissolve the Seym and the Senate. The President would rule by decree between parliamentary sessions, which he could delay at will. Furthermore, the freedom of the press was to be limited.

Economic Progress and the End of the Trade War

In 1928-1929, Polish lands reached their prewar level of industrial production on the eve of the Great Depression.

Twelve years of trade war between Germany and Poland ended on March 17, 1930 with the signing of a commercial agreement between Poland and Germany in Warsaw. The trade war was initiated by the Germans, who demanded to expand the German territory at the expense of Poland.

President Mościcki dissolved the Seym and Senate on Aug. 29 of that year and called for new elections. On Sept. 10, the President, working with a group of colonels, ordered the arrests and imprisonment of opposition leaders of the center-left coalition. They were shipped to the military prison in Brześć on the Bug (Brest-Litovsk). This violation of the Constitution of Poland was followed by the pacification of Eastern Galicia and by the tampering of election results.

Science and Learning in Free Poland

Institutions of higher learning were reconverted to Polish from Russian in 1915. In 1918, the Main Agricultural Academy was established in Warsaw.

In free Poland, state universities were opened in Warsaw, Kraków, Lwów, Poznań, and Wilno. The Catholic University in Lublin, founded in 1918, was a Church-finance institution. On July 13, 1920, a law was passed giving wide autonomy to schools of higher learning. The Academy of Learning in Kraków was renamed the Polish Academy of Learning. It was authorized to represent Poland abroad and establish cooperation with international scientific organizations. It joined the International Commission for the Intellectual Cooperation attached to the League of Nations.

With the national independence came a new development of the University of Warsaw and Warsaw Polytechnic. Some sixty professors came from the Universities of Kraków and Lwów to teach at the University of Warsaw. At the Warsaw Polytechnic, one-third of the faculty came from Kraków and Lwów and from foreign universities. In 1919, the Society of Scientific Courses was converted into the Free Polish University.

Warsaw became an important scientific center with many world-class scientists. The Warsaw School of Mathematics excelled in topology and logic and achieved worldwide acclaim. It published the periodical *Fundamenta Mathematicae*. The leading mathematicians in this group were topologists Kazimierz Kuratowski, Stefan Mazurkiewicz, and Wacław Sierpiński; while the leading logicians were Stanisław Leśniewski, Jan Lukasiewicz, Alfred Tarski, and Leon Chwistek, who was also a philosopher, semanticist, and an outstanding painter - one of the initiators and theoretician of Formism in painting. Polish logicians made important contributions to computer science.

At the University of Warsaw, the physics department did important research in molecular optics under Stefan Pieńkowski. Czesław Białobrzeski distinguished himself in research on the influence of radiation pressure on stellar equilibrium and on determinism in physics. Ludwik Wertenstein conducted research in radioactivity.

At Warsaw Polytechnic, Wojciech Świętosławski conducted research on the thermochemistry of chemical reactions and of the physical change of state. Outstanding work was done by Czesław Witoszyński in aerodynamics; Stanisław Zwierzchowski in the design of water turbines; Witold Wierzbicki in mechanical engineering; and Stefan Bryła in the analysis of steel structures.

Philosophers Tadeusz Kotarbinski and Waładysław Tatarkiewicz developed a strong philosophical center. Leon Petrażycki originated a broad system of philosophy of law.

The Lwów School of Mathematics led in the theory of linear operations and functional analysis. Stefan Banach, Hugo Steihaus, and Stanisław Mazur were world famous mathematicians working in Lwów. Among other outstanding scientists in Lwów was Jerzy Kuryłowicz, who excelled in comparative linguistics. He specialized in the phonetics and morphology of Indo-European and Semitic languages.

At the University of Poznań, Florian Znaniecki conducted sociological research. He founded *Przegląd Sociologiczny (Sociological Review)* and authored *The Polish Peasant in Europe and America.*

Marian Zdziechowski headed the research on the history of Slavonic culture and literature at the University of Wilno.

New orthographic rules were introduced in 1936. These rules are still valid in Poland.

Modern Literature in Free Poland

From 1919-1921, literary groups of futurists and avant-guard writers were active alongside of expressionists. *Skamander* was a group of Polish writers who expressed social criticism and pessimism, especially during the years of economic depression. While scientists were optimistically developing Polish sciences, some of the writers developed a premonition of approaching catastrophe and the disintegration of civilization.

Surrealistic philosopher, writer, playwight, and painter, Ignacy Witkiewicz, who used a pen name of Witkacy, created a theory of pure form

Stanisław Ignacy Witkiewicz
(1885-1939), Witkacy.

- a form that must give the artist and the viewer the feeling of unity and plurality in harmony with the universe. The meaning of his pure form and the novelty of his play-writing caused him to make a slow start. Witkacy expected to shock the audience and to turn his plays into a metaphysical experience. He experimented with drugs and lived in an atmosphere of social scandal. He presented a caricature of the real world expressed in pretentious jargon from the social fringe. Witkacy was the most outstanding prophet of coming catastrophic events and committed suicide upon the news that the Red Army invaded Poland on Sept. 17, 1939.

The enormous effort to restore a united country after a century of partitions caused socially radical and pessimistic writing. Catastrophism became a historical form and philosophical reflection. The most innovative writers were Witold Gombrowicz and Bruno Schulz. Despite their grotesque humor, their work was pessimistic and belonged to the "black" trend in Polish literature.

The poets of the *Skamander* group promoted ideas of simplicity, democracy, and the cult of youth. Their name originated from the literary monthly named *Skamander*. Julian Tuwim was the most prominent poet of this group. He collected satanic and Bacchanalian literature. In his work, he evolved from vitalism to reflection. Antoni Słonimski wrote reflective lyrics and, in 1919, published a collection of rebellious poetry entitled *The Black Spring*. He defended the human right to freedom of speech, feeling, and views. Jarosław Iwaszkiewicz also published in the *Skamander*. He perceived the problems of life through art. His poems are written in a sophisticated rhythmic form that enabled composers to use them as songs' texts.

Maria Pawlikowska-Jasnorzewska wrote lyrical and subtle love poetry with a sometimes shocking honesty of expression. She acquired the dignity of classical perfection, able to create dramatic tension and psychological accuracy in a few lines. Her poems were and are still called miniature masterpieces.

Kazimierz Wierzyński (1895-1976) expressed the joy of life in writing on the theme of sport for which he was awarded the gold medal at the 1924 Olympics. Later his lyrics became more reflective.

The futurist cult of technical perfection was represented by Bruno Jasieński and Anatol Stern. Their futurist cult of the irrational combined with the paradoxical was expressed through the neglect of harmony, logic, tradition, and the basic rules of orthography.

Józef Czechowicz poetically described the country landscape in the classical avant-garde style. His awareness of the tragic history gives his works catastrophic form. He was killed during the German bombing of Lublin.

Julian Przyboś wrote poetry coded in the elliptical form, which required the reader to participate in the reconstruction of his poetic vision.

Władysław Broniewski wrote communist revolutionary poetry in the style of social realism with frequent introduction of colloquialisms and prosaic expressions. His style was derived from romantic poetry.

Zofia Nałkowska wrote novels about human dependence on the environment. She illustrated the social and political relations of the 1920s and 1930s.

Maria Dąbrowska wrote a four volume epic entitled *Noce i Dnie (Nights and Days)* that covered the years 1864-1914. She was influenced by Positivism and wrote about impoverished landless Polish nobles adjusting to city life and work, while still contributing something of value to society.

The most successful playwright was Jerzy Szaniawski. His plays are known for their skillful composition and style, and many of his plays are still produced.

Architecture and Art in the 1920s and 1930s

The good quality of then current Polish architecture was displayed at the international Exposition of Architecture in Paris in 1925.

Prefabricated construction elements and the system of modules were first used in Poland in 1931.

The styles of Modernism and Historism were still used in Poland, though public buildings were built mainly in the classical style. In this style, Adolf Szyszko-Bohush constructed the Savings Bank; and Wacław Krzyżanowswki designed the Academy of Mining. Krzyżanowski built the Jagiellonian Library in the Functional style in 1938.

Monumental and tectonic sculptures were made by Tadeusz Beyer, who created the monument of General Sowiński in Warsaw. Classicism and lyricism are characteristic of portraits sculpted by Henryk Kuna. Zbigniew Pronaszko was a representative of formism, which he expressed in synthetic forms reduced to geometric figures. His best work is the sculpture of the poet Adam Mickiewicz. August Zamoyski sculpted an excellent portrait of the poet Antoni Słonimski, and also created classical nudes.

Avant-garde sculptors, Katarzyna Kobro-Strzemińska and Maria Jarema, evolved from more expressive to more abstract delicate forms. Stanisław Szukalski was a sculptor born in Kraków who worked in the United States. He attempted to create the Polish national style and sculpted symbolic compositions used in architectural decorations.

Jan Rembowski and Leopold Gottlieb followed the style of Wyspiański in their paintings of the Polish Legions of Józef Piłsudski. Eventually, their paintings showed the concrete forms of classicism. There were over thirty different artistic associations in Poland whose foci ranged from the esthetic interpretation of color to the pure construction and technique to trends developed in the 19th century, including specific styles of folk art. Some of the works in the neo-Realist style were very close to Naturalism. However, artists that tried to convey political ideologies through their art failed because it was not intelligible to the general public. The Polish variety of Expressionism was known as Formism: a combination of Cubism and Futurism. Andrzej Pronaszko painted in a post-cubist style and specialized in stage design.

The best classical paintings were painted in Wilno, where Zbigniew

Pronaszko was a professor of fine arts. The Wilno classical school of painting included Ludomir Sleńdziński, who was fascinated with the Renaissance art collections in museums and derived from them inspiration for his stylized nudes.

The dominant style of Polish painting was more pictorial than cubist. The painters of the Young Poland movement started in the period of modernism. Very

B. Pniewski, Villa "Patria" Krynica, Poland (1934).

dynamic painting inspired by the Polish folk art was created by Zofia Stryjeńska.

Władysław Strzemiński created his own theory of "unism" after trying constructivism and utilitarianism in his abstract paintings.

Monumental and severe paintings were created in "romantic-classicist" style by Szczęsny Kowarski. He decorated the ceilings of the Wawel Castle in Kraków in a style derived from the Baroque. Later, he turned to Realism in his collective portrait of *The National Government of the* 1863 national uprising in the Kingdom of Poland.

The esthetics of color dominated the Polish version of Colorism, which originated from Impressionism. Jerzy Fedkowicz was a colorist who displayed a perfect technique in his landscapes, portraits, and still lives. The colorists considered the process of painting and textures to be the most important in colorist style. Jan Cybis used pure color in his paintings. The aggressive colors of Zygmunt Waliszewski (1897-1936) were used in all his paintings ranging from landscapes, portraits, historical scenes, and satire. He also worked on the decorations of the Wawel Castle in Kraków. Waliszewski belonged to group of "Kapists" named after the Committee of Paris (K.P.) of Polish colorists. The use of pure color from the solar light spectrum was attempted by members of another group named Pryzmat (from the word "prism").

There was a great diversity of styles in Polish paintings of the 1920s and 1930s. An abstract style of painting was called "formal art." Ironically, some of its practitioners were leftists who, in the 1950s, would be told to paint in the Socialist-Realist style. The surrealist paintings of Bronisław Linke were often grotesque as he attacked the middle class, capitalism, fascism, and Nazism.

Leonard Pękalski painted in post-classical monumental figures in the Royal Castle on the Wawel Hill in Kraków.

Wacław Wąsowicz made primitive woodcuts of many Polish towns. Władysław Skoczylas executed his woodcuts in the style of the Young Poland, which promoted unity and modernity combined with national tradition and folk art.

Theater in Free Poland

The network of theaters expanded as censorship disappeared. Most of the theaters were in Warsaw. New troupes initiated new theatrical forms under the leadership of Leon Schiller, Juliusz Osterwa, and Stefan Jaracz. They renewed the performing arts in Poland. Actors were to experience their roles. Osterwa asked his actors to give up individual displays. He directed an actors school attached to the theater *Reduta* in Warsaw. At first, the repertoire was exclusively Polish.

Leon Schiller directed the Bogusławski Theater in Warsaw from 1924-1926. He was a great lover of Polish theatrical tradition; at the same time, he had a good knowledge of the European theater. Earlier he produced shows in Kraków in the *Green Baloon Cabaret*. He developed the principles of the Monumental Theater and produced great spectacles on national themes, staging them with great expression. His productions of Romantic dramas, *Kordian* (by Słowacki) and *Forefather's Eve* (by Mickiewicz), were shown in several theaters. He harmoniously combined the text, light, and rhythm with sets designed by Andrzej Pronaszko, one of the best Polish stage designers.

By 1936, twenty-six permanent professional theaters were active in major Polish towns – ten of them were located in Warsaw. Generally, the Polish stage had been a great success in the art of stage design and ingenuity of individual producers.

In 1921, the world premiere of Witkacy's *Tumor Mózgowicz (Tumor the Brainard)* was staged in Kraków. It was directed by Teofil Trzciński.

Polish Film in the 1920s and 1930s

Cinematography started to develop rapidly in free Poland. Each year, dozens of films were produced and their length increased to over 10,000 feet. About forty adaptations of Polish novels were produced as silent films. With the advent of the talkie revolution, the adaptations of novels continued. Some experimental films were also made.

In 1924, Karol Irzykowski wrote an outstanding theoretical book entitled *The Tenth Muse* in which he defines the cinema as "a visualization of man's association with matter."

In 1929, START –*Stowarzyszenie Propagandy Filmu Artystycznego (Association of the Dissemination of Artistic Films)*- was formed in Warsaw. After the show of an artistic movie, the audience was invited to take part in a discussion and an evaluation of the film shown.

The artistic quality improved in 1932 with a picture about newspaper boys entitled *Legion ulicy (The Legion of the Street)* by Aleksander Ford, who, together with Jan Zarzycki, produced the film *Ludzie Wisły (The People of the Vistula)*. Polish films slowly reached a world-class quality. The breakthrough came with the presentation of contemporary social problems. There was a parallel improvement in situation comedies.

There were over 800 movie theaters in Poland in 1939. Some seventy of them in Warsaw alone. By the same time, 300 feature films were produced in 150 studios.

Music in Free Poland

Karol Szymanowski followed Chopin's styled piano compositions in preludes, etudes, and variations. He also composed impressionistic pieces for the piano and violin, combining elements of folk music with modern techniques of composition. Fascinated by the Tatra Mountains, he composed a ballet *Harnasie (The Tatra Outlaws)*, and mazurkas for the piano. He liked the originality of Kurpie region north of Warsaw and honored it with the *Pieśni Kurpiowskie (Kurpie Songs)*. Szymanowski formulated the duties of

music critics and composers in a series of articles entitled *My Splendid Isolation,* in which he explained the most modern trends in European music. Orchestra music and operettas were written in neo-Romanticist style. Music flourished in independent Poland. Research on the history of Polish music was conducted at the University of Kraków and at the University of Lwów. The Old Polish Music Publishers published Musicological Journals.

Karol Szymanowski (1882-1937).

The Press in Free Poland

In 1930, over one million copies of daily papers shaped the public opinion of thirty million inhabitants of Poland. Quality professional journals of great repute were published - many of them reflected a high standard of Polish intellectual life. On the other hand, complaints were made about the partisan and provincial press, as well as about the semi-pornographic and anti-Semitic papers.

The center-right ruling coalition published *Kurier Poranny, Polska Zbrojna,* the *Gazeta Polska,* and *Pion.* The right-wing National Democratic Party published *Gazeta Warszawska, Warszawski Dziennik Narodowy,* and *Kurier Poznański.* Business enterprises published *Kurier Polski;* the clergy edited *Mały Dziennik*; Christian Democracy had the *Polonia*; the conservatives published *Czas, Słowo, and Dziennik Poznański*; and the socialists had the *Robotnik, Naprzód,* and *Gazeta Robotnicza.* The radical right had *Prosto z Mostu.*

The Peasant Party published *Zielony Sztandar (The Green Banner),* *Wyzwolenie,* and *Piast*; the Communist Party illegally published the *Czerwony Sztandar (The Red Banner)* and *Nowy Przegląd.* The anti-Nazi press of the People's Front published *Dziennik Popularny* in 1936-1937, as well as *Oblicze dnia, Lewar, Poprostu* and *Sygnały.* The liberals published

Wiadomości Literackie. Illustrated weeklies included *Świat, Tygodnik Ilustrowany, Tęcza*, and *Światowid.* Periodicals for children were published by *Nasza Księgarnia,* owned by the Union of Polish Teachers.

The main press syndicates were the *Dom Prasy* in Warsaw and *Ilustrowany Kurier Codzienny* in Kraków, which published two dailies and seven weeklies. The national minorities published 125 periodicals in Ukrainian, 105 periodicals in German, and 130 periodicals in Yiddish. Jewish culture flourished. Jewish per capita the net worth in Poland was 300% higher than the national average in the 1920s and 1930s.

World's History Shaped by Poland in 1939

Germany and Japan signed the Anti-Comintern Pact. Hitler, by then in an advanced stage of the Parkinson's disease, was in a hurry to start an anti-Soviet crusade to build his 1,000 year Reich from Riga to the Black Sea. He was warned by his generals that Germany did not have sufficient manpower for his grandiose schemes of the conquest of German "living space" in central and eastern Europe. Hitler hoped to use 3,500,000 Polish soldiers. The Berlin government felt that combining German and Polish forces in Europe with Japanese forces in Asia would bring about a decisive victory over the USSR. Against the advice of the papal Nuncio, Poland repeatedly withstood German pressure to join the pact. Germans pressed the Poles in 1937 and especially from Oct. 25, 1938 to Jan 27, 1939, (See page 18). Minister Józef Beck followed the strategic advice of the late Marshal Piłsudski, which was to hold both the Germans and the Soviets at bay as long as possible, then, by all means, get the rest of the world involved. Thus, Polish refusal to join the Anti-Comintern Pact derailed Hitler's plans and caused him to lose a chance to join Japan in the attack on the USSR in 1939.

On March 31, 1939, Poland obtained a guarantee of independence and the inviolability of its borders from Great Britain and France - a preliminary step to the signing of a common defense treaty. On April 11, Hitler signed the *Fall Weiss* order that laid out the September invasion of Poland. Germany terminated its non-aggression treaty with Poland on April 28, and immediately demanded the annexation of Gdańsk, as well as a German-controlled highway and railroad line through Poland to East Prussia. These demands were rejected by Poland.

During May-Aug. 1939, Moscow tried to take advantage of

Poland's troubles with Germany to get rid of the Japanese front in Asia. The Soviets asked permission to enter Poland. However, the Warsaw government refused to permit the passage of Soviet Army through its territory. The Poles felt that this would have meant an inevitable Soviet takeover through the subversion and pacification of Poland by the Soviet terror apparatus. Meanwhile, negotiations between Germany and the USSR finalized their plans for a joint invasion of Poland and a new partition of its lands. At the time Soviet-Japanese battle raged at Khalkhim-Gol.

Polish Solution of the *Enigma* Given to Great Britain

On July 25, 1939, Poland gave Great Britain and France each a copy of a linguistic deciphering electro-mechanical device for the German secret military code system *Enigma*, complete with specifications, perforated cards, and updating procedures. Thanks to the Polish system for breaking the *Enigma,* the British project Ultra was able to interpret German secret messages during the entire war of 1939-1945. The solving of German *Enigma* eventually became one of the most important Polish contributions to the Allied's victory over Germany in World War II. In 1999, the American code expert David A. Hatch of the Center of Cryptic History, NSA, Fort George G. Meade, Maryland wrote that *"the breaking of the Enigma by Poland was one of the cornerstones of the Allied victory over Germany."*

German Betrayal of Japan and the German-Soviet Pact

In the Soviet-Japanese battle on Aug 20 - 25, 1939 on the Khalka River at Khalkhim-Gol, near the trans-Siberian railroad, 25,000 Japanese soldiers and 10,000 Soviets were killed. Just when Japan expected German help against the USSR, Germany was instead signing a pact with the Soviets.

On Aug. 22, Hitler ordered his generals to use utmost ferocity against all ethnic Poles; but he said nothing about Polish Jews. The following day, the Soviet-German non-aggression pact set the stage for the outbreak of World War II. The secret clauses on the partition of Poland were the opening stage of the Hitler-Stalin partnership in the obliteration of Poland, and the genocide of Polish citizens. The full

212

content of the Soviet-German pact was immediately revealed to the government of the United States by agents in Moscow. The United States did not warn Poland about the secret content of the Hitler-Stalin pact.

Japan felt betrayed by Germany and lodged a sharp protest in Berlin. (The Japanese never forgave the Germans for this betrayal. Japan did not renew its attacks on the USSR in 1941, even

The Crane Gate - the Symbol of Gdańsk, Engraving 1735.

after Germany declared war on the United States four days after Japanese attack on Pearl Harbor on Dec. 7, 1941. Germany desperately needed the help of a Japanese offensive against the Soviet Siberian Army, in order to take Moscow. Thus, Hitler's declaration of war against the United States was a suicidal blunder that hopelessly aggravated the situation of Germany in its conduct of a two-front war.

The Polish-British Pact - Poland's Decision to Defend Itself
On Aug. 25, 1939, the Polish-British Common Defense Pact against German aggression was signed. It was followed on Aug. 31, by the German ultimatum to Poland delivered by the media - not formally. Hitler, certain of Soviet cooperation against Poland, demanded a plebiscite in Pomerania, and the annexation of the free city of Gdańsk. Poland mobilized 1,500,000 soldiers for the coming defensive war. Following Marshal Piłsudski's strategy, Poland committed itself to fight a defensive war that was to bring the participation of France, Britain, and a full-fledged World War.

OF THE PEOPLE KILLED IN W. W. II, 50% WERE UNARMED VICTIMS
DISTRIBUTION OF GERMAN CAMP SYSYTEM IN OCCUPIED EUROPE BY THE END OF 1943
(C) 1991 Iwo Cyprian Pogonowski
GERMAN WARTIME DEATH MACHINE SYSTEM OF OVER 8500 CAMPS
MAIN CAMPS
DEATH CAMPS
USSR
JAN. 20, 1942 Berlin-Wannsee Conference
The German Government, facing defeat in the World War, planned "The Final Solution of the Jewish Problem", and ordered competitive bids for the equipment to kill 11,000,000 Jews and Gypsies, and under "The Plan Ost" 51,000,000 Slavs living in the "Future Reich" were to be killed.
Dec.10, 1942 an urgent request was made by the Polish Government-in-Exile in London for Allieds' bombing of gas chambers, crematoria and access railroads to stop the industrialized process of genocide.
Polish demand was ignored by Roosevelt while Churchill made empty promises.
GERMAN CIVILIAN CAMP SYSTEM HELD TOTAL OF 18,000,000,
IT KILLED 11,500,000 WHILE OTHER VICTIMS WERE KILLED IN EXECUTIONS ELSEWHERE.
GERMAN METHOD OF EXTERMINATION OF THE JEWS
AN ESTIMATE OF VICTIMS:
EINSATZGRUPPEN 1,200,000
DEATH CAMPS 3,060,000
MAIN CAMPS 500,000
GHETTOS & TRANSPORT 500,000
OVER 20% OF CITIZENS OF POLAND WERE KILLED, NEARLY HALF OF THEM JEWS
ATLANTIC
NORTH SEA
SWEDEN
NEUTRAL
BALTIC
Einsatzgruppe A
Einsatzgruppe B
Einsatzgruppe C
Einsatzgruppe D
CASPIAN SEA
BLACK SEA
TURKEY
Apr. 19 – May 16, 1943 Warsaw Ghetto Uprisin by 600 Jews against 2000 German Police.
SPAIN
MEDITERRANEAN SEA
OTHER VICTIMS:
GERMAN ARMY KILLED 3,500,000 P.O.W.
1,200,000 JEWSAND SOME 7,000,000 OTHER UNARMED CIVILIANS
WHILE THE GESTAPO KILLED 11,500,000 PEOPLE OR A TOTAL OF APPROX.: 25 MILLION PEOPLE KILLED OUT OF COMBAT

Germany's Wartime Death Machine (1939-1945).

WORLD WAR II (1939-1945)

(German-Nazi Devastation)

Germany and Soviet Attack; France and England at War

When World War II began on Sept. 1, 1939, the German cruiser Schleswig-Holstein (while on a "good will" visit) opened fire on Polish positions in the port of Gdańsk with its sixteen-inch guns. Despite the massive German attacks that followed, two hundred Polish soldiers held the Westerplatte until Sept. 7. Massive German air raids on the open Polish cities, airports, and railroads began on the first day of the war. The Germans attacked Polish fortified positions with seventy divisions - twice as many men as the Poles could muster in forty incomplete divisions.

On Sept. 2, 1939, the Germans started construction of the Concentration Camp Stutthof in Sztutowo near Gdańsk. It was equipped with gas chambers in which 65,000 Polish Christians would be poisoned. Long before the invasion, the Gestapo prepared extensive lists of members of the Polish leadership community who were to be arrested and executed.

The following day, during the battle on Poland's frontiers, Great Britain and France declared the war on Germany. However, they let the Polish Army fight alone.

On Sept. 14, the Army of Pomerania successfully counter-attacked near Łowicz and Skierniewice. Polish attacks caused the Germans to withdraw their forces from the battle on the Vistule River, in order to face the Army of Pomerania. The decisive German air superiority ended the battle on Sept. 17, though twenty-five major German-Polish battles continued to rage on. It was amidst this chaos that the Red Army attacked Poland with sixty divisions. (Stalin achieved the armistice with Japan by unleashing Germany against Poland, France, and Great Britain.) The largest Polish-German tank battle of the campaign lasted from Sept. 18 to Sept. 20, as a result of the counterattack of the Army of Krakow near Tomaszów Lubelski.

Losses in the Polish Campaign of 1939

The partition of Poland along the Hitler-Stalin Line on the Bug River was agreed upon on Sept. 28. Germany annexed 90,000 sq. km. with ten million citizens as part of the German Reich. The Germans then formed the General Government of 100,000 sq. km. with twelve million Poles. The Soviet Union annexed 200,000 sq. km. with a population of fifteen million, with the Wilno region incorporated into the future Soviet Republic of Lithuania. Polish military losses were as follows: 66,300 troops killed; 133,700 wounded; 587,000 captured by the Germans; and 452,536 by the Russians - the total number of Polish prisoners of war taken in the 1939 Fall Campaign was about 1,040,000 according to German and Soviet official statements. Poland's total mobilization numbered about 1,500,000 men, of which 100,000 escaped to Romania, Hungary, and the Baltic Republics. German losses were: 16,000 killed, and 32,000 wounded. The Polish Army destroyed one-third of the German tanks and one-fourth of the airplanes used against it. The Polish Navy arrived intact to England, and on Apr. 8, 1940, it sank the first German ship during the Second World War.

German records indicate that their war machine used over 402 million rounds of rifle and machine gun ammunition; over 2 million artillery shells; and about 70,000 aerial bombs. In the 1940 defeat of the British and French armies, the Germans used less than half as much ammunition, artillery shells, and bombs.

The mass murder of Polish civilians by the German army and security forces was committed from the beginning of the attack on Poland. It was the beginning of a five-year German reign of terror in occupied Poland. Mass deportations to the Soviet Union of a total of up to two million Polish citizens started immediately. A high mortality rate among deportees eventually led to some 750,000 to one million dead. In the Spring of 1940, the Soviets executed 21,857 Polish officers and other members of the intelligentsia at Katyń, Kharkov, Tver, and other localities. At the same time, and in coordination with the Soviets, the Germans executed 20,000 Polish professionals in the *Aktion AB* (the Extraordinary Pacification).

Learning and Science Under Occupation, 1939-1945

Hitler's Plan East to obliterate Poland and other Slavic countries included the genocide of 51,000,000 Slavs in order to open the fertile lands between Riga and the Black Sea for German colonization. The extermination of the Polish intellectual community started from the first days of war. Both the Germans and the Soviets had long lists prepared before the war of Polish citizens who were to be executed. Forty percent of all university faculty members were killed by the Germans. Twenty seven universities and institutes of higher learning were destroyed, together with 50% of high schools and grade schools and most of the libraries.

Germans immediately imposed a ban on the publication of Polish books and periodicals. The Polish language was suppressed as a medium of literary expression. The Germans closed middle and higher educational programs and made them illegal. Consequently, the Polish resistance organized clandestine education, including university and polytechnic courses that were taught in hiding to some 4,500 students in Warsaw, 1,100 in Kraków, 150 in Lwów, 265 in Wilno, and 660 in provincial towns. Under the disguise of vocational schools, an additional 5,800 students were enrolled. The learned societies continued their underground work. The Polish Government-in-Exile of Gen. Władysław Sikorski, who also served as Commander-in-Chief, organized financial help for scholars in occupied Poland and abroad. Despite the losses suffered during the course of the German

General Władysław Sikorski (1881-1943).
Prime Minister of Polish Government-in-Exile (1939-1943); Commander-in Chief (1939-1943); and Proponent of the Confederation of States on Soviet Western Border.

extermination policy, many textbooks and monographs were published in Poland shortly after the end of combat in 1939.

During the war, the Polish Medical Faculty was attached to the University of Edinburgh; and in Liverpool, the Polish School of Architecture was activated in 1942. The Polish Pedagogical College was organized in 1943. Polish soldiers interned in Switzerland studied in Zurich, Fribourg, and at St. Gallen. About 640 students took advantage of these programs.

University level courses were taught secretly in POW camps in Germany. In 1941, the Polish Institute of Arts and Sciences in Amerca was organized and had branches in Chicago, Montreal, Brazil, and Mexico. Its first president was the socilologist, Bronisław Malinowski.

German occupation caused far less damage to the Polish language than to other aspects of Polish culture. A few new German words like *lager*, *kapo*, and *kennkarta* passed temporarily into the Polish language that then had over 100,000 words; of these, about 10% were in use by an average Pole (of this everyday vocabulary, one-fourth was of Old Slavic origin).

Literature and Art Under Occupation

Forty percent of Polish artists were either killed or died in concentration camps. Many works of art, monuments, and architecture were destroyed. Some artists recorded scenes of German terror in Poland including mass arrests, deportations, and executions. Authentic illustrations by prisoners survived the war and are exhibited in such museums as Auschwitz and Majdanek.

The most outstanding Polish poet of the 20th century, Krzysztof Kamil Baczyński (1921-1944), wrote Romantic poetry describing the tragic events of German occupation. He and his wife Barbara were killed fighting as soldiers in the Polish Home Army in the Warsaw uprising in 1944. Andrzej Trzebiński (1922-1943) wrote poetry and drama *Aby podnieść różę (To Pick up a Rose)*. He was executed in Warsaw for his resistance activities. He and Tadeusz Gajcy (1922-1944) were editors of *Sztuka i naród (The Art and the Nation)*. Gajcy expressed his immense imagination in poetry and a play, *Homer i orchidea (Homer and the*

Orchid). Other poetry was written anonymously by Słonimski, Staff, Broniewski and others.

The Press Under Occupation

German Nazis replaced the Polish press with their own propaganda papers printed in Polish in Warsaw, Kraków, Częstochowa, Kielce, Radom, and, after 1941, in Lwów and Wilno. The Polish clandestine press of 1,400 newspapers led all the resistance press in occupied Europe. Twenty-three literary periodicals were secretly published. The underground press reported that 14,000 civilians and 110,000 Polish soldiers under Gen. Władysław Anders were evacuated from the USSR in March 18-Aug. 30, 1942. To confuse the German occupational forces, Poles published fifteen German language diversion and propaganda papers designed to counter Nazi propaganda. These papers also included also factual information such as that from May 11-18, 1944, the 2nd Polish Corp of Gen. Anders won the battle of Monte Cassino and opened the road to Rome from the south for the Allies. Soviet propaganda was spread by the communist fringe press of the Polish Workers Party.

Polish People's Republic and the Warsaw Uprising

The communist government of Poland was formed in Moscow on July 21-22, 1944. However, for propaganda reasons, the official communique referred to Chełm Lubelski as the site in Poland where the Soviet puppet government was created. Immediately, the Public Security Office (Urząd Bezpieczeństwa, the UB) was created as a part of the Soviet terror apparatus in Poland in the new postwar frontiers.

The Polish Home Army proclaimed an independent Poland and fought from Aug. 1 to Oct. 2, 1944 against Germans in Warsaw. Hitler ordered the complete destruction of Warsaw. Stalin stopped the offensive of Marshal Konstanty Rokossowski. However, the Second Soviet Armored Army pretended to mount an assault on the Warsaw suburb Praga. During the uprising, over 150,000 civilians were killed; in the suburb of Wola alone, 40,000 civilians were massacred. Eighteen thousand insurgents were killed. Among the wounded were over 100,000 civilians and

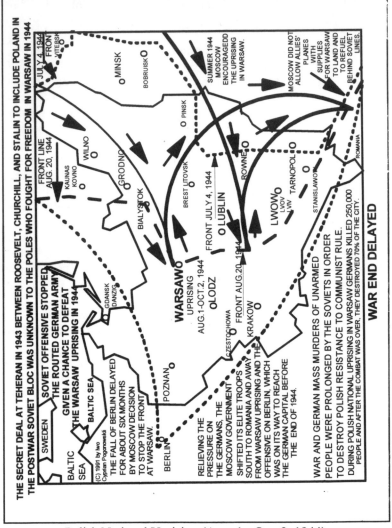

THE SECRET DEAL AT TEHERAN IN 1943 BETWEEN ROOSEVELT, CHURCHILL, AND STALIN TO INCLUDE POLAND IN THE POSTWAR SOVIET BLOC WAS UNKNOWN TO THE POLES WHO FOUGHT FOR FREEDOM IN WARSAW IN 1944

SOVIET OFFENSIVE STOPPED THE ROUTED GERMAN ARMY GIVEN A CHANCE TO DEFEAT THE WARSAW UPRISING IN 1944

THE FALL OF BERLIN DELAYED FOR ABOUT SIX MONTHS BY MOSCOW DECISION TO STOP THE FRONT AT WARSAW.

RELIEVING THE PRESSURE ON THE GERMANS, THE MOSCOW GOVERNMENT SHIFTED ITS ELITE TROOPS SOUTH TO ROMANIA AND AWAY FROM WARSAW UPRISING AND THE OFFENSIVE ON BERLIN, WHICH WAS ON ITS WAY TO REACH THE GERMAN CAPITAL BEFORE THE END OF 1944.

WAR AND GERMAN MASS MURDERS OF UNARMED PEOPLE WERE PROLONGED BY THE SOVIETS IN ORDER TO DESTROY POLISH RESISTANCE TO COMMUNIST RULE. DURING POLISH NATIONAL UPRISING IN WARSAW GERMANS KILLED 250,000 PEOPLE AND AFTER THE COMBAT WAS OVER, THEY DESTROYED 70% OF THE CITY.

SUMMER 1944 MOSCOW ENCOURAGEDD THE UPRISING IN WARSAW.

MOSCOW DID NOT ALLOW ALLIES' PLANES WITH SUPPLIES FOR WARSAW TO LAND AND TO REFUEL BEHIND SOVIET LINES.

WAR END DELAYED

FRONT LINE AUG. 20, 1944

JULY 4 1944 FRONT

FRONT JULY 4, 1944

FRONT AUG. 20, 1944

WARSAW O
UPRISING
AUG. 1-OCT. 2, 1944

BERLIN O

POZNAN O

OLODZ

KRAKOW

CZESTOCHOWA

GDANSK DANZIG

BALTIC SEA

SWEDEN

BALTIC SEA

MINSK O

BOBRUISK O

VITEBSK

PINSK O

WILNO O

KAUNAS KOVNO O

GRODNO O

BIALYSTOK O

BREST LITOVSK O

LUBLIN O

ROVNE O

LWOW O
LVOV
LVIV

TARNOPOL O

STANISLAWOW O

ROMANIA

(C) 1991 by Iwo Cyprian Pogonowski

Polish National Uprising (Aug. 1 - Oct. 2, 1944);
Its Influence on Soviet Strategy.

220

25,000 insurgents.

Losses to the First Polish People's Army were 3,764 officers and soldiers, while the Germans lost 26,000 men. Eighty-seven percent of Warsaw was destroyed. Most of the destruction was done after the combat by German Army Engineers. The Soviet Army stood by across the Vistula River. The deadly struggle between the Germans and Russians did not prevent them from again joining hands against the Poles. On Oct. 2, 1944, Warsaw was surrendered by Gen. Tadeusz Bór Komorowski who, like most of the Poles, was unaware that the Allies had already betrayed Poland in Teheran (Nov. 28.- Dec.1, 1943), as they secretly placed Poland in the Soviet postwar zone of influence.

On Aug. 2-20, 1944, The First Polish Armored Division won the decisive battle of Falaise, important in the liberation of France.

The End of the War and Polish Losses
Berlin fell on May 2, 1945. Germany surrendered unconditionally six days later. It was the end of the Second World War in Europe. 6,028,000 or 22.2 percent of Polish citizens were killed by the Germans, including 644,000 in combat; an additional 1,000,000 perished as a result of the deportation of 1,900,000 to the Soviet Union. It is not certain whether this total includes all Polish citizens murdered by the Germans and Soviets in their respective genocidal campaigns. The fact that, despite the horrible conditions of the war, some 400,000 children were born each year in the Polish ethnic area tends to diminish the estimates of the human losses in war-torn Poland. Nearly three million Polish Jews were killed by the Germans, a total of over eleven million people of different nationalities were killed by the Germans in Poland and in Polish lands annexed by Germany during the war.

On June 17 - 21, 1945, Representatives of the Big Three (USA, UK, and USSR) met in Moscow to finalize the composition of the Provisional Government of National Unity of the Republic of Poland.

During the Second World War, Poland was devastated and plundered by the Germans and the Soviets. The Polish population was systematically robbed by the Germans and the Soviets. Eventually, there was hardly a person in Poland, Jew or Gentile, whose property was not

221

destroyed or taken over either by the German Nazis or the Communists

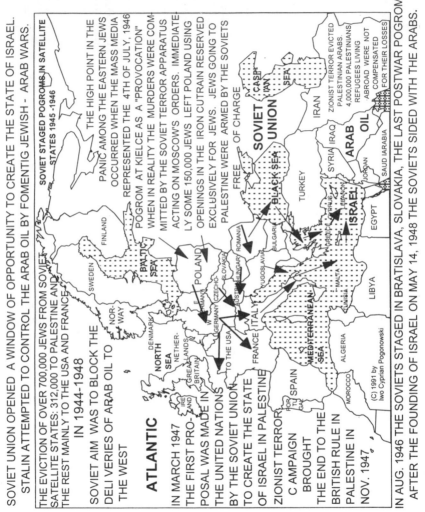

SOVIET UNION OPENED A WINDOW OF OPPORTUNITY TO CREATE THE STATE OF ISRAEL. STALIN ATTEMPTED TO CONTROL THE ARAB OIL BY FOMENTIG JEWISH - ARAB WARS.

THE EVICTION OF OVER 700,000 JEWS FROM SOVIET SATELLITE STATES: 312,000 TO PALESTINE AND THE REST MAINLY TO THE USA AND FRANCE IN 1944-1948

SOVIET AIM WAS TO BLOCK THE DELIVERIES OF ARAB OIL TO THE WEST

IN MARCH 1947 THE FIRST PROPOSAL WAS MADE IN THE UNITED NATIONS BY THE SOVIET UNION TO CREATE THE STATE OF ISRAEL IN PALESTINE

ZIONIST TERROR CAMPAIGN BROUGHT THE END TO THE BRITISH RULE IN PALESTINE IN NOV. 1947.

SOVIET STAGED POGROMS IN SATELLITE STATES 1945-1946

THE HIGH POINT IN THE PANIC AMONG THE EASTERN JEWS OCCURRED WHEN THE MASS MEDIA REPRESENTED THE 4TH OF JULY, 1946 POGROM AT KIELCE AS A "PROVOCATION" WHEN IN REALITY THE MURDERS WERE COMMITTED BY THE SOVIET TERROR APPARATUS ACTING ON MOSCOW'S ORDERS. IMMEDIATELY SOME 150,000 JEWS LEFT POLAND USING OPENINGS IN THE IRON CURTAIN RESERVED EXCLUSIVELY FOR JEWS. JEWS GOING TO PALESTINE WERE ARMED BY THE SOVIETS FREE OF CHARGE

ZIONIST TERROR EVICTED PALESTINIAN ARABS 4,000,000 PALESTINIANS REFUGEES LIVING ABROAD WERE NOT COMPENSATED FOR THEIR LOSSES

ARAB OIL

(C) 1991 by Iwo Cyprian Pogonowski

IN AUG. 1946 THE SOVIETS STAGED IN BRATISLAVA, SLOVAKIA, THE LAST POSTWAR POGROM. AFTER THE FOUNDING OF ISRAEL ON MAY 14, 1948 THE SOVIETS SIDED WITH THE ARABS.

Eviction of Jews from Eastern Europe by the Soviets (1939-1947).

POLISH PEOPLE'S REPUBLIC
A PART OF THE SOVIET BLOC

(Socialist-Realism and Modernism, 1944-1989)

New Frontiers, Soviet Occupation, and Arrests
On March 1, 1945, Stalin ordered to start the transfer of 105,000 sq. km. of the Soviet zone of the occupation of Germany to the Polish administration - this area was added to the 207,000 sq. km. left of the prewar area of Poland after the Soviet annexation of Polish provinces east of the Bug River. Despite Soviet plunder, the former German areas, together with what was left of prewar Polish territory, represented a 50% larger economic potential than Poland possessed before the war.

In March 1945, *Catholic Weekly (Tygodnik Powszechny)* began publication in Kraków after the authorization from the NKVD.

On March 27, Gen. Leopold Okulicki, the last Commander-in-Chief of the Home Army (AK), and Jan Stanisław Jankowski, former vice-premier and delegate of the Government-in-Exile, were arrested by the Soviets in Poland. They were sentenced to ten years imprisonment in Moscow in June 1945 in the show trial of sixteen Polish leaders.

On Apr. 22, E. Osóbka-Morawski (an NKVD agent), acting as the Prime Minister of the Provisional Government of the Republic of Poland, signed a twenty-year treaty of friendship, mutual assistance, and post-war cooperation with the USSR. Poland formally became a part of the Soviet zone of interest, which soon became known as the Soviet Bloc. Stalin's policy of accomplished facts in Poland was backed by the presence of 3,000,000 Red Army men and NKVD and NKGB troops, who were equipped with 50,000 artillery pieces and mortars, 10,000 tanks and self-propelled guns, and 10,000 airplanes. At the same time, the American army of 2,500,000 men was stationed throughout Europe.

Polish Culture under Soviet Control

The consolidation of Soviet control over Poland by the pacification of anti-Communist resistance was mostly completed by 1948. The mobilization of Poland's and other satellite countries' resources was of strategic importance to Moscow as it entered the Cold War and strove for world domination. The organization of education, science, and research was to follow the Soviet model established before the war. The Soviet approach to all subjects was called "progressive." However, Soviet aims had to be reconciled with the reality of the devastation of Poland and the population losses. Germans destroyed most of the cadres of Polish universities and schools of higher learning. Thousands of Polish scholars remained in the West, unwilling to work under the Soviets. Contacts with foreign scientists were broken. School buildings were destroyed.

Selected foreign scientific and professional periodicals had to be made available however, at the same time, measures "had to be taken" to prevent "anti-Communist contamination." The Soviets had a chance to take advantage of the Polish need and will to rebuild Poland and to make up for the lost time. Thus, the Soviets intended to control the process of reconstruction. All press and books published were subject to severe censorship. Polish writers had to "smuggle" their thoughts through the censorship and the public soon learned to read "between the lines." Irony was one of the weapons of self-defense. Endless jokes were created to ridicule the enforcement of Communist ideology and the imposition of the "socialist realism."

In 1951, the First Congress of Polish Science called for the establishment of a Soviet-style Polish Academy of Sciences (PAN) as a supreme scientific institution for the coordination, planning, and implementation of research and cooperation with the armament and other industries. The Soviets wanted to take stock of the situation in the Polish science and to lay out plans for state-controlled development. Communist style socio-economic development was important for the control and exploitation of the population. The progress in science and technology was strategically important for the Soviets. State supervision of these activities was also to give the Soviets a chance to solidify their power over Poland; and, eventually, to take over any successfully advanced technical or scientific project for completion and exploitation in the USSR. All Soviet satellite states were subject to the same Moscow policy. Communist propaganda was to permeate all socio-economic activities in order to consolidate the Soviet grip on the satellites.

All students enrolled in higher learning received a stipend from the government and did not have to pay the tuition. However, "proletarian" criteria were applied to promote admission of students from families of communist party members, peasants, and workers and to discriminate against the offspring of the prewar intelligentsia and civil service, business people, property owners, and politicians who opposed communism. The enrollment was much larger than before the war.

In 1944, Maria Skłodowska-Curie University was founded in Lublin; Catholic University was reopened two years later. The universities of Warsaw, Kraków, and Poznań were reopened after having worked underground during German occupation. Nicolas Copernicus University was founded in Copernicus' birthplace in Toruń in 1945. It was staffed with the surviving professors of the University of Wilno. Polish Wilno became Vilnius, the capital of Lithuania and most of its Polish inhabitants were forced to emigrate to Poland. Surviving professors of the University of Lwów and Lwów Polytechnic moved to Wrocław in Silesia and were employed at the University of Wrocław. The University of Łódź was created out of the Polish Free University.

Warsaw Polytechnic, Wrocław Polytechnic, and the Academy of Mining and Metallurgy in Kraków were soon followed by the conversion of higher schools of engineering into Polytechnic institutes in Gliwice, Łódź, Gdańsk, Poznań, Szczecin, and Częstochowa. Separate academies were created by separating the Departments of Medicine, Theology, Agriculture, Physical Education, and Economics from existing universities.

Polish Literature in 1945-1948, Socialist Realism

The official reason for the strict control of the press and all publications was the need to protect communist state secrets against western espionage. Thus, an objective description of any mishap was treated as an act of espionage in service of a foreign intelligence, and therefore a criminal offence. Any dissemination of information unfavorable to the communist regime was treated as an anti-state action equal to the sabotage and was therefore severely punishable. The only people who had access to any objective information were high ranking communists who regularly received a confidential bulletin that could not be seen by any unauthorized person.

There was an awareness of the scrutiny of everything published in Poland under the Soviet control. This had an eroding effect on the authenticity of the literary output produced in such an atmosphere of uneasiness and often an outright fear of the consequences of any printed statements. Some tried to compromise by claiming belief in Marxism-Leninism and all the high ideals usurped by the Soviets. A few chose to work for the communist propaganda machine. Even works of high artistic value written before or after the Soviet takeover were often published with introductions following the current party line. The introductions and additions were not signed and appeared to contain the views of the author. Any objections by the authors were disposed of by intimidating threats. Few had the courage to face the terror apparatus and, thus, the mendacity of communist propaganda permeated practically all literary output, the press, and anything else published under the Soviet control.

Any printed announcement had to be approved by the office of the censor. That covered even death notices. All typewriters had to be registered and sample printing had to be deposited at the Office of the Press Control. These controls extended to the use of stencil paper, which was sold to people who registered their stencil cutting typewriter. The formalities related to the registration of the typewriters resembled gun registration in the free world. All samples of any rubber stamps had to be registered before they could be legally used. Any sermon or public speech had to be approved before it could be delivered. The dissemination of the information from western radio broadcasts was punishable with a prison term. The frequencies of Radio Free Europe and Voice of America were jammed with powerful signals.

War experiences understandably occupied an important place in Polish prose. Zofia Nałkowska (1884-1954) unmasked the bestiality of German Nazis in an objective narrative in *Medaliony (Medallions, 1946)*. Her motto was "men have prepared this fate for men." Perfectly truthful descriptions of the crimes of the Germans were, of course, easily approved for publication as were criticisms of prewar Poland. Any texts describing crimes of the Soviets were forbidden and, if illegally published, were punishable with prison terms. The Soviet version of events in the world was the only acceptable one. There were taboos which could not be mentioned such, as the Soviet invasion of Poland in 1939, the Soviet-German pacts, and the joint German-Soviet program of the destruction of the Polish leadership community. The Soviets insisted that the Polish officers murdered by the NKVD in the Katyń forest were executed by the Germans; however, any mention of the word "Katyń" was strictly forbidden. On the other hand, the topic of German concentration camps in Poland was most welcomed by the communist-controlled publishing houses.

The Auschwitz memoirs of Tadeusz Borowski (1922-1951) show a merciless vision of the world with shocking frankness. He published his short stories under the title *Pożegnanie z Marią (Farewell to Maria, 1948)* and *Kamienny Świat (World of Stone, 1948)*. In them, he describes with bitter realism the inner stupor which he developed during the daily activities of trading, dating, and working under constant fear of arrest, and then his years in Auschwitz. After 1948, he turned to Soviet mandated "socialist realism" and wrote in the spirit of Marxist-Leninist ideology.

Adolf Rudnicki (1912-1990) wrote about the martyrdom of Jews in short stories entitled *Epoka Pieców (Times of the Ovens, 1948)* and other works, in which he showed the Jews in a biblical perspective as a chosen people and a doomed people as seen by a Jewish survivor.

A soldier's version of the war was described by former war correspondent in Spain, Ksawery Pruszyński (1907-1950), who wrote *Droga wiodła przez Narvik (The Road through Narvik, 1941, 1945)*.

Jerzy Andrzejewski (1909-1983) wrote *Popiół i diament (Ashes and Diamonds, 1948)*, on which Andrzej Wajda based the script of the film of the same name. This film earned awards at the Cannes Festival in 1957. At this point in time, Andrzejewski expressed the hope for an understanding between the Catholics and the communists in Poland.

A talented poet, Wisława Szymborska (b. 1923), wrote about the "concerned eyes of Joseph Stalin." Later, she was embarrassed by her poetic collaboration with the Soviets when she was given the 1996 Nobel

Prize for Literature.

Socialist Realism in Polish Theater

City theaters started staging plays immediately after the war ended in 1945. In devastated towns, makeshift means were used by newly formed companies. Actors evicted by the Soviets from Wilno (now Vilnius) moved to Toruń and Łódź. Those evicted from Lwów (now Lviv) moved to Katowice. In the areas east of the Odra River, new Polish theaters were organized.

Drama schools were opened in Łódź, Kraków, and Warsaw. The Soviets viewed theater as a propaganda tool and for this reason permitted their regime in Warsaw to grant funds to theaters through city budgets. Some producers such as Andrzej Wajda and Krzysztof Zanussi worked simultaneously in theaters and in the movies. Among the actors were only a few survivors of the prewar period. Soon, they were joined by young graduates of the drama schools. Musicians and composers worked for the needs of the theaters, as music became increasingly more important in Polish postwar theater.

The city of Kraków was the only one which was not seriously damaged during the war. In 1945, it became the main Polish theatrical center with the Słowacki Theater, Stary Theater, Rhapsody Theater, and the Grotesque Theater of Puppets and Actors. Łódź became the leading theater center with its Polish Army Theater, the Scena Theater, the Poetic Estrada Theater, and the Theatr Kameralny. Warsaw had to be rebuilt after near complete devastation by the Germans. The first to open was the Teatr Polski in 1946, which helped organize Teater Kameralny. It was followed by the arrival from Łódź of the Contemporary Theater. The National Theater was rebuilt in 1949.

A large number of Polish and Russian comedies were staged. In 1947, a Festival of Shakespeare's Plays was held. It was followed in 1949 by a Festival of Russian Plays. Until the mid-1950s, Polish producers and actors were ordered to adopt socialist-realism and to show the heroes of socialist labor. A fiasco resulted from this Soviet initiative.

Socialist Realism in Polish Film

In 1945 the entire production of films was nationalized because "...films should not be governed by financial profit but by social and educational criteria only... [because] a necessary condition for the creation of good and fully valid films is a definite break from private enterprise" (wrote Jerzy Toepliz, 1909-1995). In other words, state control and communist propaganda was to dominate film production in Poland. This meant that Polish producers had to make sure that their films were acceptable to the censors or see their films either altered, or not shown in the theaters. However, the communist regime used the film industry as a potent propaganda weapon.

State Enterprise Film Polski produced films, distributed them, and organized teaching programs for all aspects of cinematography.

In 1947, the Film Maker's Union included only twenty-eight experienced cinematographers. There was a lack of equipment and only 220 cinemas had survived the war - half of them in the city of Łódź and its vicinity.

The film, *The Last Stage,* by W. Jakubowska was a documentary on the Auschwitz concentration camp made by a Polish Catholic survivor in 1948. It was exploited in a Soviet peace offensive. This film was awarded the Grand Prix in Czech Marianske Lazne in 1948; the Grand Prix at Gotwaldov in 1949; as well as the Soviet-sponsored Award of the World Peace Council in 1951.

The film, *Border Street,* by A. Ford on the extermination of the Warsaw Ghetto was produced in 1948; it was subsequently awarded the Golden Medal at the Festival in Venice.

The Congress of Film Makers, held in Nov. 1949 in Wisła, Poland, tried to make films into "weapons for fighting for [Soviet-style] socialism and for hastening the process of socialist construction and preventing of the action of class enemy." The films of the Stalinist period were produced in the style of socialist realism. In 1950-1954 produced Polish films were the worst in the history of the industry; the producers were said not to have understood the principles of socialist realism and committed the "sin of superficiality."

The Press as Communist Propaganda Tool

In People's Poland the press became "public property" - a euphemism for it being a tool of Soviet propaganda. The press had to be reorganized from the bottom up. Some 4,000 professional newsmen were killed during the war. The paper industry was 70% destroyed. Broadcasting systems did not exist. Thus, the communists organized their unified socialist press. Within limits acceptable to the Soviets, a few church periodicals were allowed to publish under strict censorship.

The number of periodicals grew steadily. There were 61 in 1944; 600 in 1945; 1050 in 1947; 431 in 1954; 800 in 1956; and 1,013 in 1961.

Stalin Dies, but Stalinism Stays

Stalin died on March 5, 1953. The death of Stalin occurred amidst a new purge at the top of the Politburo for the purpose of re-consolidating Soviet control over its terror apparatus in Poland. At the same time, Moscow ordered a new anti-church offensive throughout the satellites. Show-trials of priests were staged throughout Poland. Communist authorities took over the Catholic press. The city name of Katowice was changed to Stalingrad.

During Stalinism abortion was strictly banned and a very high demographic increase occurred in Poland. Despite political murders, show trials, and terror there was no hunger in Poland. In fact, the proceeds from monopolized state sales of alcohol and tobacco were used to subsidize food; and during the communist period, the Polish population attained the highest average body height in its history. Later, these subsidies came from international borrowing and resulted in heavy indebtedness.

Poland became over 90% Roman Catholic and eventually produced the first non-Italian pope in centuries.

The end of German repatriation from Poland was ordered by the USSR to be completed on Aug. 24, 1953.

The Spontaneous Reconstruction

In the reconstruction of Poland, the spontaneous effort of the Polish population was a reaction to years of terror and depravation under German occupation and its planned destruction of Polish society. Thus, despite the controlling role of the USSR over Poland's geopolitical situation, the accomplishments of the Polish nation under the communist rule increasingly became Polish national achievements.

The reconstruction of Warsaw was accomplished despite economic hardship, which resulted not only from war destruction but also from ever-growing armament programs imposed by the Soviets. During Sept. 1953, an act was issued by the government on the reconstruction and expansion of the port city of Gdańsk.

Revelations by Col. J. Flajszfarb-Światło

On Dec. 5, 1953, Col. J. Flajszfarb-Światło asked for asylum in West Berlin. He was an NKVD officer, vice-director of the Tenth Dept. in the Ministry of Public Security, and an active Stalinist who tortured prisoners. He could have been included in the anti-Semitic purge ordered by Moscow in the satellites. However, it is not quite clear why Col. Józef Flajszfarb-Światło defected to the West. He publicly exposed communist corruption on Radio Free Europe after an initial press conference in Washington, DC. However, he did not expose the role of "Soviet ádvisors" who were the real rulers of People's Poland. His criticism was directed against Bierut and other Polish agents of the Soviet Stalinist regime, who had outlived their usefulness to Moscow under the new regime of Nikita Khrushchev. Thanks to the propaganda value of his revelations during the Cold War, Światło escaped prosecution for the crimes he committed on his victims in Poland. Światło's public appearances ended in the Spring of 1955.

On Feb. 12, 1955, the balloon operation "Spotlight" started and eventually delivered 3,000,000 copies of Col. Swiatlo's reports to Poland.

Treaty of Warsaw, Propaganda War, and the "Thaw"

The Treaty of Warsaw was signed on May 11-14, 1955, integrating the military and economic forces of the entire Soviet bloc. It was the next phase of the Cold War and the Soviet reaction to the re-militarization of West Germany within NATO by the United States. People's Poland accordingly severed relations with the Vatican.

The Polonia Association for the relations with Poles abroad was founded on Oct. 18, 1955. Two million Poles, persecuted and under Russification pressure in the USSR, were excluded from the activities of Polonia.

From Feb. 14 to Feb. 25, 1956, the Twentieth Congress of the Soviet Communist Party was held in Moscow. N. Khrushchev's "Secret Speech" described some of the Stalin's crimes, especially those committed against fellow communists.

Death of Bierut and the "Rehabilitation" of Gomułka

On March 12, 1956, Bolesław Bierut died while visiting Moscow, like many communist leaders who were at the end of their usefulness to the Soviets. He was an old NKVD hand. He had been the head of Polish National Council, then the president of Polish People's Republic, and was currently the First Secretary of the Communist Party (PZPR). He was apparently executed because of the lack of an orderly succession procedure, because he knew "too much," and, above all, because he compromised the Soviets by failing to insure the secrecy of the details of Communist rule by methods of organized crime. Some of these methods were disclosed by Beirut's right-hand-man, Col. Swiatło, in 141 reports on Radio Free Europe.

On Apr. 10, 1956, W. Gomułka was officially rehabilitated and was soon summoned to Moscow to prepare him for a political career as a "patriot persecuted by the Soviets." Over 35,000 prisoners were released by the communist government in Poland following the passage of the amnesty law by the rubber-stamp parliament on Apr. 23, 1956.

On May 1, 1956, the first television station started broadcasting from Warsaw.

The "Bread and Freedom" Riots and Collectivization Failure

The "Bread and Freedom" labor uprising was provoked in Poznań on June 28, 1956. The two days' fighting of workers and communist government forces resulted in the death of 53 men. Communist party offices were destroyed and the files of the secret police burned. Hungarian demonstrations, organized in sympathy of events in Poznań, led to an uprising and the Soviet invasion of Hungary. Moscow ordered the purge of Hilary Minc, the Stalinist tsar of the Polish economy. His demotion was part of the Soviet drive to stop all criticism of "Soviet advisors" and to blame only their Jewish subordinates.

The political upheaval in the USSR after Khrushchev's attack on Stalinism was reflected in the events in Poland and then in Hungary. Both of them were constantly manipulated by Moscow.

During Aug. 25 - 27, 1956, a pilgrimage of over one million Poles visited the Catholic Monastery of Częstochowa.

Krushchev's Approval of Gomułka

Some increase of Poland's internal autonomy was permitted by Moscow. It was conditioned on purging the armed forces of nationalists. The beginning of the "Polish Road to Socialism" was announced. It was the end of Stalinist terror - other versions of Soviet terror were to follow.

On Oct. 21, 1956, W. Gomułka was appointed the First Secretary of the communist party (PZPR). Thanks to his earlier arrest by the Soviets, he was the most popular man ever to hold the top office in People's Poland.

With the reduction of the intensity of communist terror, there were widespread public demands to bring back the large number of Poles still imprisoned in the Soviet Union. Meanwhile, the Hungarian uprising started

On Oct. 23, 1956, W. Gomułka spoke at the rally of about 400,000 cheering people on the Parade Square in Warsaw. On Oct. 28, Stefan Cardinal Wyszynski returned from the internment in Komańcza.

On Nov. 1, the Red Army invaded Hungary.

Victimization of Former Executioners and Anti-Semitism

On Nov. 11, 1957 the Warsaw Provincial Court sentenced R. Romkowski (Menasz Grynszpan) - former Deputy Minister of Public Security - to 15 years imprisonment. Józef Goldberg-Różański, the former Director of the Investigations Dept. in the Ministry of Public Security was sentenced to 14 years; and the former Director of the Tenth Dept. in the Ministry of Public Security, A. Feign was given twelve years. All three were Jewish agents of the NKVD/KGB, used by the Soviets as scapegoats for communist crimes in Poland. It was a part of continued Soviet propaganda aimed at converting anti-communist sentiments into anti-Semitism.

The Soviets continued to flood Poland with successive waves of anti-Semitism in the tsarist tradition, in order to disrupt the relations between Christians and Jews, who were still full of memories of common suffering under the Nazi-German terror.

On Feb. 9, 1958, the repatriation figures for 1955-1957 were published: 131,000 former prisoners from the USSR, and 6,000 returnees from other countries.

Economic interdependence of the Soviet bloc was tightened. The agreement to build an oil pipeline from USSR to Poland and East Germany, in order to supply them with Soviet oil, was signed in Moscow on Dec. 18, 1959. The United States gave Poland the "most favored nation" status on Nov. 17, 1960; and on Nov. 18, Poland was admitted to the General Agreement on Tariffs and Trade (GATT).

On Dec. 6, the national census counted 29,776,000 inhabitants in Poland. On Dec. 16, Poland's yearly production of coal exceeded 100,000,000 tons.

Berlin Wall, Isolation, and Economic Data

On Aug. 13, 1961, the Berlin Wall was erected. The isolation of Poland increased amidst growing tension between the United States and the USSR. It was the end of the hopes for liberation of the captive nations held under the Soviet domination.

On Nov. 11, the production of the 100,000th ton of Polish sulfur made Poland the sixth largest producer of sulfur in the world.

Postwar building of ships in the Gdańsk shipyard reached 1,000,000 deadweight ton.

During 1961-1965 trade school education was expanded from 764,200 students to 1,535,000 by 1965.

Andropov's Anti-Semitic Program and Riots in Poland

The program of Jiri Andropov (1914-1984), the head of the KGB, was lanched in Poland in June of 1968. In a meeting with Andropov in Russia, Mieczysław Demko-Moczar learned the specific details. Anti-

Semitism in the satellites was used by the Soviets to help their propaganda in the Middle East.

Apparently the Soviets ordered Dubcek to stage the "Prague Spring" in order to justify Soviet military "police action," which, in turn was to serve as a cover for secretly moving Soviet rockets with nuclear warheads to the Czech border with Bavaria.

Thousands of Jews and Poles of Jewish descent were forced to emigrate. Andropov's terror was in full swing. However, no one was executed, as had been the case during the Stalinist years when many Jews were appointed to serve as executioners. Some of them were turned into victims in 1968.

The purge ordered by Andropov reached the security service. Numerous Jews were fired from the terror apparatus, and so were the people who would not speak against Jews.

On July 20, 1969, an American man stepped on the moon. The Soviets lost face in the space race, and there was rejoicing in Poland.

In Dec. 8-12, 1970, the third postwar census established a population of 32.6 million in Poland. On Dec. 12, the prices of basic foodstuffs were increased by the communist government. The Soviets ordered an increase in food prices to be accompanied by a decrease in the prices of luxury items. The purpose was to provoke riots, that would serve as an excuse to remove Gomułka from office. The very next day strikes and protest marches spread in Gdańsk, Gdynia, and Sopot. On Dec. 14, workers of Lenin Shipyards in Gdansk demonstrated; students did not participate because workers did not support them in 1968. Dec. 15 was "Bloody Tuesday" in Gdańsk. Officially, 48 people were killed and 1,165 injured in the battle of workers against security forces. The strike then spread to Paris Commune Shipyards in Gdynia and Waryński Shipyards in Szczecin. Protest marchers attacked police headquarters and set fire to the local PZPR District Committee in Gdańsk. Many shipyard workers were killed in Gdynia on their way to work. On Dec. 16, tanks and helicopters were used against workers, while riots continued in Elbląg, Pruszcz Gdański, and Tczew. On Dec. 17, a state of siege was declared in Poland as the battle against workers spread to Gdynia and Szczecin (Stettin); a total of 300 workers were killed and 4,500 injured. On Dec. 18, W. Gomułka was reported to have suffered a stroke.

Amendment of Constitutions in the Satellites and Show Trials

On June 24, 1971, Gierek instituted a new economic policy that was to expand the consumer sector and bring a small car and a TV set to every Polish household. Gierek's "economic maneuver" (as he called it) was based on massive foreign loans that were to be repaid out of the production of industrial plants financed by the same loans; the Five-Year-Plan for 1971-75 was revised. A crackdown on leaders of the December labor strikes was ordered.

In Sept. 1971, Soviet Bloc members, including Poland, were pressed by the Soviets to amend their constitutions and to proclaim their socialist character; emphasize the leading role of their Communist parties; and to commit themselves to friendship and cooperation with the Soviet Union.

Helsinki Pact and Constitutional Amendments

Poland, along with 34 other nations, signed the Helsinki Pact on Aug. 1, 1975. It recognized existing boundaries as inviolable and guaranteed freedom of thought, conscience, religion, and belief. A gradual linkage was established between Western credits and the compliance with the Helsinki Pact. Guidelines were formulated for the next congress of the Polish Communist Party. They called for the affirmation, in an amendment to the Polish constitution, that Poland is a socialist state in which the Communist Party is a "leading force" cooperating with USSR. The Church protested the "totalitarian nature" of the proposed amendments.

Protests and Show Trials

Police conducted mass arrests of strike leaders in Radom, Ursus, Płock, Łódź, Starachowice, Grudziądz, and Nowy Targ.

On July 2, 1976, E. Gierek and P. Jaroszewicz spoke at a communist rally at Katowice. On July 17, show trials of Radom strikers started in Warsaw, while numerous protest letters were addressed to the government, which imposed the rationing of sugar on Aug. 13.

On Sept. 23, The Workers' Defense Committee (*Komitet Obrony*

Robotników), the KOR, was founded to help brutally suppressed strikers and their families with legal, financial, and medical matters, as well as new jobs for the unemployed. KOR received an initial subsidy of $10,000 from the American United Auto Workers' Union.

On Nov. 2, 1976, Jimmy Carter defeated Gerald Ford in the race for the presidency of the U.S. President Carter stated that his national security advisor will be Polish-born Dr. Zbigniew Brzeziński.

In Feb. of 1977, Wajda's film, *Man of Marble,* was shown. It described the tragic fate of a workers' hero exploited by the Stalinists and killed in the 1970 Gdańsk massacre. On March 25, 1977, the Movement for the Defense of Human and Civil Rights (ROPCiO) was established. Organized opposition to communist rule and Soviet domination grew.

NOWA, an underground publishing house, was founded in May of 1977. Among its publications were the works of Czesław Miłosz, Aleksander Sołzhenitsyn, Orwell's *1984*, and 50,000 copies of *What to Do in Contacts with the Police.* The house also published the bi-weekly *Robotnik (The Worker)*.

S. Pyjas, a student and KOR member, was killed on May 7, 1977.

Human Rights and the Polish Pope

From Dec. 29-31, 1977, President Carter visited Warsaw and emphasized human rights. Gierek limited arrests of KOR and NOWA activists to 48-hours in order to obtain American debt financing.

On Apr, 29, 1978, a Baltic Coast Committee of Free Trade Unions was formed by Andrzej Gwiazda, Anna Walentynowicz, and Lech Wałęsa in Gdańsk.

On June 27, the first Polish cosmonaut, H. Hermaszewski, was sent in orbit on the Soyuz 30 spaceship.

In July a Provisional Committe for the Self-Defense of Farmers was formed in the Lublin region.

On Oct. 5, 1978, the Nobel Prize for Literature was given to Isaac Bashevis Singer, a Polish-born writer of the Yiddish subculture.

On Oct. 16, Karol Wojtyła, Archbishop of Kraków, was elected as Pope John Paul II. This fact strengthened the position of Polish Catholics. (It also helped to stop derisive anti-Polish jokes in the U.S.)

On Dec. 7, a national census counted 35 million people.

In Dec. of 1978 the hard currency debt of Poland reached $15 billion.

During June 2-10, 1979, Pope John Paul II made a pilgrimage to Poland on the nine-hundredth anniversary of the martyrdom of St. Stanislaus. The Pope delivered sermons on spiritual freedom to the largest field masses in the history of Christianity.

On Dec. 12, 1979, a NATO decision was made to place Pershing II and Cruise rockets in Europe in response to the introduction of Soviet SS-20 (RSD-10) rockets in East Germany. The three-warhead SS-20 near Berlin could have reached Chicago when used with one warhead. Suspicion spread that the Soviets, while losing the arms race, might be preparing for a preventive assault on the West.

In Dec. 27, 1979, Soviet attention was drawn away from Poland, when the USSR invaded Afghanistan. The invasion resulted in an American-led boycott of the Moscow Olympics and an embargo on grain sales to the USSR.

Strike in Gdańsk Shipyard

On Aug. 14, 1980, a celebration was held in Warsaw at the Tomb of the Unknown Soldier. It was the sixtieth anniversary of the victory of the Polish Army, led by Marshal Józef Piłsudski, over the Soviet invasion (the battle involved over 1.5 million soldiers and prevented a Soviet linkup with German Communists in 1920).

The following day, a total of 50,000 workers went on strike in Gdańsk in a communication blackout, as all telephone lines were cut. Gierek returned to Poland and cited Soviet "concern." Soviet TASS announced "routine maneuvers" of Warsaw Pact armies in the Baltic area, including East Germany.

On Aug. 31, the final agreement was signed. Wałęsa used a souvenir pen with an image of the Pope and signed under a crucifix hanging on the wall. The agreement, a first in the Soviet Bloc, sanctioned a free and independent union with the right to strike.

On Sept. 17, the national union Solidarność (*Solidarity*) was made official. On Sept. 21, the first radio transmission of the Sunday Mass in postwar Poland was allowed.

Birth of Solidarity, an Escalating Crisis, and Martial Law

The following day marked the birth of Solidarity in Gdańsk, when thirty-six regional independent unions united themselves. On Sept. 24, Solidarity applied for registration with the Warsaw court. Tension built up as the court delayed.

On Oct. 24, Solidarity's membership reached eight million industrial workers, including over one million Communist Party members.

On Nov. 10, the charter of Solidarity was legalized by Polish Supreme Court, without making a reference to the leading role of the Communist Party. The text of the Gdańsk Agreement was added as an appendix to the charter of Solidarity.

On Dec. 13, the USSR eased the tension. The Soviets preferred that Polish Communists handle the situation in Poland. Gen. Jaruzelski enforced a "State of War." The USSR accused the United States of making a false alarm. In reality, American disclosures helped prevent a Soviet invasion of Poland.

On Dec. 14, Rural Solidarity started a registration drive and eventually had 4 million members, in addition to the eight million in the industrial Solidarity.

On Dec. 20, the Polish ambassador to the United States, Romuald Spasowski, resigned his post in protest against the military takeover in Poland; a few days later, he was followed by Zdzisław Rurarz, the Polish ambassador to Japan and Philippines. Both received political asylum in the United States, and later were sentenced to death in absentia and stripped of their Polish citizenship by a Warsaw court.

Papal Visit, Wałęsa's Nobel Prize

The second pilgrimage to Poland by the Pope John Paul II occurred June 16-23, 1983. The Pope reminded the communist government that joining unions is a natural right of workers; victims of recent repression were mentioned by name.

On July 22, Martial Law was finally abolished.

On Oct. 5, Lech Wałęsa received the Noble Peace Prize. It was an international approval of Solidarity.

During Oct. of 1983 the government took a still stiffer attitude towards the opposition. On Oct. 19, 1984, the secret police abducted, tortured, and murdered the Chaplain of Solidarity, Fr. Jerzy Popieluszko of the St. Stanisław Church in Warsaw.

On Nov. 3, hundreds of thousands attended the funeral of Fr. Popiełuszko. There was a consolidation of the support for the Solidarity.

Gorbachov in Power, Food Prices Raised

On March 11, 1985, Mikhail Gorbachov assumed power in the USSR and initiated moves "to deprive Washington of the Soviet adversary" - the Soviets attempted to end the open adversarial relations with the United States and to pursue Moscow's interests by political means, in the recognition of the nuclear stalemate and the economic weakness of the USSR.

Soviet military doctrine followed Lenin's belief that war was the essence of domestic and international politics as a product of the class struggle. For this reason, up to 40% of Soviet gross domestic product was spent for the Red Army, while the United States under President Reagan spent no more than 8% of its GDP on defense. When Gorbachev tried to salvage the economy and to reform the Soviet system of government, he reduced the activities of the Soviet terror apparatus and downsized the military spending. The Russian war industry was difficult to retool for peacetime production. Ethnic struggle broke out throughout the Soviet territory when terror was reduced in order to prove to the United States that the USSR had ended its mobilization for war. However, on Apr. 26, 1985, the Warsaw Pact was renewed for the next twenty years.

In Oct. of 1985, the participation in parliamentary elections was 56%. There was a general apathy, as the arrests and raises in food prices continued. Solidarity ineffectually urged a boycott. The regime claimed 66% participation.

On Nov. 12, 1986, Gen. Jaruzelski, the first secretary of the communist party, became the head of the State Council.

Gorbachov's Visit and the Proposed "Roundtable"

On July 11, 1988, Mikhail Gorbachov, the First Secretary of the Communist Party of the USSR, visited Poland - even as the persecution of Solidarity continued.

Police General and Minister of the Interior Minister, C. Kiszczak, headed the terror apparatus of about two million people. Following Moscow's orders, Kiszczak called for preliminary "Roundtable Negotiations" with "representatives of the Polish society." The Soviet purpose in authorizing the "Roundtable" was to avoid military pacification of the type used in Hungary in 1956.

On Aug. 31, 1988, a Kiszczak-Wałęsa meeting was moderated by Archbishop Dąbrowski. After it ended, Wałęsa convinced the strikers to stop the strikes without any guarantees from the government.

Meanwhile, West German leaders like Helmut Kohl and Helmut Schmidt believed that the unification of Germany was at least one or two generations away.

Towards Power-Sharing and the End of the People's Republic

John R. Davis, who served as an Ambassador to Poland from 1983 to 1990, wrote in *the Polish Review,* 1999, No. 4, (p.389): "The historic political earthquake of 1989 was the product of Polish actions and initiatives. The Polish people and the Polish diaspora took inspiration from Solidarity and the election of a Polish Pope, and pushed determinately for their freedom....Solidarity crafted a careful agreement which opened the door to real democracy and, within six months, to the end of communism in Poland and its Eastern European neighbors....the Poles achieved it through their own efforts. The Cold War on which the West had spent trillions of dollars was won at no cost to the West by Polish wisdom and perseverence."

Walter Raymond, Jr., of the CIA, served as Assistant Director and Coordinator of President Bush's Support for Eastern Europe's Democracy (1987-1992). He wrote (p.397) in *Poland - The Road to 1989,* "Poland is the classic case of victory of ideas over tanks. In Poland, when the potent formula of W+I (workers and intellectuals) joined together, a revolutionary mix emerged... The dissidents stressed basic democratic themes, protection for human rights of workers. They fought a psychological war..."

Thomas W. Simons , Jr., Deputy Assistant Secretary of State for European Affairs and United States Ambassador to Poland (1990-1993), wrote (p.401): "Poland's liberation from communism was very much a Polish process, but American policy was helpful to this process, because of reasons that had little to do with Poland - American reasons and NATO reasons - United States policy happened to track closely Solidarity's approach. This excellent basis for communication between Solidarity and the United States Government ...allowed Solidarity and the United States Government to reinforce each other. Solidarity's position was "no taxation without representation.'... under the slogan 'Let Poland be Poland' Christmas candles were lit for Poland all over America. (In protest of the Martial Law.)...Poland offers two lessons....First, there can be no progress without significant political and economic liberalization. ....the pace of political progress in Poland has been so stupendous that the tiny benefits announced April 17 had grown to over $1 billion in the United States assistance....The United States ... continued to be at the Poland's side..."

Roundtable Negotiations "with Representatives of the Polish Society" Chaired by a Police General   (1988-9).

THE THIRD REPUBLIC OF POLAND 1989 -

(Post-Modernism in Poland)

Negotiations Led by the Head of the Terror Apparatus

From Feb. 6, - Apr. 5, 1989, "Roundtable Negotiations" met in committees for political, social, and economic reforms and for labor union pluralism, known as an "anti-crisis understanding," between the communist authorities and the "constructive opposition." The negotiations were conducted under the chairmanship of Gen. Kiszczak.

Legalization of Solidarity and an Election Contract

At the conclusion of the Roundtable, the Solidarity Labor Union became legalized and an election contract was signed. In the Seym, the Communists and their allies (PZPR, ZSL, SD, and Pax) were guaranteed 65% of the seats. Thus, the Senate was to be elected freely, and so were 35% of its seats in the house of representatives. Both houses were to elect the President of Poland in a joint session called the National Assembly.

The changes in Poland were to serve as a model for the smaller satellite states and were to assure the West that the Soviets have given up preparation for war and really meant peace.

On Feb. 12, 1989, the end of one-party rule was announced by the government in an official proclamation in Warsaw.

On Feb. 21, the provision for the "leading role" of the communist party was removed from the Polish constitution.

On Mar. 7, the Polish government officially stated that the USSR executed thousands of Polish officers, prisoners of war, in 1940 at Katyń.

On Mar. 15, trading in foreign currency, without the disclosure of its origin, was legalized. The first private Currency Exchanges were opened.

On Apr. 7, constitutional amendments were passed, including the recreation of the Senate (earlier eliminated by the communists).

Apr. 25, marked the partial evacuation of Soviet forces from Hungary. The Soviets ordered the removal of barbed wire and mines from the Hungarian-Austrian border, thus preparing an opening in the Iron Curtain for East Germans to travel to West Germany, where these refugees were covered by a generous social security system. Apparently, the Soviets made preparations for flooding West Germany with refugees from East Germany as a bargaining chip in shaping the "New Europe."

In Apr. of 1989, Rural Solidarity was legalized. The *Weekly Solidarity* was reestablished. Solidarity television programs were permitted. The Constitution of 1952 was amended; the office of the president was reestablished, and the bicameral parliament was recreated by adding the Senate to the Seym.

On June 4, some 62% of voters participated in restricted elections to the lower house (the Seym) and in the free elections to the Senate, which had been reestablished with Soviet approval. The opposition gained 160 seats out of 161 allowed in the lower house, and 92 seats out of 100 in the Senate. Former Communist Party member Bronisłw Geremek became the head of the Opposition Club in the lower house.

On June 18, there was a 25% participation in the runoff elections. The opposition gained 99% of the Senate. Mikołaj Kozakiewicz of the Communist Controlled Small Holders Party became the House Speaker, and Andrzej Stelmachowski was elected the Marshal of the Senate. A State Supreme Tribunal was also established.

On July 3, a Soviet-approved solution was voiced: "Communist President and Opposition Prime Minister." Three day later, M. Gorbachev assured the Council of Europe that the USSR would not interfere with reforms in Poland and Hungary.

During July 9 - 11, U.S. President G. Bush visited Poland and met L.Wałęsa; on July 17, diplomatic relations between Poland and the Vatican were reestablished.

A Change after 45 Years of Open Soviet Domination
On July 19, the National Assembly elected Gen. Wojciech Jaruzelski the President of Poland by a one vote majority. Gen. Jaruzelski resigned as

the First Secretary of Polish Communist Party and was replaced by Mieczysław Rakowski (on July 29).

On Aug. 1, the end of all price controls and food rationing resulted in a panic on the market.

The next day, President Jaruzelski designated Police Gen. Kiszczak, the head of the terror apparatus in Poland, as the Prime Minister. His candidacy was opposed by Solidarity.

On Aug. 19, Police Gen. Kiszczak resigned as designated Prime Minister. Tadeusz Mazowiecki was designated as the first non-communist candidate for the office of prime minister in the former Soviet Bloc.

On Aug. 24, the Seym nominated the first noncommunist head of government in Poland in 40 years.

On Sept. 12, a government of 23 people was formed and sworn in under Prime Minister Tadeusz Mazowiecki, with the Citizen's Parliamentary Club (OKP) taking the most important departments such as economy, culture, media, security, foreign policy, and defense. Leszek Balcerowicz, once a member of the communist party, was in charge of the conversion to market economy. Mazowiecki recommended a wide dividing line to separate his regime from the communist past. Post-communist propaganda successfully interpreted "the wide dividing line" as a recommendation to forget about the past and to legalize the participation of the communist elite in the political life of the Third Polish Republic.

In Sept. of 1989, Soviet security chief and the head of KGB, Vladimir Kruichkov, was the first foreign visitor to come to meet the new Polish Prime Minister.

On Sept. 19, a trade agreement between Poland and the European Economic Community was signed.

On Sept. 22, the Independent Student Association (NZS) was registered.

On Sept. 29, ZOMO, the motorized riot "peoples' police," was disbanded.

Soviets Permit the Removal the Berlin Wall

On Oct. 3, the Soviets permitted the removal of the Berlin Wall. The Soviets played the card of the unification of Germany, based on the immediate integration of the economies of both Germanies. The equal exchange value of the West German mark and the East German mark was artificial because, in reality, theses currencies were exchanged one to four respectively. The economic drainage of West Germany was to end its subsidies for the European Union.

From Nov. 9 - 14, German Chancellor Helmut Kohl's visited Poland. A symbolic reconciliation of Poland and Germany took place during the Catholic Mass at Krzyżowa, in Silesia.

Prime Minister Mazowiecki visited the USSR and was told by Gorbachev that Poland should join NATO. During the visit the Prime Minister paid an official tribute at Katyń to the 21,957 Polish intelligentsia executed by the Soviets in the Spring of 1940. Papal Nuncio Archbishop Józef Kowalczyk arrived to Poland. Germany was unified, and the communist regimes in East-Central Europe disintegrated.

On Nov. 17, the monument of Feliks Dzierżyński was destroyed in Warsaw. Dzierżyński was the Polish founder of the Soviet terror apparatus, intelligence establishment, and Soviet command economy. He was the head of the Supreme Council of Soviet Economy from 1921-1924.

Two days later Lech Wałęsa delivered a speech to a joint session of the United States Congress. He received repeated standing ovations.

Austerity Program and an Amended Constitution

On Dec. 8, an austerity program was announced by Premier T. Mazowiecki to end the economic crisis in Poland caused by departing communists.

On Dec. 29, the parliament amended the constitution and approved the austerity economic program; and the country's official name became "The Republic of Poland," instead of the communist Polish People's Republic. Poland proclaimed a democratic republic with the parliament as the supreme political power in the country. Freedom of assembly and the formation of political parties were proclaimed. The competence of the Constitutional Tribunal was broadened. The statements about the leading role of the communist party, planned economy, socialism, and the eternal alliance with the USSR were eliminated from the constitution.

On Jan. 1, 1990 the złoty was devalued, and the prices increased sharply as the austerity program entered a stage of "shock therapy." Thus, widespread unemployment and economic suffering came before any review was made of the communist crimes made in service of the USSR and at the expense of Polish poeple. As a result, the population lost the chance to eliminate the communist elite from the political life of Poland.

Belated Demands to Eliminate Communist Elite from Politics

During Jan. 25 - 28, the Polish Communist Party (PZPR) self-dissolved during its final eleventh congress. Party members reorganized themselves as the (post-communist) Social Democracy of the Polish Republic (SdRP). It was led by Aleksander Kwaśniewski and Leszek Miller.

On Jan. 27, the name of Lenin Shipyard was changed back to Gdańsk Shipyard.

On Feb. 9, the crowned white eagle was reestablished as the emblem of Poland, as it had been during the Second Polish Republic (1918-1945). The communist police (MO) and (SB) were dissolved. The new State Police (PP) and the Office of State Security was organized, including many former members of the communist terror apparatus.

On Feb. 15, 1990, Solidarity demanded early free parliamentary and presidential elections, the removal of the communists from government positions, and the creation of new jobs for people unemployed because of economic restructuring.

On March 8, the West German Parliament renounced all claims to Polish provinces east of the Oder-Neisse River Line, established at Potsdam in 1945.

On Apr. 6, Constitution Day on the 3rd of May was reestablished as a national holiday, instead of the July 22nd date commemorating the founding of the satellite communist regime in Poland.

Five days later, the parliament abolished censorship in Poland.

Admission of Soviet Guilt and a Split in Solidarity

On Apr. 13, the president of the USSR, Mikhail Gorbachev, officially admitted Soviet guilt in the NKVD execution of the 21,857 members of Poland's leadership community captured by the Red Army.

During Apr. 19-25, the second convention of Solidarity Labor Union took place. Lech Wałęsa was chosen as the union leader and announced his intent to run for the office of the president of Poland.

On May 2, during his official visit to Poland, the West German President stated that Poland's borders were permanent.

Public Depressed by "Shock Therapy"

On May 27, only 42% of the voters participated in the municipal elections, the first completely free elections in postwar Poland. The electorate was discouraged by economic "shock therapy" and a lack of any review of communist crimes. The post-communist SdRP acquired an important strategic position.

The presidential campaign began in June 1990. A divided Solidarity was represented by Lech Wałęsa and Tadeusz Mazowiecki.

On June 21, a joint resolution by West and East German Parliaments confirmed the borders of Poland.

On July 13, the Law on Privatization of State Estates passed. On Aug. 2, religious education was reintroduced to schools by the Minister of National Education, H. Samsonowicz.

On Sept. 5, Solidarity withdrew its logo from the first page of *"Gazeta Wyborcza" (The Electoral Gazette)* in response to its publisher's support for the post-communists.

One week later, the Western Big Four and the two Germanies met in Moscow to settle the terms of German unification.

The Unification of Germany; Wałęsa as President

Moscow agreed to the admission of a united Germany to into NATO under the condition that no NATO forces would be stationed east of the Elbe River, and that the German army (the Bundeswehr) on the territory of former East Germany should not exceed 50,000 men (without offensive weapons).

On Nov. 14, the foreign ministers of Poland and a united Germany signed a treaty guaranteeing Poland's borders. The Polish-German Border Treaty recognized the Odra-Nysa line as the permanent border between Poland and Germany.

On Nov. 20, coal miners went on a protest strike against the austerity program.

Five days later, only 56.7 % participated in presidential elections. Mazowiecki (18%) was eliminated by Wałęsa (40%) and an unknown candidate from Canada Stanisław Tymiński (32%).

On Nov. 26, T. Mazowiecki resigned as Prime Minister of Poland.

`On Dec. 9, only 53% participated in the runoff election won by Lech Wałęsa (74%) over Stanisław Tymiński (23%).

On Dec. 22, L. Wałęsa was inaugurated as the first postwar democratically elected President of Poland. Polish President-in-Exile, R. Kaczorowski, surrendered the state insignia to L. Wałęsa. President Wałęsa received the Soviet Ambassador to Poland before talking to any other ambassadors in Warsaw.

Five days later, President L.Wałęsa nominated J. K. Bielecki as the new Prime Minister.

The Dissolution of the Warsaw Pact

On Feb. 15, 1991 the Presidents of Poland, Hungary, and Czechoslovakia signed "the declaration of cooperation in European integration," known as the Visegrad Triangle.

On Feb. 23, M. Krzaklewski was elected to head Solidarity. He succeeded L. Wałęsa. Krzaklewski was much better educated than Wałęsa. He gave a new hope to Solidarity which, so far, had been ineptly led by Wałęsa amidst quarrels and innuendos

Two days later, the foreign and defense ministers of the Warsaw Treaty Organization countries signed an agreement to dissolve the Pact. Moscow implied that NATO should do likewise.

On March 9, the "Round Table Contract Parliament" dissolved itself. On March 17, seventeen Western countries canceled half of Poland's $33 billion foreign debt or $16.5 billion.

During March 19 -26, 1991, President L.Wałęsa visited the United States to the disappointment of many American Poles. A public television interview exposed Wałęsa's ignorance and crude manners, which diminished his popularity and fame as a Noble Price laureate.

Deepening Recession; Start of the Red Army Withdrawal

In March of 1991, the unemployment rate grew to over seven

percent amidst a deepening recession. Poland's foreign debt also reached 46.2 billion dollars.

On Apr. 1, the Soviet-dominated "Warsaw Pact" was officially dissolved. Three days later, the Red Army began its withdrawal from Poland, after 47 years of continuous presence.

In Nov. 1991 began the negotiations for the admission of Poland into the European Economic Community. Poland joined the Council of Europe.

On Dec. 2, Poland was the first country to recognize the independence of Ukraine.

Presidential Politics and Prospects

On Nov. 19, 1995, some sixty-eight percent of the electorate participated in the presidential elections. A post-communist candidate, Aleksander Kawśniewski (SLD), obtained fifty-two percent of the vote. He won mainly because of the strength of his post-communist political machine, which was able to outmaneuver and split the new fledgling political parties. Many of them were too small to have any representation at all. Kwaśniewski displayed more intelligence, better manners, and by far better understanding of public relations than did his opponent, Lech Wałęsa. There was a widespread yearning in Poland for a return to traditional Polish civility, which Wałęsa sadly lacked.

The dissolution of the USSR proceeded by replacing it with the Commonwealth of Independent States. The act of establishing CIS was signed in Belarus, near the Polish border, by Boris Yeltsin and a number of practically unknown individuals, apparently acting as figureheads for the General Staff and the Military Intelligence (the GRU) of the Red Army - the core of the Russian military-police complex. The Commonwealth of Independent States was suspected to be a strategic deception aimed at the depriving the United States of the Soviet enemy, while Moscow kept its nuclear arsenal. It changed Moscow's relations with NATO. Moscow's apparent aim was to peacefully remove American forces from Europe, while Russia remained a nuclear superpower.

Poland's economy underwent a shock therapy in order to achieve a conversion from a command economy to free market. This happened when the country suffered from high inflation and unemployment. At that time, the Poles missed the chance to expose the crimes of the communist puppet regime and to bar the communist party elite from politics.

The post-communist elite, members of the *nomenklatura*, continued to dominate the mass media and were able to continue their propaganda. They also profited from having dealt with the West for nearly 50 years, while the people of Poland were oppressed by communist terror apparatus and isolated behind the Iron Curtain.

There were no personality clashes at the top of the post-communist political machine, while their opponents were plagued with quarrels at the top of each party. The frequency of these personality conflicts suggest that many of them occurred as a result of activities of agents provocateurs - a notorious tactic used by communists in People's Poland.

Economic hardship discouraged many voters from participation in elections. This low election turnout gave post-communists a chance to make a strong political comeback. However, the Polish economy, freed from communist restrains, had been growing faster than any other in Europe. The Russian economic crisis in the mid-nineties did not weaken the economy of Poland. Once dominant, export to Russia fell to nine percent of the total exports from Poland.

The population of Poland supported joining both the NATO alliance and the European Union. Poland joined NATO in 1999. The disproportion of sizes of the German and Polish economies poses a threat of German economic domination and massive purchases of land in Poland by the Germans. Hopefully, Poland will be able to conclude political agreements limiting German purchases of land similar to those concluded between Germany, Austria, and Denmark.

Poland is here to stay, judging by the performance of Polish culture which is of considerable importance to Europe, flourishing as it does in the physical center of the European continent. The cultural history of Poland constitutes an uninterrupted and original achievement which, unfortunately, has not been reflected in her political history. However, the spirit of the Polish nation lives on with the knowledge that the Poles have done great things together and have the will to do them again.

NOBEL PRIZE WINNERS BORN IN POLAND

Maria Skłodowska-Curie	1903 Physics
Henryk Sienkiewicz	1905 Literature
Albert Abraham Michelson	1907 Physics
Maria Skłodowska-Curie	1911 Chemistry
Walther Herman Nernst	1920 Chemistry
Władysław Stanisław Reymont	1924 Literature
Tadeusz Reichstein	1950 Medicine
Maria Goepert-Mayer	1963 Physics
Andrew V. Schally	1977 Medicine
Isaac Bashevis Singer	1978 Literature
Monachem Begin	1978 Peace
Czesław Miłosz	1980 Literature
Ronald Hoffman	1981 Chemistry
Lech Wałęsa	1983 Peace
Klaus von Klitzing	1985 Physics
Georges Charpak	1992 Physics
Shimon Peres	1994 Peace
Joseph Rotblat	1995 Peace
Wisława Szymborska	1996 Literature

Note: Polish writers won Nobel Prizes for Literature: in 1905 Henryk Sienkiewicz; in 1924 Władysław Reymont; in 1980 Czesław Miłosz; in 1999 Wisława Szymborska and Polish born Yiddish writer Bashevis Singer in 1978. Henryk Sienkiewicz (1846-1916) wrote Polish historical novels. His novel *Quo Vadis*, about early Christians in Nero's Rome won him the Noble Prize and was, by far, the greatest bestseller worldwide at the time. It was adapted into several movies.

The early Noble Prizes for science were won: in 1907 Albert Michelson (born in Strzelno,1852-1931)in physics for determining the speed of light with high accuracy and providing the basis for the development of the theory of relativity; and in 1903 and in 1911 by Maria Skłodowska-Curie (born in Warsaw, 1867-1934) in physics and chemistry respectively.

Maria Curie named Polonium the first radioactive element discovered by her. Her daughter Irene Curie-Joliot also won Nobel Prize (1935) for chemistry for her synthesis of new radioactive elements.

CHRONOLOGY OF POLAND'S HISTORY

623 The first Slavonic state of Samon
740 The height of the success of Slavonic tribal military democracies
840 The beginning of the first Polish dynasty the Piasts (c.840-1370)
966 The establishment of Western Christianity in Poland
1025 Poland becomes an independent kingdom
1241 The first of three devastating Mongol invasions
1374 The taxing authority of regional legislatures is introduced
1385 The union of Poland and Lithuania at Krewo
1410 Poland's victory at Grunwald over the Teutonic Knights
1422 Private property legally protected in Poland
1433 The due process law established in Poland
1454 Polish national parliament established
1493 The bicameral parliament established in Poland
1505 The constitutional law "nothing new about us without us"
1569 The establishment of the Polish Nobles' Republic
1573 The general elections viritim established in Poland-Lithuania
1683 The defeat of the Turkish invasion by King John III at Vienna
1697 The sovereignty crisis – the fraudulent inauguration of August II
1717 The sovereignty crisis deepening – the "Saxon night" in Poland
1768 The Bar Confederacy – the war of the first partition
1772 The first partition of Poland by Austria, Prussia, and Russia
1789 The Constitution of May 3 (the first in Europe)
1792 The war of the second partition (in defense of the constitution)
1793 The second partition of Poland by Prussia and Russia
1794 The war of the third partition – the Kościuszko Insurrection
1795 The third partition of Poland by Austria, Prussia, and Russia
1795 The treaty of destruction of Poland signed in St. Petersburg
1815 The establishment of the Kingdom of Poland within Russia
1830 The war with Russia for the independence of Poland
1863 The uprising against Russian domination
1918 Poland becomes independent
1920 The defeat of Soviet invasion by Józef Piłsudski at Warsaw
1926 The coup by Józef Piłsudski and semi-dictatorship
1939 The invasion of Poland by Germany and the Soviet Union
1939 The partition of Poland by Germany and the Soviet Union
1944 People's Poland in Soviet Bloc
1958 The election of Archbishop Karol Wojtyła as Pope John Paul II
1989 The Third Polish Republic

The Piast Dynasty

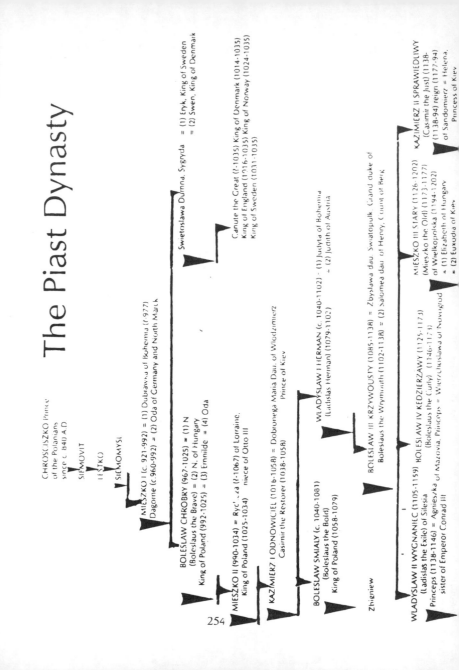

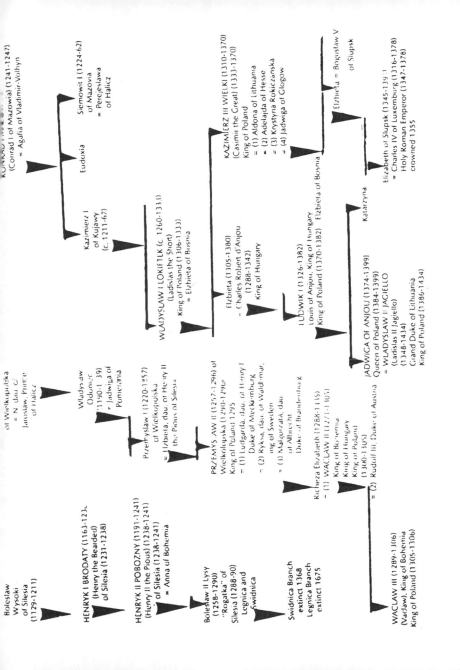

KONRAD I MAZ.?.?
(Conrad I of Mazowia) (1241-1247)
= Agafia of Vladimir-Volhyn

Bolesław
Wysoki
of Silesia
(1129-1211)

of Wielkopolska
= N. dau. of
Jarosław, Prince
of Halicz

Siemowit I (1224-62)
of Mazovia
= Perejeslawa
of Halicz

Eudoxia

HENRYK I BRODATY (1163-123.
(Henry the Bearded)
of Silesia (1231-1238)

Władysław
Odonicz
(1190-1239)
= Jadwiga of
Pomerania

Kazimierz I
of Kujawy
(c. 1211-67)

HENRYK II POBOZNY (1191-1241)
(Henry II the Pious) (1238-1241)
of Silesia (1238-1241)
= Anna of Bohemia

Przemysław I (1220-1257)
of Wielkopolska
= Elżbieta, dau. of Henry II
the Pious of Silesia

WŁADYSŁAW I ŁOKIETEK (c. 1260-1333)
(Ladislas the Short)
King of Poland (1306-1333)
= Elżbieta of Bosnia

KAZIMIERZ III WIELKI (1310-1370)
(Casimir the Great) (1333-1370)
King of Poland
= (1) Aldona of Lithuania
= (2) Adelajda of Hesse
= (3) Krystyna Rokiczanska
= (4) Jadwiga of Głogów

Bolesław II Łysy
(1258-1290)
"Rogatka" of
Silesia (1288-90)
Legnica and
Świdnica

PRZEMYSŁAW II (1257-1296) of
Wielkopolska (1290-1296)
King of Poland 1295
= (1) Ludgarda, dau. of Henry I
Duke of Meckłemburg
= (2) Ryksa, dau. of Waldemar,
King of Sweden
= (3) Małgorzata, dau.
of Albrecht,
Duke of Brandenburg

Elżbieta (1305-1380)
= Charles Robert d'Anjou
(1288-1342)
King of Hungary

LUDWIK I (1326-1382)
Louis of Anjou, King of Hungary
King of Poland (1370-1382)

Elżbieta of Bosnia

Katarzyna

Elżbieta = Bogusław V
of Słupsk

Elizabeth of Słupsk (1345-139.?)
= Charles IV of Luxemburg (1316-1378)
Holy Roman Emperor (1347-1378)
crowned 1355

Świdnica Branch
extinct 1368
Legnica Branch
extinct 1675

Richeza Elizabeth (1288-1335)
= (1) WACLAW II (1271-1305)
King of Bohemia
King of Poland
(1300-1305)
= (2) Rudolf III, Duke of Austria

JADWIGA OF ANJOU (1374-1399)
Queen of Poland (1384-1399)
= WŁADYSŁAW II JAGIEŁŁO
(Ladislas II Jagiello)
(1348-1434)
Grand Duke of Lithuania
King of Poland (1386-1434)

WACLAW III (1289-1306)
(Vaclav) King of Bohemia
King of Poland (1305-1306)

MAP OF POLAND

German genocide of the Jews (1942-1944), eviction of the Germans and mass resettlement of the Poles resulted in the loss of multinational character of Poland's towns for the first time in history.

Territorial shift to the western frontier on the Oder-Neisse enabled Poland to overcome economic debilitation caused by the century of partitions, 1795-1918.

256

INDEX

265

266

269

Forthcoming Illustrated Histories from Hippocrene Books
FALL 2000

France: An Illustrated History
Lisa Neal

Encompassing more than 500,000 years from primordial times to the 21st century, French history is a vast body run through by manifold and, often turbulent, currents. This volume provides a succinct panorama of these cultural, political, and social currents, as well as concise analyses of their origins and effects. Complemented by 50 illustrations and maps, this text is an invaluable addition to the library of the traveler, the student, and the history enthusiast.

150 pages • 5 X 7 • 50 b/w photos/Illus./maps • $14.95hc • 0-7818-0835-9 • W • (105)

Korea: An Illustrated History from Ancient Times to 1945
David Rees

Koreans call their country *Choson*, which is familiarly translated as "The Land of the Morning Calm." From the time of the legendary Tan-Gun in the third millennium B.C. until the middle of the twentieth century, however, Korea was forced to weather many military and political storms. This volume concisely depicts these political and social events, as well as Korea's profound spiritual and cultural heritage—all enriched by 50 illustrations and maps.

150 pages • 5 X 7 • 50 b/w photos/Illus./maps • $14.95hc • 0-7818-0785-9 • W • (152)

Spain: An Illustrated History
Fred James Hill

This concise, illustrated history explores the remarkable history of Spain—a thriving center of Islamic civilization until its eventual conquest by Catholic kings—from the first millennium B.C. to the 21st century. With its succinct portrayal of the country's political and social history, along with the concomitant cultural developments and achievements, this volume is perfect for the traveler, student, and history enthusiast.

150 pages • 5 X 7 • 50 b/w photos/Illus./maps • $14.95hc • 0-7818-0836-7• W • (113)

Other Illustrated Histories from Hippocrene Books. . .

The Celtic World: An Illustrated History
Patrick Lavin

From the valleys of Bronze Age Urnfielders to the works of 20th century Irish-American literary greats Mary Higgins Clark and Seamus Heaney, Patrick Lavin guides the reader on an entertaining and informative journey through 182 captivating pages of Celtic history, culture, and tradition. Complemented by 50 illustrations and maps, this concise yet insightful survey is a convenient reference guide for both the traveler and scholar.

185 pages • 5 x 7 • 50 b/w Illus./maps • $14.95hc • 0-7818-0731-X • W • (582)

England: An Illustrated History
Henry Weisser

English history is a rich and complex subject that has had a major influence upon the development of the language, laws, institutions, practices and ideas of the United States and many other countries throughout the world. Just how did all of this originate over the centuries in this pleasant, green kingdom? This concise, illustrated volume traces the story from England's most distant past to the present day, highlighting important political and social developments as well as cultural achievements.

166 pages • 5 x 7 • 50 b/w Illus./maps • $11.95hc • 0-7818-0751-4 • W • (446)

Ireland: An Illustrated History

Henry Weisser

Erin go bragh! While it is easy to appreciate the natural beauty of Ireland, the Emerald Isle's history is also a rich and complex subject of study. Spanning prehistoric and Celtic Ireland to modern times, this concise, illustrated volume examines the people, religion, social changes, and politics that have evolved into the tradition of modern Ireland.

166 pages • 5 x 7 • 50 b/w illus./maps • $11.95hc • 0-7818-0693-3 • W • (782)

Israel: An Illustrated History

David C. Gross

Israel has always been a major player on the world stage. This concise, illustrated volume offers the reader an informative, panoramic view of this remarkable land, from biblical days to the 21st century. With topics exploring art, literature, sculpture, music, science, politics, religion and more, here is a wonderful gift book for travelers, students, or anyone seeking to expand their knowledge of Israeli history, culture, and heritage.

160 pages • 5 x 7 • 50 b/w illus./maps • $11.95hc • 0-7818-0756-5 • W • (24)

Mexico: An Illustrated History

Michael Burke

This convenient historical guide traces Mexico from the peasant days of the Olmecs to the late 20th century. With over 150 pages and 50 illustrations, the reader discovers how events of Mexico's past have left an indelible mark on the politics, economy, culture, spirit, and growth of this country and its people.

183 pages • 5 x 7 • 50 b/w illus. • $11.95hc • 0-7818-0690-9 • W • (585)

Poland in World War II: An Illustrated Military History

Andrew Hempel

This illustrated history is a concise presentation of the Polish military war effort in World War II, intermingled with factual human-interest stories and 50 black-and-white photos and illustrations.

117 pages • 5 x 7 • 50 b/w illus. • $11.95hc • 0-7818-0758-1 • W • (541)

Russia: An Illustrated History

Joel Carmichael

Encompassing one-sixth of the earth's land surface—the equivalent of the whole North American continent—Russia is the largest country in the world. Renowned historian Joel Carmichael presents Russia's rich and expansive past—upheaval, reform, social change, growth—in an easily accessible and concentrated volume. From the Tatar's reign to modern-day Russia, the book spans seven centuries of cultural, social and political events.

252 pages • 5 x 7 • 50 b/w illus. • $14.95hc • 0-7818-0689-5 • W • (781)

Prices subject to change without notice. **To purchase Hippocrene Books** contact your local bookstore, call (718) 454-2366, or write to: HIPPOCRENE BOOKS, 171 Madison Avenue, New York, NY 10016. Please enclose check or money order, adding $5.00 shipping (UPS) for the first book and $.50 for each additional book.